ENVIRONMENTAL GOVER

This is an important examination of how China is currently dealing with environmental problems and challenges, and of its successes, failures and dilemmas.

This new book gives special attention to the development of 'environmental governance' in contemporary China, especially in the urban, industrial and infrastructure sectors, showing how the rapid economic growth that has transformed China in recent years has major implications for the environment, as well as future economic development.

Leading international scholars explore a range of key issues, including:

- economic growth and the environment

- the environmental policy process

- the legal framework for environmental protection

- the role of environmental NGOs

- energy policy

- water issues

- biotechnology and GMOs

- and the international dimension

This new volume shows how environmental policy, politics and governance are core issues posed by China's accelerated economic development. At the same time it analyzes, illustrates and argues that major steps are under way in taking up these challenges. In doing so the book provides an in-depth, balanced and comprehensive assessment of contemporary environmental reforms in China.

This book was previously published as a special issue of *Environmental Politics*

Neil Carter is Senior Lecturer in Politics at the University of York, UK.

Arthur P. J. Mol is Chair and Professor of Environmental Policy at Wageningen University, The Netherlands.

90 0789817 2

ENVIRONMENTAL GOVERNANCE IN CHINA

Edited by
Neil T. Carter and
Arthur P. J. Mol

LONDON AND NEW YORK

First published 2007 by Routledge
2 Park Square, Milton Park, Abingdon, Oxon, OX14 4RN

Simultaneously published in the USA and Canada by Routledge
270 Madison Ave, New York NY 10016

Routledge is an imprint of the Taylor & Francis Group, an informa business

Transferred to Digital Printing 2008

Typeset in Times by KnowledgeWorks Global Limited,
Southampton, Hampshire, UK

British Library Cataloguing in Publication Data
A catalogue record for this book is available
from the British Library

Library of Congress Cataloging in Publication Data
A catalog record for this book has been requested

ISBN 10: 0-415-37169-4 (hbk)
ISBN 13: 978-0-415-37169-8 (hbk)

CONTENTS

1. China's Environmental Governance
   in Transition   1
   ARTHUR P. J. MOL AND NEIL T. CARTER

2. Environmental Governance: the Emerging Economic Dimension   23
   ELIZABETH ECONOMY

3. Institutional Reform, Economic Changes, and Local
   Environmental Management in China: the case of Guangdong
   Province   42
   CARLOS WING-HUNG LO AND SHUI-YAN TANG

4. Public Participation with Chinese Characteristics: Citizen
   Consumers in China's Environmental Management   63
   SUSAN MARTENS

5. Same Longitude, Different Latitudes: Institutional Change in
   Urban Water in China, North and South   83
   JAMES E. NICKUM AND YOK-SHIU F. LEE

6. Environmental Implications of Energy Policy in China   100
   NATHANIEL T. ADEN AND JONATHAN E. SINTON

7. China's Environmental Governance of Rapid Industrialisation   123
   HAN SHI AND LEI ZHANG

8. Balancing Technological Innovation and Environmental
   Regulation: an Analysis of Chinese Agricultural Biotechnology
   Governance   145
   JAMES KEELEY

9. China, the WTO, and Implications for the Environment   162
   ABIGAIL R. JAHIEL

10. China and the Environment: Domestic and Transnational
    Dynamics of a Future Hegemon   182
    NEIL T. CARTER AND ARTHUR P. J. MOL

Index   197

China's Environmental Governance in Transition

ARTHUR P. J. MOL & NEIL T. CARTER

Introduction

China has been witnessing an almost unprecedented period of continuous high economic growth during the last 15 years. The modernisation and transition process set in motion in the mid 1980s, started to accelerate and mature in the early 1990s, showing average national economic growth percentages of around 8 per cent and more (Figure 1). During the same time frame the Chinese economy opened to the global market, resulting in increasing international trade, growing Foreign Direct Investment inflows (and recently also outflows), and greater international travel by Chinese citizens. Economic development has been quite uneven, both sectorally and regionally. The eastern provinces and the industrial sectors have made the most contribution to the country's economic acceleration, while economic development in the agrarian sectors of the west has been much less pronounced and in places is even stagnating. Modernisation patterns and technological innovations differ significantly between regions and between sectors. At the same time, not all groups in society have profited to the same extent from these developments. In general, a

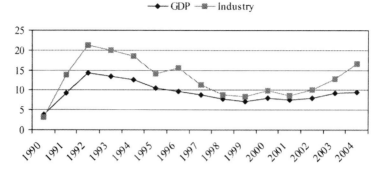

Figure 1. Economic and industrial growth percentages in China, 1996–2004. *Source*: World Bank data.

growing inequality can be witnessed in the country, where a new rich upper middle class has profited from economic development and access to the global economy, while significant parts of the Chinese population have suffered from rural marginalisation, the closing of inefficient state factories and reductions in the state bureaucracies.

As Shapiro's (2001) impressive study illustrates, neither imperial nor Maoist China avoided environmental degradation, and the repression of human beings at least paralleled violence by humans towards nature. But rapid economic and industrial modernisation and development ushered in a new phase of continuous pressure on the environment. In this new phase there is no simple mono-causal and one-directional way in which economic development relates to the environment. On the one hand, economic growth, industrialisation (including some agricultural sectors), further urbanisation caused by a migrating rural population, increasing consumption levels, accelerated extraction of minerals and ores, and growing air and car transportation have resulted in increases in resource use and higher pollution levels. The increases (and predicted trends for the next decade) in car ownership, the penetration of durable consumer goods such as televisions, mobile phones, refrigerators and personal computers, and energy use are regularly reported in western journals and newspapers. On the other hand, technological and management innovations and developments, the entry into global markets, the increasing capacity of environmental state institutions, the commitments to international environmental treaties and the growing environmental awareness of China's new middle class and ruling elites[1] have contributed to increased efficiencies in resource use, the adoption of environmental technologies, cleaner products, lower emission intensities per unit of product, and the closing down of some inefficient (and thus heavily polluting) factories.

The overall impact of these contrasting tendencies differs, as can be expected in such an enormous country, between provinces and regions, between economic sectors, and among the social groups confronted with the positive and negative economic, environmental and social consequences of these developments. As in many countries, there is no one clear tendency in China. We can observe neither an overall tendency towards environmental decay jeopardising the global sustenance base, nor a general trend towards greening the economic, political and social institutions and practices. Understanding and interpreting current environmental developments in China in terms of a national environmental Kuznets curve, makes little sense. To evaluate the way that China is currently dealing with environmental problems and challenges, and the successes, failures and dilemmas it faces, we are in need of much more detailed analyses and insight into various institutional developments and social practices. These analyses are further complicated by the fact that China's system of environmental governance is both very much in the making and under constant change and transition due to a fluid social environment, both nationally and internationally.

This introduction sets the stage for such dynamic analyses by first describing the historic development of what we might call China's environmental state, including its successes and failures (some of which will be further elaborated in other contributions). The subsequent sections introduce the developments in those Chinese institutions that aim to contribute to diminishing the environmental burden produced by China's unprecedented economic growth path.

The Birth of China's 'Environmental State'

In the birth period of environmental management (in the 1970s and early 1980s) China's environmental protection system showed characteristics similar to those of other centrally planned economies, such as those in Europe before the fall of the Berlin Wall in 1989. These included limited citizen involvement; no independent environmental movement or NGOs; little response to international agreements, organisations and institutions; a strong focus on central state authority and especially the Communist Party of China (CPC) with restricted freedom of manoeuvre for both decentralised state organisations, para-statals and private organisations; an obsession with large scale technological developments (in terms of hard technology); problems with coordination between state authorities and departments, together with a limited empowerment of the environmental authorities (see Ziegler, 1983; DeBardeleben, 1985; Lothspeich & Chen, 1997). The further development of China's environmental reform strategy was not a linear process; there was no simple unfolding of the initial model of environmental governance invented thirty years ago under a command economy. Two main factors are behind a certain degree of discontinuity in Chinese environmental reform. First, the economic, political and social changes that China witnessed during the last two decades also affected the original 'model' of environmental governance. Economic transformations towards a market-oriented growth model, decentralisation dynamics, growing openness to and integration in the outside world, and bureaucratic reorganisation processes have shifted China's environmental governance model away from those common to centrally planned economies. Second, China also witnessed the inefficiencies and ineffectiveness of its initial environmental governance approach, not unlike the 'state failures' (Jänicke, 1986) that European countries witnessed in the 1980s before they transformed their environmental protection approach.

The start of serious involvement by the Chinese government in environmental protection more or less coincides with the introduction of economic reforms in the late 1970s. Pollution control was initiated in the early 1970s, especially following the 1972 United Nations Conference on the Human Environment in Stockholm. In 1974 a National Environmental Protection Office was established, with equivalents in the provinces, although its main development occurred after the enactment and implementation of the environmental laws and regulations since the late 1970s, with particularly rapid acceleration in the 1990s. Following the promulgation of the state Environmental Protection Law in 1979 (revised in 1989), China began systematically to establish her environmental regulatory system. In 1984 environmental protection was defined as a national basic policy and key principles for environmental protection in China were proposed, which include 'prevention is the main, then control', 'polluter responsible for pollution control' (already introduced in the 1979 environmental law), and 'strengthening environmental management'. Subsequently, a national regulatory framework was formulated, composed of a series of environmental laws (on all the major environmental sectors, starting with marine protection and water in 1982 and 1984), executive regulations, standards and measures. At a national level China has now some 20 environmental laws adopted by the National People's Congress, around 140 executive regulations issued by the State Council, and a series of sector regulations and environmental standards set by the State Environmental Protection Agency (SEPA).

Institutionally, the national regulatory framework is vertically implemented through a four-tier management system, i.e., national, provincial, municipal and county levels. The latter three levels are governed directly by their corresponding authorities in terms of both finance and personnel management, while SEPA is only responsible for their substantial operation. The enactment of the various environmental laws, instruments and regulations through the last two decades was paralleled by a stepwise increase of the bureaucratic status and capacity of these environmental authorities (Jahiel, 1998). For instance, the NEPA, was elevated via the National Environmental Protection Bureau to the National Environmental Protection Agency (in 1988), and in 1998 it received ministerial status as SEPA. By 1995, the 'environmental state' had over 88,000 employees across China and by 2004 it had grown to over 160,000 (see Figure 2).[2] Jahiel (1998: 776) concludes on this environmental bureaucracy: 'Clearly, the past 15 years ... has seen the assembly of an extensive institutional system nation-wide and the increase of its rank. With these gains has come a commensurate increase in EPB authority – particularly in the cities'. Although the expansion of the 'environmental state' sometimes met

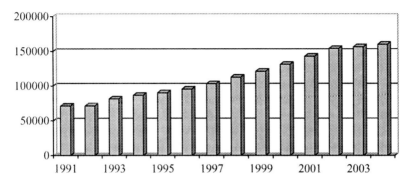

Figure 2. Governmental staff employed for environmental protection in China. *Source*: *China Environment Statistical Report* (1991–2004).

stagnation (e.g. the relegation of Environmental Protection Bureaux (EPBs) in many counties from second-tier to third-tier organs in 1993–94), over a period of 20 years the growth in quantity and quality of the officials is impressive (especially when compared with the shrinking of other state bureaucracies). Besides SEPA, the State Development Planning Commission (SDPC) and the State Economic and Trade Commission (SETC) are crucial national state agencies in environmental protection, especially since the recent governmental reorganisation in 1998.

In between State Successes and State Failures

Arguably, these administrative initiatives have contributed to some environmental improvements, although the widespread information distortion, the discontinuities in environmental statistics and the absence of longitudinal environmental data in China should made us cautious about drawing any final conclusions.[3] Total suspended particulates and sulphur dioxide concentrations show an absolute decline in most major Chinese cities between the late 1980s and the late 1990s (Lo & Xing, 1999; Rock, 2002), which is, of course, remarkable given the high economic growth figures during that decade. By the end of 2000 CFC production decreased 33 per cent compared to mid 1990s levels, due to the closure of 30 companies (SEPA, 2001). It is reported (but also contested) that emissions of carbon dioxide have fallen between 1996 and 2000, despite continuing economic growth (Sinton & Fridley, 2001, 2003; Chandler *et al.*, 2002). Most other environmental indicators show a delinking between environmental impacts and economic growth; for example, water pollution in terms of biological oxygen demand (World Bank, 1997). Many absolute environmental indicators (total levels of emissions; total energy use) show less clear signs of improvements (see Zhang & Chen, 2003, on air emissions; ASEAN, 2001; SEPA, 2005).

More indirect indicators that suggest similar relative improvements are the growth of China's environmental industry, indicated by the proportion of sales to GDP: an increase from 0.22 percent in 1989 up to 0.87 percent in 2000. This is even more spectacular when taking into account the rapid economic growth over these years (average 9.4 per cent annually). Also the increase in governmental environmental investments is astonishing, rising from 0.6 per cent of GDP in 1989 to 1.0 per cent of GDP in 1999 and 1.4 per cent in 2004 (see Figure 3). The increase of firms certified with ISO14001 standards, from nine (in 1996), to around 500 (in 2000) to over 8800 (in 2004) (http:// www.iso.ch/iso/), and the closing of heavily polluting factories following influential environmental campaigns during the second half of the 1990s (Nygard and Guo, 2001) point in a similar direction.

Obviously, these positive signs should not distract us from the fact that overall China remains heavily polluted, that emissions are often far above (and environmental quality levels far below) international standards, that only 25 per cent of the municipal wastewater is treated before discharge (although 85 per cent of industrial wastewater according to SEPA data; SEPA, 2001), and that environmental and resource efficiencies of production and consumption processes are overall still rather low. While relative improvements can certainly be identified, absolute levels of emissions, pollution, resource extraction and environmental quality often do not yet meet standards.

Environmental Governance: State and Market

How is contemporary China dealing with these current and prospective environmental threats and risks? What mechanisms, dynamics and innovations can we identify in China's system of environmental governance? In setting the research agenda for such an analysis we have to bear in mind that

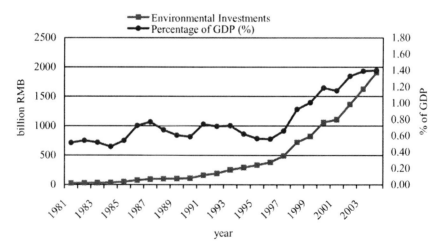

Figure 3. Governmental environmental investments, 1981–2004: absolute (in billion RMB) and as proportion of GDP. *Source*: *China Statistical Yearbook* (1981–2004).

we are trying to understand a moving target, quite unlike the more stable contemporary (environmental) institutions of European and other OECD countries. We will group our analyses of innovations and transitions in China's environmental governance system in four major categories: political transitions, and the role of economic actors and market dynamics (this section), emerging institutions beyond state and market, and processes of international integration.

Transitions in the 'Environmental State'

The state apparatus in China remains of dominant importance in environmental protection and reform. Both the nature of the contemporary Chinese social order and the character of the environment as a public good will safeguard the crucial position of the state in environmental protection and reform for some time. Environmental interests are articulated in particular by the impressive rise of Environmental Protection Bureaux (EPBs) at various governmental levels. However, the most common complaints from Chinese and foreign environmental analysts focus precisely on this system of (local) EPBs. The local EPBs are heavily dependent on both the higher level environmental authorities and on local governments. However, as little importance is given to environmental criteria in assessing the performance of local governments, they often display no interest in stringent environmental reform, yet they play a key role in financing the local EPBs (see Lo & Tang, this volume). There are also poor (financial) incentives for both governments and private actors to comply with environmental laws, standards and policies. Not surprisingly, therefore, there is a significant level of collusion between local officials and private enterprises which 'employ' them in order to get around strict environmental monitoring. Finally, local EPBs are criticised for their poor environmental capacity (in both qualitative and quantitative terms) and, more generally, for the lack (and distortion) of environmental information.

Yet the environmental state in China is clearly undergoing a transitional process that elsewhere is labelled political modernisation (see Jänicke, 1993; Mol, 2002), where traditional hierarchical lines and conventional divisions of power are transformed. Although processes of political modernisation in China's environmental policy have different characteristics from those that are found in European countries, the direction of those reforms is nevertheless similar: greater decentralisation and flexibility whilst moving away from a rigid, hierarchical, command-and-control system of environmental governance. Increasingly local EPBs and local governments are given – and taking – larger degrees of freedom in developing environmental priorities, strategies, financial models and institutional arrangements (Lo & Tang, this volume). This parallels broader tendencies of decentralisation in Chinese society, but it is also specifically motivated by state failures in environmental policy. The tendency is one towards larger influence and decision-making power by the local authorities and diminishing control by Beijing, both by the central state structures and by the CPC (for instance, on decentralisation in energy policy (Andrews-Speed *et al.*, 1999)). Decentralisation and greater flexibility may result in environmental policies that are better adapted to the local physical and socio-economic situations. But, in China, as elsewhere, decentralisation does not automatically result in better protection of the environment, as local authorities typically give preference to economic growth and investments over the progressive development of environmental policies and stringent enforcement of environmental regulation and standards. As both an active civil society and accountability mechanisms are poorly developed, decentralisation in China's environmental policy is weakened by the absence of critical correction mechanisms.[4] But a larger degree of freedom for local authorities does result, for better or for worse, in a growing diversity amongst the Chinese provinces and towns in how they deal with local and regional environmental challenges. It also contributes to differences in success and failure, which divide not only along lines of economic prosperity, where the richer eastern provinces and towns are systematically more concerned with, and prepared to invest in, environmental reform, but also within the eastern part of China, where environmental prioritisation differs among towns (Zhang, 2002).

Not unlike other countries, decentralisation tendencies in China come along with counter tendencies. Environmental protection projects, for instance, are increasingly financed centrally. The central state has also responded to the growing relative autonomy of local authorities by refining their system of evaluating towns and town governments, and including environmental indicators in it, such as the Urban Environmental Quality Examination System and the National Environmental Model City (Rock, 2002; Economy, this volume). Via such mechanisms, local leaders are no longer only judged according to political and economic criteria, but also according to environmental results. Mayors are often required to sign documents guaranteeing that they meet certain environmental targets.

A second transition in environmental governance follows the separation between state owned enterprises (SOE) and the line ministries and local governments (in the case of Town and Village Enterprises) that were originally responsible for them (see Shi and Zhang, this volume).[5] There is a slow but steady process of transferring decision-making on production units from the political and party influence to economic domains, where the logics of markets and profits are dominant.[6] Although local level governments in particular are often reluctant to give up direct relations with successful enterprises because of the linkages to financial resources, there is an unmistakable tendency for enterprises to secure growing autonomy from political agents. This development opens opportunities for more stringent environmental control and enforcement as the 'protection' of these SOEs by line ministries and bureaux at all government levels is less direct. It also sets preferential conditions for the stronger rule of – environmental – law (see below). But it does not solve one of the key problems of environmental governance: the low priority given to environmental state organisations vis-à-vis their economic and other counterparts. The progress in strengthening and empowering China's environmental authorities is ambivalent, as is common elsewhere around the world. While the national environmental authority in Beijing has strengthened its position vis-à-vis other ministries and agencies, this is not always the case at the local level, where more than incidentally the EPBs are part of – and thus subservient to – an economic state organisation (see Vermeer, 1998; Zhang, 2002; Lo & Tang, this volume). Also, at the central level interdepartmental struggles continue to fragment environmental authority (Jahiel, 1998; Lo & Xing, 1999). For instance, the State Economic and Trade Commission (SETC) is the primary responsible party for the new 2002 Cleaner Production Promotion Law, rather than SEPA. The former is also responsible for energy conservation policy (Chen & Porter, 2000). The Ministry of Science and Technology won the battle over the coordination of China's Agenda 21 programme from SEPA, despite heavy influence and lobbying from UNDP (Buen, 2000). And Keeley reports in this volume on the struggles around GMO regulation.

Lastly, the strengthening of the rule of law can be identified as a modernisation in environmental politics, closely tied to the emergence of a market economy. The system of environmental laws has led to the setting of environmental quality standards and emission discharge levels, and the establishment of a legal framework for various implementation programmes.[7] But usually the environmental programmes themselves, the administrative decisions related to the implementation of standards, and the bargaining between administrations and polluters on targets have been more influential for environmental reform than the laws and regulations *per se*. Being in conflict with the law is usually still less problematic than being in conflict with administrations and programmes, and most of the massive clean-up programmes were not so much derived from environmental laws (although they were not in conflict with them), but rather based on administrative decisions taken at the top.[8] The same is true for enforcement of national environmental laws at the local level. The rather vague laws are interpreted in very different ways by EPBs, often under strong administrative influence from the local mayor's office (see Ma & Ortolano, 2000). Courts have been marginally involved in enforcement and EPBs use them only as a last resort to enforce environmental laws to which polluters refuse to adhere (Jahiel, 1998). More recently, there are signs that the rule of law is taken more seriously in the field of environment, which has been triggered by the opening up of China to the global economy and polity. This is paralleled by stronger (financial) punishments and legal procedures initiated by, for instance, environmental NGOs such as the Centre for Legal Assistance to Pollution Victims (CLAPV) in Beijing. One of the potential threats to the environment is, of course, the institutional void that can emerge when the administrative system loses its power over environmental protection, while the rule of law has been only weakly institutionalised in the field of environment.

Market Incentives and Economic Actors

Traditionally, centrally planned economies did a poor job in setting the right price signals for a sustainable use of natural resources and a minimisation of environmental pollution. With a turn to a market-oriented growth model one would expect this to change. In contemporary China, environmental interests are indeed being slowly institutionalised in the economic domain of prices, markets, and competition, in three ways.

First, subsidies on natural resource prices are increasingly being abandoned and prices for natural resources tend to move to cost prices (see Aden & Sinton on energy, this volume). That these changes differ regionally is shown by the example of water prices: in 1996 it cost 0.843 yuan to supply a ton of water, while the average price of water in Hebei province was 0.6–0.9 yuan/ton, 0.637 yuan in Beijing and only 0.013 yuan in Hetao region (Lo & Xing, 1999; see also Nickum and Lee, this volume). To date, we have only witnessed relative improvements, as the cost prices rarely include costs for repair of damage and environmental externalities (and we know from the major flooding caused by forest felling that these externalities can be quite significant in monetary terms).

Second, clear attempts are being made to increase environmental fees and tax reductions[9], so that they do influence the (economic) decision-making of polluters. In particular, discharge fees (on water and air), first introduced in the 1980s, have become more common, both because they are an important source of income for local EPBs and a significant trigger for the implementation of environmental measures, albeit not to the same extent everywhere. Wang and Wheeler (1999) found that the fees are higher in heavily polluted and economically developed areas and that they do influence air and water emission reductions within companies. Fees are often only paid for discharging above the standard (see Ma & Ortolano, 2000). Notwithstanding the rhetoric of 'pollution prevention pays' and 'cleaner production' that have entered modern China since the 1990s, fees are still so low and monitoring is so weak that many enterprises risk payment, rather than installing environmental protection equipment or changing production processes. Many small and rural industries, in particular, have managed to escape payment due to lack of enforcement. The introduction of higher fees is by no means a smooth process. In 1992 NEPA proposed an increase of 0.20 yuan per kg of discharged sulphur dioxide following coal burning (an increase of less than 1 per cent), to cover at least part of the environmental costs of desulphurisation.[10] Implementation was postponed first to 1996 and then only introduced as a pilot programme, which – in an extended version – was still the situation in 2000.

Third, market demand has started to take the environmental and health dimensions of products and production processes into account, especially in international markets that have increased so dramatically in the wake of China's accession to the WTO (see Shi & Zhang, and Jahiel, this volume). As far back as 1990 the import of Chinese refrigerators to the EU was restricted due to the use of CFCs as a cooling agent (Vermeer, 1998), but that was still an exception. Today, these kinds of international (especially European, North American, and Japanese) market trends towards greener products and production processes are felt in many more product categories, pushing for instance to higher levels of ISO certification, and growing interest for cleaner production, eco-labelling systems and industrial ecology initiatives (Shi, 2003; Shi *et al.*, 2003). Like most developing economies, the Chinese domestic market still poorly articulates environmental interests, and green or healthy labelling is underdeveloped. SEPA (2003) reports, however, on the establishment of eight organic food certification institutions and there is labelling of GMO products.

In general, domestic economic actors hardly articulate environmental interests. Insurance companies, banks, public utility companies, business associations, general corporations and others do not yet play any significant role in environmental governance. Sometimes they even impede environmental improvements. For instance, local banks are not eager to lend money to polluters for environmental investments, according to a World Bank study (Spofford *et al.*, 1996). There are three major exceptions to the absence of economic actors in the ecological modernisation of the Chinese economy: large Chinese firms that operate in an international market, the environmental industry and R&D institutions.

- Large Chinese and joint venture firms that operate for and in a global market articulate stringent environmental standards and practices, but also try to pass these new standards and practices on to their customers and state organisations, pushing the domestic level playing field towards international levels (Jahiel, this issue; Shi & Zhang, this volume). The Chinese petrochemical company Petrochina, for instance, is currently investing in several countries and has joint venture operations in China with several western oil multinationals. It strongly feels the need to acquire international recognised environmental management knowledge, standards and emission levels, allowing it to compete on a global market. The involvement of the multinational Shell in the development of the east–west oil pipeline resulted in significant environmental and democratic improvements, also affecting its Chinese counterpart (Seymour *et al.*, 2005).
- The expanding environmental industry presses for the greening of production and consumption processes, as it has a clear interest in growing environmental regulation and reform (Sun, 2001; Liu *et al.*, 2005; Figure 3). Also, foreign environment and utility companies and consultancies (such as the French water company Vivendi) are increasingly entering the Chinese market, bringing about an upward push towards more stringent environmental standards.
- Research and development institutions, from the ones linked to universities to those related to the line ministries and bureaux, are increasingly focusing their attention on environmental externalities, and articulate environmental interests among decision-making institutions within both the economic and

the political domains. In universities a growing number of environmental departments, centres and curricula were established in the late 1990s.

Beyond State and Market: Civil Society

Besides an emerging NGO sector and increasing local activism and complaints, civil society's contribution to environmental reform is to be found in two other arrangements: the rise of critical environmental coverage in the media, and the importance of unwritten social norms, rules and codes of conduct.

Environmental Protests and (GO)NGOs

China has a very recent history of environmental NGOs and other social organisations that articulate and lobby for environmental interests and ideas of civil society amongst political and economic decision-makers (see Qing & Vermeer, 1999; Ho, 2001; Guobin Yang, 2005; Martens, this volume). As the first environmental NGO was only established in the mid 1990s the history of this sector is rather short. For a long time Government-Organised NGOs, such as the Beijing Environmental Protection Organisation and China Environment Fund, dominated the environmental 'civil society' sector.[11] They had, and still have, more freedom of registration and manoeuvre due to their close links with state agencies. Through closed networks with policy-makers and their expert knowledge, these GONGOs articulate environmental interests and bring them into state and market institutions. In doing so GONGOs play a role in bridging the gap between NGOs and civil society on the one hand and the state on the other, thus 'becoming an important, non-state arena for China's environmental politics' (Wu, 2002: 48). Recently, these GONGOs have gained more organisational, financial and political independence and autonomy from the state, and are (thus) evaluated more positively by Western scholars. At the same time, environmental NGOs are developing rapidly, although these NGOs remain embedded in the Chinese state. Figures on the number of NGOs are unreliable. Economy (2005) estimates around 2,000 registered NGOs and an equal amount of unregistered ones, while Guobin Yang (2005) provides more moderate (though rapidly increasing) numbers.[12] These – mostly local or provincial – NGOs are often not very adversarial or confrontational, but rather expert or awareness-raising organisations, such as Global Village. The 'political room' for a western-style environmental movement still seems limited, but compared to a decade ago this room is expanding. While in some of the Central and East European centrally planned economies environmental NGOs played a role in articulating environmental and other protests against the ruling social order, in China environmental NGOs have been marginal until now in pushing for environmental reform of the Chinese economy or polity. International NGOs such as Greenpeace and WWF have invested major efforts in further stimulating the environmental movement in China, with ambivalent successes.

Together with economic liberalisation, decentralisation of decision-making and experiments with local democratisation there is also growing pressure from – often unorganised – citizens on local (environmental) authorities to reduce environmental pollution. Dasgupta and Wheeler (1996) estimated that local and provincial authorities responded to over 130,000 complaints annually in the period 1991–1993, while Chinese data show lower figures for these years but a sharp increase from the mid 1990s onward, to over 600,000 in 2004 (Figure 4). In most of the cities and towns systems of complaints and hotlines have been installed, albeit with varying levels of use and effect.[13] In China, this system of complaints and the growing attention of (state-owned and state-controlled) media to environmental pollution and environmental mismanagement are more important than NGOs in influencing economic and political decision-makers. But the complaints system is a poor form of 'participation' by civil society in environmental governance, as Martens (this volume) explains in more detail. It focuses only on (sensible) monitoring after pollution has happened, at a time where the 'expropriation of the senses' needs a preventive and precautionary approach. A more systematic involvement of citizens and civil society in the stage of project development with full access to information is largely missing, although the recent revision of the Environmental Impact Assessment regulations seems to enable larger participation by the public.

Media and Environment

In an interesting analysis De Burgh (2003) explains the recent major changes in Chinese journalistic practices and media. After decades of state-ownership and full control, parts of the media have been given economic independence, whilst some competition has emerged between newspapers (but not yet on television). These changes created new pressures to secure a major share of newspaper funding from advertisements (up to 60 per cent in newspapers) and more attention to consumer preferences.[14] Media staff are increasingly recruited

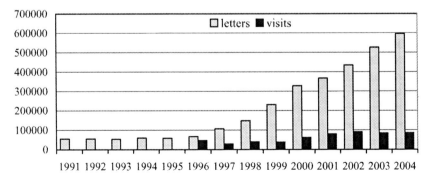

Figure 4. Environmental complaints by letters and visits to EPBs. *Source: China Environment Statistical Reports* (1991–2004).

outside party control and financial incentives are used to attract good professionals (Fang, 2002). In addition, state controls have been relaxed somewhat and reporting freedom has increased, although state and party control remains tight, especially over more sensitive issues.[15] The Chinese media clearly serve two masters, the Party and the market (Hong Lui, 1998; Latham, 2000), and seem constantly to test the limits of what the Party will allow (Li Junhui, 2005), which seems to be a moving target. Within this transitional state the global media, such as satellite TV, are still very much dependent on the Chinese authorities, and can only broadcast and sell under specified conditions for certain markets (Sparks, 2005).

Environmental issues are increasingly considered non-sensitive issues, which has turned the reporting of environmental accidents, disasters and routine cases of pollution breaching standards into a more regular practice in China.[16] Research by Li Junhui (2005) on newspaper reporting on dams, arguably one of the most sensitive environmental issues in China, and of Wang (2005) on industrial parks, illustrate that local newspapers in particular feel the pressure from local state authorities to refrain from reporting critically, while national bans on reporting emerge when minority issues and national (security and economic) interests are involved. Based on several sources Guobin Yang (2005) concludes that environmental NGOs and their campaigns have been treated favourably in the Chinese newspapers from their emergence in the mid 1990s onwards. There are close ties between the Chinese conventional media (newspapers, radio, television) and environmental NGOs (Hu Kanping, 2001; Xie & Mol, 2006), and, perhaps not coincidentally, several green NGOs are led by (former) professional journalists. These close ties arise also from the fact that environmental NGOs are a source of news, and pollution victims and environmental NGOs need the media to build up pressure.[17] While this freedom has caused greater uncertainty among journalists and media decision-makers about what is and what is not allowed, by the same token most journalists and media are decreasingly willing to accept simple top-down Party directions. Especially since SARS the scope for revealing environmental information has expanded.[18] The emerging 'investigative journalism' also focuses on scrutinising authority, although journalists and media seldom touch upon 'Chinese leaders in action' or challenge the (local) state legitimacy, unless it is allowed from above. Transparency has increased in environmental governance, but governmental control is still felt and transparency in environmental governance through these media is a far from routine matter.

The Internet has further expanded the possibilities for free media access and production, but here also the state is present. The Chinese government tries to remain in control of the Internet, for instance by monitoring Internet use of consumers, requiring registration at local security agencies and limiting links or gateways between national and international networks. It puts cameras in internet cafes, imposes temporary bans on them and requests identification from users. It closes websites, limits access to and production of news sites and weblogs, blocks access to 'undesirable' websites, intimidates actual and potential users, imposes restrictive policies on internet service providers. Not surprisingly, the government strongly backs international calls for further state control of the world wide web, for instance at the Tunis UN World Summit on the Information Society in November 2005.[19]

Social Norms, Rules and Codes of Conduct

Informal social norms, rules and unwritten codes of conduct play an important role in structuring human action. These rules are strongly anchored in Chinese civil society, rather than in the formal institutions of state and market, and may play an important role in environmental reform. Ma and Ortolano (2000) mention three major non-formal rules: respect for authority and status even if it conflicts with the formal institutions; the social connections or *guanxi* that play a major role in organising social life in China; and the moral authority and social capital that is included in the concept of (losing, maintaining or gaining) 'face'. With the growing importance attached to environmental protection, these and other 'informal' rules and institutions are put to work for environmental goals and rationalities. *Guanxi* and 'face' play a role in environmental protection, where informal networks of social relations are formed around environmental programmes and dispute resolutions, and social capital is built via environmental awards, prices, and media coverage. If we are to understand environmental reform dynamics in China, we have to understand how and to what extent these informal institutions, networks, and connections articulate environmental rationalities via, for instance, the inclusion of environmental norms in social capital and moral authority and the increase of the status of environmental authorities. These dynamics of course do not operate either in the same way or with equal strength in a rich modern metropolitan city such as Shanghai, as they do in poor western rural regions.

Global Integration

The increasing (especially economic, but also political) integration of China in the world has its influence on domestic environmental governance. But compared to the significant influence of foreign pressure and assistance that is sometimes exerted on national environmental policy in other Asian countries, China has been reluctant to accept assistance under stringent environmental conditions. The Three Gorges Dam is a clear example, where China ignored both foreign pressure against the dam and threats to withhold international loans for this project.[20] Moreover, in international negotiations for Multilateral Environmental Agreements, Chinese authorities are often hesitant to support stringent environmental policies that could rebound on domestic efforts (see Johnston, 1998; McElroy *et al.*, 1998; Chen & Porter, 2000), although China has signed and ratified most of the important MEAs.

However, on less controversial issues foreign assistance programmes have made a clear contribution to and/or influenced China's environmental policies and programmes. Between 1991 and 1995 US$1.2 billion foreign capital was invested in environmental protection in China (Vermeer, 1998). More recently, China has become an object of considerable international attention as well as environmental funding, via several MEAs and multilateral institutions such as the World Bank, Asian Development Bank (ADB) and the Global Environment Facility (see Huq *et al.*, 1999) and the United Nations Environment Programme. By the end of the 1990s the World Bank and the ADB together provided US$800 million for environmental loans in China annually. Asuka-Zhang (1999) illustrates the significance of Japanese environmental official development assistance (ODA) and environmental technology transfer to China. It is estimated that by the end of the 1990s around 15 per cent of China's total environment-related spending originated from bi- and multilateral lending and aid (Tremayne & De Waal, 1998). Foreign projects and international experts had a significant influence on the development and introduction of ISO 14001 certified environmental management systems and of cleaner production, resulting finally in the 2002 Cleaner Production Promotion Law (Mol & Liu, 2005). The phasing-out of CFC use following the Montreal Protocol has been another example. Directly after the Montreal Protocol negotiations (1987) China increased its CFC production – by some 100 per cent between 1986 and 1994 (Held *et al.*, 1999) – becoming the world leader in CFC production and consumption in 1996. Then, in response to international aid and potential trade bans by OECD countries, from the mid 1990s it stabilised CFC production and saw consumption fall, before production began to decline in 2000.[21]

The recent growing openness to and integration in the global economy and polity will only increase international influence on China's domestic environmental reform. For instance, China's membership of the WTO will enhance the importance of the ISO and other international standards in international, but also increasingly in domestic, business interactions (see Jahiel, this issue). And it will make China more vulnerable to international criticism of its domestic environmental performance. But international integration will also result in a growing role for China in setting the agenda and influencing the outcomes of international negotiations and agreements, including those affecting the environment. China will become increasingly important in international environmental negotiations and will exercise increasing power in directing the outcomes of these negotiations, for better or for worse.

This Volume

It is against the background of immense (national and global) environmental challenges, a future world hegemonic power in transition and a national system of environmental governance that is still in development, that this issue should be placed. All the contributions brought together start their analysis from the huge environmental challenges China and the world are facing, following

China's ongoing economic development. But instead of reinforcing the apocalyptic environmental portraits that seem to have become dominant in the international policy and scientific circles (see Liu and Diamond, 2005), this volume focuses on and analyses the unprecedented dynamics in environmental governance that China is developing today. Whether or not these institutional, social and economic innovations and transformations in environmental governance will form a sufficient answer to the current and future environmental challenges cannot yet be answered. But the various contributions in this volume illustrate the significant level of reflexivity that has become institutionalised in today's modern world. The times of denying or trivialising environmental challenges have passed. Having said that, a whole set of new questions emerges: on successful forms and institutions of environmental governance in a transitional economy, on the democratic underpinnings of major environmental transitions, on the international interdependencies of environmental reform programmes, on the changing power relations that come along with a programme of ecological modernisation, both domestically and internationally. These kinds of question form the heart of the analysis in the various articles.

The first three contributions deal with the institutional changes in the economy, the political–administrative system and civil society, respectively. Elizabeth Economy analyses how innovative economic mechanisms and institutions are being developed in China to deal with environmental challenges. Carlos Lo and Shui-Yan Tang look into the changes in local systems of environmental authorities and institutions, taking Guangdong province as a case study area. Susan Martens investigates the various Chinese environmental frames through which citizen consumers are, and will be, involved in environmental reforms. Subsequently, four articles assess environmental governance developments in four major areas or sectors. Through a comparative analysis of two major watersheds, James Nickum and Yok-Shiu Lee investigate the similarities and differences in water governance in China. Nathaniel Aden and Jonathan Sinton analyse one of the major environmental challenges of China: the greening of its energy system to cope with greenhouse gas emissions and ever growing natural resource demands. Han Shi and Lei Zhang report on the industrial transformations of what is often labelled the world's workplace: the ongoing modernisation and environmental reform of what used to be one of the most inefficient and backward industrial systems in the world. In the last sectoral analysis, James Keeley looks at one of the key environmental challenges of the future: genetic modification. Finally, Abigail Jahiel sets developments in China into a wider context by investigating what the ongoing liberalisation of the Chinese economy, and especially its inclusion in the World Trade Organisation scheme, means for the environment and environmental institutions.

In the concluding article, we bring the various contributions together to assess the major developments that are currently taking place or are in development with respect to China's environmental governance.

Acknowledgements

The authors would like to thank Richard Edmonds for his helpful comments on an earlier version of this paper.

Notes

1. See amongst others the various polls that are regularly organised in China on environmental awareness and problem definitions: Fang (1999); SEPA (1999); Stockholm Environmental Institute (2002); Lee (2005).
2. In 2000 there were over 80,000 environmental staff at the county level (in more than 7000 institutions), 35,000 staff at the city level (in 1700 institutions), almost 11,000 staff at the provincial level and some 3000 staff at the national level (together in some 300 institutions) (SEPA, 2001).
3. The annual 'Report on the State of the Environment in China' by SEPA usually contains data on emissions and environmental quality, but there are major inconsistencies in data presentation between 1997 and 2004 (see: www.zhb.gov.cn/english/SOE for the various annual national environmental reports and the related statistics). The voluminous annual China Environment Statistical Report provides more detailed environmental data (and appears from 2005 onwards also in English).
4. One can, however, witness increased opportunities for public involvement in policy making processes, such as the new Environmental Impact Assessment Law of 2003. Nevertheless, these levels of, and opportunities for, public involvement fall far short of western practices and standards (see Wang *et al.*, 2003).
5. From research on steel enterprises, Fisher-Vanden (2003) reports that within Chinese state-owned enterprises decentralisation in firm management improves the incorporation of new and more energy and environmentally efficient technology.
6. By the end of the 1990s many state owned enterprises had full decision-making power for production, sales, purchasing and investments. But in most cases relations between these enterprises and state authorities are still intricate and local agencies still succeed in extracting funds from profitable enterprises for public works or other purposes, in subsidising inefficient enterprises and in influencing decisions at enterprises. This is also valid in the case of TVIEs, as Zhang (2002) has shown for counties in Anhui and Jiangsu provinces.
7. The major eight national environmental programmes are: environmental impact assessment; three synchronizations; pollution discharge fee system; pollution control with deadlines; discharge permit system; assessment of urban environmental quality; centralised control of pollution and the environmental responsibility system. The first three date from the late 1970s, the last three were implemented later to manage problems the first three could not handle (for further details see Ma & Ortolano, 2000).
8. Most sinologists who aim to understand the state environmental protection system pay only marginal attention to environmental laws and the enforcement of environmental laws, preferring to concentrate on administrative measures and campaigns (see Jahiel, 1998; Vermeer, 1998; Ma & Ortolano, 2000).
9. Tax reductions are sometimes offered if environmental goals are reached, such as in the case of energy saving in steel plants and other heavy energy consuming industries (cf. Chen & Porter, 2000).
10. 'Notification on Implementation of Pilot Programme of Levy on Industrial Sulphur Dioxide Pollution by Coal Burning'. State Council Letter (1996#24) agreed on the pilot implementation via SEPA's 'Report on Pilot Programme of Sulphur Dioxide Discharge Fee'.
11. There are many kinds of GONGO, including foundations, education centres, research institutions, and industry associations. They are able to play a major role due to their less restrictive institutional structure, their expertise and the personal connections.

12. In China, NGOs need to be registered. Registration can be in different forms, but usually it means that these NGOs function under the umbrella of another, existing organisation (a governmental organisation, a university, a research institute or a private business).
13. Dasgupta and Wheeler (1996) show that the average number of environmental complaints of major cities and provinces in one year ranges from 55.0 per 100,000 inhabitants in Shanghai to 1.7 per 100,000 inhabitants for the northwestern province Gansu. According to Chinese official sources most provincial EPBs respond to over 80 per cent of these (telephone, letter and face-to-face visits) complaints (China Environment Statistical Reports, 1991–2004).
14. In 2002 there were some 2100 newspapers in China, some of them organised in groups (data from the World Association of Newspapers, 2003; http://www.wan-press.org/). Few are national newspapers. Most are either regionally restricted (provincial, major cities), for special target groups (e.g. Youth League) or published by special organisations and agencies (such as for instance SEPA).
15. As Fang (2002) and Li Junhui (2005) explain Chinese news media are regulated and controlled via five mechanisms, of which the first two are the most important: government administrative system; Party committees; the legal system; social surveillance of other parties and social groups; (self)regulation from associations in the news industries.
16. A survey by the Chinese NGO Friends of Nature amongst a significant number of national, provincial and local newspapers showed that coverage of environmental items in these newspapers especially increased in the second part of the 1990s (Friends of Nature, 2000). This seems no different in the other traditional media.
17. Shang Hongbo (2004) studied how pollution victims in four cases of industrial pollution in different parts of China used the media to build up pressure once the (local and national) authorities proved unreceptive to their complaints. Alongside these strategies of informational governance, litigation, protesting and mediation with the polluters are other strategies used by these victims.
18. Interview Tsinghua University professor, October 31, 2005; interview deputy director EMC, November 4, 2005; interview Chinese Academy of Sciences division head, November 3, 2005.
19. See for instance Sinclair (2002); Wilson (2004); Downing (2005).
20. Of course, China is big enough to shift international loans to less environmentally and socially controversial projects, setting free national finances for the more controversial ones.
21. Data from the Ozone secretariat of UNEP: http://www.unep.org/ozone

References

Andrews-Speed, P., Dow, S. & Gao, Z. (1999) 'A provisional evaluation of the 1998 reforms to China's government and state sector: the case of the energy industry', *Journal of the Centre for Energy, Petroleum and Mineral Law and Policy* 4(7): 1–11 (www.dundee.ac.uk/cepmlp/journal).

ASEAN (2001) *Second ASEAN State of the Environment Report* (Jakarta: ASEAN).

Asuka-Zhang, S. (1999) 'Transfer of environmentally sound technologies from Japan to China', *Environmental Impact Assessment Review* 19(5–6): 553–67.

Buen, J. (2000) 'Challenges facing the utilisation of transferred sustainable technology in China: the case of China's Agenda 21 Project 6–8', *Sinosphere* 3(1): 13–23.

Chandler, W., Schaeffer, R., Dadi, Z., Shukla, P., Tudela, F., Davidson, O. & Alpan-Atamer, S. (2002) *Climate Change Mitigation in Developing Countries. Brazil, China, India, Mexico, South Africa, and Turkey* (Arlington, VA: Pew Center on Global Climate Change).

Chen, Z. & Porter, R. (2000) 'Energy management and environmental awareness in China's enterprises', *Energy Policy* 28: 49–63.

Dasgupta, S. & Wheeler, D. (1996) 'Citizen complaints as environmental indicators: evidence from China'. World Bank Policy Research Working Paper, Washington, DC.

De Burgh, H. (2003) *The Chinese Journalist* (London: Routledge).

DeBardeleben, J. (1985) *The Environment and Marxism–Leninism – the Soviet and East German Experience* (Boulder, CO: Westview Press).

Downing, J. (2005) 'Activist media, civil society and social movements', in W. de Jong, M. Shaw & N. Stammers (eds.) *Global Activism, Global Media* (London: Pluto Press), pp. 149–64.

Economy, E. (2005) 'China's environmental movement'. Testimony before the Congressional Executive Commission on China Roundtable on Environmental NGOs in China: Encouraging Action and Addressing Public Grievances, Washington, DC.

Fang, H. (2002) *The History of Journalism and Communication in China* (Beijing: Renmin University Press).

Fang, Y. (1999) 'Zhongguo shimin de Huanjing yishi diaocha: Beijing he Shanghai' (A survey of Chinese residents' environmental consciousness in Beijing and Shanghai), in Xi Xiaolin & Xu Qinghia (eds.) *Zhongguo gongzhong huanjing yishi diaocha (A survey of China's public environmental consiousness)* (Beijing: Zhongguo huanjing kexue chubanshe (China Environmental Science Press)), pp. 109–30.

Fisher-Vanden, K. (2003) 'Management structure and technology diffusion in Chinese state-owned enterprises', *Energy Policy* 31: 247–57.

Friends of Nature (2000) *Chinese Newspapers' Environmental Awareness* (Beijing: Friends of Nature).

Guobin Yang (2005) 'Environmental NGOs and institutional dynamics in China', *China Quarterly* 181: 47–66.

Held, D., McGrew, A., Goldblatt, D. & Perraton, J. (1999) *Global Transformations. Politics, Economics and Culture* (Stanford, CA: Stanford University Press).

Ho, P. (2001) 'Greening without conflict? Environmentalism, NGOs and civil society in China', *Development and Change* 32(5): 893–921.

Hong Lui (1998) 'Profit or ideology? The Chinese press between party and market', *Media, Culture and Society* 20: 31–41.

Hu Kanping (2001) 'Harmony in diversity: the relationship between environmental journalism and green NGOs in China', in J. Turner & F. Wu (eds.) *Green NGOs and Environmental Journalist Forum: a Meeting of Environmentalists in Mainland China, Hong Kong and Taiwan* (Washington, DC: Woodrow Wilson Centre), pp. 30–1.

Huq, A., Lohani, B., Jalal, K. & Ouano, E. (1999) 'The Asian Development Bank's role in promoting cleaner production in the People's Republic of China', *Environmental Impact Assessment Review* 19(5–6): 541–52.

Jahiel, A. (1998) 'The organization of environmental protection in China', *China Quarterly* 156: 757–87.

Jänicke, M. (1986) *Staatsversagen. Die Ohnmacht der Politik in die Industriegesellshaft* (Munich: Piper).

Jänicke, M. (1993) 'Über ökologische und politieke Modernisierungen', *Zeitschrift für Umweltpolitik und Umweltrecht* 2: 159–75.

Johnston, A. (1998) 'China and international environmental institutions: a decision rule analysis', in McElroy, Nielsen & Lydon (eds.), pp. 555–99.

Latham, K. (2000) 'Nothing but the truth: news media, power and hegemony in south China', *China Quarterly* 163: 633–54.

Lee, Y. (2005) 'Public environmental consciousness in China: early empirical evidence', in K. Day (ed.) *China's Environment and the Challenge of Sustainable Development* (Armonk, NY: M. E. Sharpe), pp. 60–5.

Li Junhui (2005) 'The position of Chinese newspapers in the framing of environmental issues', MSc thesis, Wageningen University.

Liu, J. & Diamond, J. (2005) 'China's environment in a globalizing world', *Nature* 435: 1179–86.

Liu, Y., Mol, A. & Chen, J. (2005) 'Environmental industries in China: barriers and opportunities between state and market', *International Journal of Environment and Sustainable Development* 4(3): 269–89.

Lo, F.-C. & Xing, Y.-Q. (eds.) (1999) *China's Sustainable Development Framework. Summary Report* (Tokyo: United Nations University).

Lothspeich, R. & Chen, A. (1997) 'Environmental protection in the People's Republic of China', *Journal of Contemporary China* 6(14): 33–60.

Ma, X. & Ortolano, L. (2000) *Environmental Regulation in China. Institutions, Enforcement, and Compliance* (Lanham, MD: Rowman and Littlefield).

McElroy, M., Nielsen, C. & Lydon, P. (eds.) (1998) *Energizing China. Reconciling Environmental Protection and Economic Growth* (Newton, MA: Harvard University Press).

Mol, A. (2002) 'Political modernisation and environmental governance: between delinking and linking', *Europæa. Journal of the Europeanists* 8(1–2): 169–86.

Mol, A. & Liu, Y. (2005) 'Institutionalizing cleaner production in China: the Cleaner Production Promotion Law', *International Journal of Environment and Sustainable Development* 4(3): 227–45.

Nygard, J. & Guo, X. (2001) *Environmental Management of Chinese Township and Village Industrial Enterprises (TVIEs)* (Washington, DC/Beijing: World Bank and SEPA).

Qing, D. & Vermeer, E. (1999) 'Do good work, but do not offend the "old communists": recent activities of China's non-governmental environmental protection organizations and individuals', in W. Draguhn & R. Ash (eds.) *China's Economic Security* (Richmond, VA: Curzon Press), pp. 142–62.

Rock, M. (2002) 'Getting into the environment game: integrating environmental and economic policy-making in China and Taiwan', *American Behavioral Scientist* 45(9): 1435–55.

SEPA (1999) 'Quanguo Gongzhang Huanjing yishi diaocha baogao' (A survey of the nation's public environmental consiousness (summary)), *Huanjing jiaoyu (Environmental education)* 4: 25–7.

SEPA (2001) *Report on the State of the Environment in China 2000* (Beijing: State Environmental Protection Agency).

SEPA (2003) *Report on the State of the Environment in China 2002* (Beijing: State Environmental Protection Agency).

SEPA (2005) *Report on the State of the Environment in China 2004* (Beijing: State Environmental Protection Agency).

Seymour, M., Beach, M. & Lasiter, S. (2005) 'The challenge of positive influence: managing sustainable development on the West–East Pipeline Project', *China Environment Series* 7: 1–16.

Shang Hongbo (2004) 'The tactics and strategies used by collective pollution victims to defend their rights and interests in industrial pollution conflicts in China', MSc thesis, Wageningen University.

Shapiro, J. (2001) *Mao's War against Nature: Politics and the Environment in Revolutionary China* (Cambridge: Cambridge University Press).

Shi, H. (2003) 'Cleaner production in China', in A. Mol & J. van Buuren (eds.) *Greening Industrialization in Transitional Asian countries: China and Vietnam* (Lanham, MD: Lexington), pp. 63–82.

Shi, H., Moriguichi, Y. & Yang, J. (2003) 'Industrial ecology in China, part 1 and 2', *Journal of Industrial Ecology* 7(1): 5–8.

Sinclair, G. (2002) 'The internet in China: information revolution or authoritarian solution?' Available at http://www.geocities.com/gelaige79/intchin.pdf (Accessed 5 December 2005).

Sinton, J. & Fridley, D. (2001) 'Hot air and cold water: the unexpected fall in China's energy use', *China Environment Series* 4: 3–20.

Sinton, J. & Fridley, D. (2003) 'Comments on recent energy statistics from China', *Sinosphere* 6(2): 6–11.

Sparks, C. (2005) 'Media and the global public sphere: an evaluative approach', in W. de Jong, M. Shaw & N. Stammers (eds.) *Global Activism, Global Media* (London: Pluto Press), pp. 34–49.

Spofford, W., Ma, X., Ji, Z. & Smith, K. (1996) *Assessment of the Regulatory Framework for Water Pollution Control in the Xiaoqing River Basin: a Case Study of Jinan Municipality* (Washington, DC: World Bank).

Stockholm Environmental Institute (2002) *Making Green Development a Choice: China Human Development Report* (Oxford: Oxford University Press).

Sun, C. (2001) 'Paying for the environment in China: the growing role of the market', *China Environment Series* 4: 32–42.

Tremayne, B. & De Waal, P. (1998) 'Business opportunities for foreign firms related to China's environment', *China Quarterly* 156: 1016–41.

Vermeer, E. (1998) 'Industrial pollution in China and remedial policies', *China Quarterly* 156: 952–85.

Wang, H. & Wheeler, D. (1999) *Endogenous Enforcement and Effectiveness of China's Pollution Levy System* (Washington, DC: World Bank).

Wang, Q. (2005) 'Transparency in the grey box of China's environmental governance: a case study of print media coverage of an environmental controversy from the Pearl River Delta region', *Journal of Environment and Development* 14(2): 278–312.

Wang, Y., Morgan, R. & Cashmore, M. (2003) 'Environmental impact assessment of projects in the People's Republic of China: new law, old problems', *Environmental Impact Assessment Review* 23: 543–79.

Wilson III, E. (2004) *The Information Revolution and Developing Countries* (Cambridge, MA: MIT Press).

World Bank (1997) *Clear Water, Blue Skies* (Washington, DC: World Bank).

Wu, F. (2002) 'New partners or old brothers? GONGOs in transitional environmental advocacy in China', *China Environment Series* 5: 45–58.

Xie, L. & Mol, A. (2006) 'The role of *guanxi* in the emerging environmental movement in China', in A. McCright & T. Clark (eds.) *Community and Ecology* (Amsterdam: Elsevier/JAI) (in press).

Zhang, L. (2002) 'Ecologizing industrialization in Chinese small towns'. PhD thesis, Wageningen University.

Zhang, T. & Chen, J. (2003) 'Industrial environmental management in China', in A. Mol & J. van Buuren (eds.) *Greening Industrialization in Asian Transitional Economies: China and Vietnam* (Lanham, MD: Lexington), pp. 23–38.

Ziegler, C. (1983) 'Economic alternatives and administrative solutions in Soviet environmental protection', *Policy Studies Journal* 11(1): 175–88.

Environmental Governance: the Emerging Economic Dimension

ELIZABETH ECONOMY

Introduction

Chinese scholars through the centuries have provided detailed accounts of the impact of economic development on their country's environmental landscape. By the mid-1800s, wide swaths of northern China were desert; deforestation and poor agricultural practices had degraded vast tracts of land; overuse had depleted fish stocks; and small-scale factories had begun to pollute the country's water resources. Compounding the challenge of development were the pressures of China's burgeoning population and frequent wars, which took their own serious toll on the environment.

Nothing, however, could have prepared the world for the explosive growth of the Chinese economy at the end of the 20th and beginning of the 21st centuries. A raft of new government policies encouraged the privatisation of agriculture, the wholesale urbanisation of China's rural population, the development of tens of thousands of small-scale rural industries and an influx of international investment. The results have been staggering: hundreds of millions of Chinese have been lifted out of poverty; China's economy continues to grow at a rate of 8–12 per cent annually, as it has for two decades; and by the end of 2005, China was the fourth largest economy and third largest exporting nation in the world, after the United States and Germany.

Still, China's environment has paid a steep price for this economic success. The tens of thousands of small-scale factories – paper and pulp, electroplating, dyeing and chemical, among others – have brought unforeseen wealth to many rural communities, but have also polluted the water and poisoned the air. China's reliance on coal to fuel its economic growth has made the country home to five of the 10 most polluted cities in the world, as well as the largest producer of sulphur dioxide (SO_2). As agricultural, household and industrial consumption of water has skyrocketed, China's cities and towns face serious challenges from lack of water: relocating households where towns are sinking beneath sea level; undertaking large-scale river diversion projects; or simply doing without access to enough water to meet their daily needs. China's continued land degradation – from overgrazing, overploughing and deforestation – contributes to desertification and the migration of millions of Chinese in northern China.

Beyond the immediate impact on the environment, there are a range of secondary challenges the Chinese government must now confront. Local economies are clearly paying the price for their disregard of the environment as factories close due to lack of water or medical costs rise due to an increasing number of health-related pollution illnesses. Chinese officials increasingly source large-scale public health problems to poor air and water quality. Most troublesome perhaps from the perspective of the Chinese leadership, if local authorities ignore, or in worst cases evade, their responsibilities to care for the environment and thereby imperil the well-being of the people, social unrest often ensues.

Yet if China's economic reforms and development are responsible for much of the country's environmental and social welfare challenges, the leadership also views the economy as an essential dimension in any effective response to the growing environmental challenges. It is not only that the Chinese government attempts to merge economic development with environmental protection, in the best traditions of Brundtland's notion of sustainable development. Increasingly economic and market mechanisms, actors, sectors and dynamics are put to work in dealing with the environmental challenges of China's rapid modernisation process. Many of the leadership's current, overarching environmental initiatives such as green gross domestic product (GDP), the National Environmental Model City programme, tradable SO_2 permits, the steep increase in environmental investments and the uptake of international standards, labels and benchmarks are only possible by embracing the growing wealth of the country, its increasing engagement with the international economy, the aggressive invitation of multinationals and its transition from a socialist to a market economy.

While it is too early to declare the success or failure of what might be called the economisation of environmental governance, this article will explore the Chinese government's initial efforts to pursue these innovations in environmental governance and attempt to draw out, at least preliminarily, the factors that are likely to contribute to or inhibit effective implementation. It starts by developing a theoretical understanding of this economic dimension of environmental governance. Subsequently four example programmes and initiatives in China are assessed: green GDP, the National Environmental Model City programme, the engagement of the international business community and tradable emission permits.

Bringing the Economy into Environmental Governance

In most Western Organisation for Economic Co-operation and Development (OECD) countries it was only in the 1980s that governments turned their attention to the economy to develop and refine their environmental policy-making and governance systems. Following the so-called state failures in environmental governance (Jänicke, 1990) environmental scientists and environmental authorities shifted their attention from a purely state-led form of environmental governance, to include among others economic and market mechanisms, actors and dynamics. The clear products of this innovation in Western environmental governance look now all too familiar: they include market-based instruments, larger responsibilities and tasks for private actors, public–private arrangements in environmental governance, economic valuation techniques and approaches, a stronger reliance on environmental taxes (e.g. on water, energy, pesticides) and the privatisation of utility companies. This development has been analysed by, among others, ecological and political modernisation theorists (Huber, 1991; Mol & Sonnenfeld, 2000; van Tatenhove *et al.*, 2000).

China has been late in introducing economic dynamics and actors into its environmental governance system, basically for two reasons. First, as a centrally planned economy that only witnessed the start of a transitional process in the late 1980s, the state and political dynamics remained dominant in environmental governance throughout most of the 1990s. While the market was slowly entering the sectors that are more traditionally seen as part of the economy (such as industrial production and consumption, pricing, agriculture and labour allocation), environmental protection remained primarily the domain of state authorities, the Party and politics. This difference in the degree of reorientation to the market between sectors can of course be explained at least partly by the 'collective good' character of the environment (Ostrom, 1990). Second, China was throughout the 1990s a developing economy, and some argue it still is. Developing economies are rarely frontrunners in innovations in environmental governance, as priorities are elsewhere, environmental pressures are usually lower and the capacity of the state infrastructure to deal with environmental problems is weaker compared to more developed economies.

However, along the path of development, the Chinese state in the 1990s was increasingly confronted with state failures in environmental policy making, as has been reported extensively by both Chinese and international scholars (Economy, 2004). Some scholars of China's environment take a rather dismal view of any Chinese effort to address the country's environmental challenges. Geographer Vaclav Smil (1993), for example, concludes: 'There are no solutions within China's economic, technical, and manpower reach that could halt and reverse these degradative trends – not only during the 1990s but also during the first decade of the new century' (pp.192–193). Other scholars, such as Mike Rock (2002a), though critical of the massive task the Chinese state is facing in addressing the growing environmental challenges, have emphasised the developments, increased capacities and innovations in China's system of environmental governance. The exploration in this contribution on the growing innovations of using economic and market dimensions in environmental governance is consistent with the latter line of argument.

Thus, in response to the increasing environmental challenges of a rapidly developing economy, state failures in commanding and controlling the Chinese economy into sustainable paths and a growing integration in – and drawing experiences and assistance from – international research, economy and polity, China's environmental officials began to experiment with a wide range of policy initiatives and innovations that were more oriented towards and made use of the economic dimension. It is of course the advancement of the transition process that made possible and even triggered such developments. So, from the mid-1990s, we see a growing number of experiments in innovative environmental governance that tap into the economy, economic actors and market dynamics. Other innovations in the Chinese environmental governance system relate to informational politics (such as, for instance, disclosures, active policies on complaint systems, increasing openness of monitoring data, the start of eco-labelling programmes, corporate disclosure programmes), partly also driven by foreign assistance (e.g. Wang *et al.*, 2002; Guo, 2005). But decentralisation, environmental auditing of governmental projects and research and technology programmes on, for instance, the circular economy are also clear innovative approaches in environmental governance.

With respect to the economisation of environmental governance, the main focus in this contribution, a number of lines can be distinguished. First, the 1990s witnessed the start of the abandonment of subsidies and a shift to cost pricing of natural resources, such as energy and water. The main aims were both economic (in terms of full cost recovery) and environmental (efficient use of scarce natural resources). Prices for water and energy have been increasing substantially during the last decade, even sometimes reflecting (part of the) abatement costs, such as for water treatment or desulphurisation. A second main category of using economics in environmental governance is the shift of tasks and responsibilities from state agencies and authorities to market actors and business. Utility companies have experienced various models of public–private arrangements, foreign direct investments, build–operate–transfer constructions and the like. Also, with respect to monitoring and measurement, environmental protection bureaux (EPBs) have shifted part of their tasks to private consultants. Or rather: some parts of the local and provincial EPBs have turned into businesses responsible, in particular, for monitoring tasks for which EPBs pay (see also the contribution of Lo and Tang to this volume). A third line of economisation in environmental governance is related to a set of market-based instruments in conventional environmental policy making, of which the experiments with tradable emission permits (as reported below) are one of the most recent examples. Less well known developments are those related to China's Urban Environmental Quality Examination System (UEQES) and the subsequent National Environmental Model City programme. Fourthly, domestic environmental governance has been shaped increasingly through the input, ideas and experiences of businesses, particularly from those Chinese and foreign companies with international experience. New ideas about standards and certification (on production processes and products), a global level playing field, voluntary agreements, company environmental reporting and auditing have to a lesser or greater degree been pushed by multinational companies. Finally, China has started experimenting with the greening of all kinds of economic categories and principles, a tendency that can be labelled external integration. In fact here we deal less with the economisation of environmental governance, but rather with the ecologising of economic governance. The development and use of green GDP (as reported below) is one example. Others include ideas on industrial ecology or the circular economy, where economic and industrial development (such as the establishment of industrial parks) is conditioned and given direction via environmental and ecological principles.

These developments around the economic dimension of environmental governance have not found an easy and smooth path into Chinese institutions and, as yet, are in no way business-as-usual in Chinese environmental governance. Some of them have almost made it into common practice, such as natural resource pricing policies, but many others are still very experimental. Conflicting interests between regulatory agencies and market actors, between state authorities at different levels and between environmental authorities and line ministries at one level are some of the causes behind the stagnation of some innovations. But often it is also a lack of institutional capacity, their poor fit with existing institutional arrangements or contradictions with other policy programmes which seriously hamper their further development and implementation.

In order to get a sense of these economic innovations and ideas about environmental governance and of their progress and future potential, four cases are examined in this article. In exploring these cases the particular focus is on how in China these new ideas and innovative experiments are perceived and introduced, rather than on the detailed programmes themselves.

Green GDP

During 2004, the Chinese leadership launched a highly publicised campaign to promote the concept of green GDP as a mechanism for integrating economic development with environmental protection in the thinking and planning of local authorities.[1] The logic behind green GDP is quite simple, as Xu Xianchun, director general of the Department of National Accounts within the National Bureau of Statistics (NBS), has argued: 'It is unreasonable for people to seek economic growth while ignoring the importance of the resources and environment' (*Asia Pulse*, 12 March 2004). While the State Council first introduced the idea of green GDP to senior Chinese officials in 1994, there was not sufficient interest at the time to pursue it (*Business Daily Update*, 30 April 2004, section 30). In 2001, however, the NBS launched a green GDP experiment in Chongqing, and based on this experience, in 2004, began collaborating with the State Environmental Protection Administration (SEPA) to develop a workable framework for calculating green GDP (*Press Trust of India*, 2 September 2004).

A number of international actors are assisting China in developing a workable methodology for calculating green GDP. The US-based non-governmental organisation (NGO) Environmental Defense and the China Council for International Co-operation on Environment and Development both have been engaged in developing models for green GDP calculation. For the first phase, China is reportedly relying on methods established by the United Nations. By 1 September 2004 SEPA had indicated that China had successfully completed an initial framework accounting system for green GDP, and that the experiment would be launched in Beijing, Jilin, Shaanxi, Guangdong, Shanghai and Shanxi (*Sinocast*, 6 September 2004). Shanxi reported as early as August 2004, before the formal onset of the experiment, that it had calculated its green GDP, concluding in the process that if one accounted for environmental costs over the past decade, GDP would have barely grown (Mallet, 2004). By February 2005, the trial had been expanded to 10 cities and provinces, including Beijing, Tianjin, Chongqing, Hubei, Liaoning, Zhejiang, Anhui, Guangdong, Hainan and Sichuan. The trials are anticipated to take a year and will measure the levels of pollution produced by certain industries and projects, as well as the costs of remediation (Cheung, 2005). They will be divided into four stages – investigation, technical preparation, overall calculation and assessment – all of which will be concluded by February 2006 (*Asia Pulse*, 1 March 2005).

The political logic of green GDP is already being promulgated extensively and has demonstrated signs of taking hold among local officials. A Xinhua commentary issued in late March 2005 (New China News Agency, 23 March 2005) suggested that green GDP will become part of a new means of evaluating local officials' performance:

> The eastern region has taken the lead in exploring the question of how to establish a brand-new concept of political performance and a scientific evaluation mechanism. Shenzhen, Ningbo, Huzhou, and Shaoxing, and other localities have taken the lead in abolishing the practice of 'putting GDP in command' in assessing cadres' political performance and, on the

basis of promoting economic growth, paid more attention to social targets, humanistic targets, resource targets, and environmental targets. After introducing a green GDP concept, Suzhou proposed that in assessing and judging achievements in development, one should not merely look at the improvement of economic targets, such as total output value, tax revenue, and the combined volume of imports and exports, but should also include strengthening of democracy and the legal system, the prosperity of social undertakings, the prosperity standards of people's lives, improvement of the ecological environment, and enhancement in the degree of civilization... When paying attention to political performance, one has to pay attention to GDP, but it is wrong to focus on GDP alone.

In addition, at a regional level, environment officials have been quick to pick up on the potential of green GDP to serve their own political interests. In Anhui province, a rainstorm forced several reservoirs to discharge at the same time during July 2004, resulting in a large body of polluted water moving downstream and causing damages of US$37 million. Xu Jiasheng, deputy director for the Anhui Provincial Environmental Protection Bureau, stated: 'The best solution is to balance the relationship between the two (economic development and environmental protection). Environmental protection should be one of the criteria used to judge the performance of government officials and a green GDP calculating system should be adopted' (*China Daily Business Update*, 23 August 2004, section 23). After the Shanxi Academy of Social Sciences calculated the costs of the depletion of coal resources, exploitation of land, water consumed and environmental pollution, Dong Jibin, the deputy director of the academy, said that pollution costs alone amounted to 10.9 per cent of the official GDP and argued that based on the significant negative influence of pollution and resource exploitation on Shanxi's GDP, the central government needed to compensate Shanxi financially for its 'contribution and sacrifice' (Kynge, 2004, p.18).

Still some Chinese officials are sceptical of the utility of the green GDP concept and its potential to be accepted among local officials. In an interview posted on Xinhuanet.com, NBS spokesman Zheng Jingping stated: 'As for the green GDP project, the concept is good but the practice will be difficult'. Zheng also claimed that green GDP is not necessarily the best way to ensure sustainable development; it will not include, for example, health costs (Hua, 2005). He claimed that while consciousness raising had occurred, 'the public has pinned too much expectation on the system' (Hua, 2005). SEPA's vice-minister for environment Pan Yue has suggested two additional challenges. First, he notes, there is the difficulty of deciding the value of natural assets. The problem is 'to decide the value of natural assets when they are not traded in the market and thus have no price. How much is the cost of felling a part of forest? We don't know, because we don't know how to count the ensuing animal extinction and soil erosion'. The second difficulty relates to overcoming the resistance of local officials. In discussing the impact on regional officials, Pan noted: 'The new index will surely lead to a drastic fall of GDP figures in some areas and in turn bring a negative influence to local officials' promotion. Therefore, resistance is to be expected' (*Asia Pulse*, 5 April 2004). Still at a May 2005 gathering with many global chief executive officers in attendance, Pan highlighted the importance of green GDP and its link to official performance as one of the most important new government initiatives (Pan, 2005).

National Environmental Model City

One of China's flagship efforts to highlight the capacity of local officials to develop the economy and protect the environment simultaneously is the National Environmental Model City programme. Over the past eight years since its inception, attainment of National Environmental Model City status has become highly desirable for local leaders, who equate the title with the ability to attract foreign investment as well as enabling their municipalities to host large-scale international gatherings. This programme builds upon the UEQES, which SEPA had already introduced in 1989. The UEQES provides an annual quantitative examination of the environmental performance of major Chinese cities, based on various sets of indicators that are weighted. Cities are ranked on the basis of this systems and the ranks and scores are published, increasingly also via newspapers, radio and television. Mike Rock (2002a, b) has provided an excellent detailed analysis of how this system affects not only city industrial environmental policy but also the personal performance and priorities of mayors and governors in cities and provinces.

Achievement of National Environmental Model City status is attained by meeting a set of highly specific environment and development targets. For example, natural gas has to supply over 90 per cent of the energy within the city; the rate of solid waste treatment has to exceed 80 per cent; more than 50 per cent of urban domestic waste water must be treated; and per capita public green area for city dwellers must be at least $10\,m^2$ (China Council for the Promotion of International Trade Guangdong Sub-council, 2004). In addition, there are requirements that the city devote at least 1.5 per cent of GDP to environmental protection, per capita GDP exceed 10,000 yuan, and the city conduct a survey of at least 1 per cent of the population and receive a satisfaction rating of higher than 60 per cent for the urban environment (Badawi *et al.*, 2004). Some cities, such as Tongxiang, Zhejiang province, which has invested as much as 2.17 per cent of local revenues in environmental protection, have far exceeded the required 1.5 per cent in an effort to achieve this environmental model city status (*China Daily*, 15 October 2004).

The programme was initially part of a 1997 agreement between China and Japan, the Japan–China Environmental Development Model City Scheme. Dalian, Chongqing and Guiyang were the test cases, and the Japan Bank for International Co-operation, along with the Japanese Ministry of Foreign Affairs, local Japanese governments and the Japan International Co-operation

Agency all supported the initial test cities with financial assistance as well as technical capacity building (Japan Bank for International Co-operation, 2000). Since the initial three test cases, the programme has blossomed. As of January 2005, 44 Chinese cities and three urban districts hold the status of National Environmental Model City (*China Daily Business Update*, 7 January 2005, section 31). International assistance continues to be an important component of the process: co-operation with Singapore assisted Zhongshan in its bid to become a National Environmental Model City, for example, and the European Union is currently working with Nanjing to develop its action plan for attaining National Environmental Model City status.

The process by which a city becomes a National Environmental Model City typically takes several years. In 1984, for example, Shenyang was ranked one of the 10 most polluted cities in China. In 2001, the city's leaders declared that they wanted the city to achieve model environmental status. During the subsequent three years, Shenyang closed down over 600 factories, upgraded 300 more, removed industries from the downtown – replacing them with residential and business districts – and increased the number of wastewater treatment plants. The change was dramatic: in 2001, Shenyang experienced 162 good air quality days; by 2003 that number had increased to 298, far exceeding, for example, that of Beijing (*China Daily Business Update*, 13 January 2005, section 13). In December 2004, it passed national inspection to win the title of National Environmental Model City. Using the city's newfound status, the mayor, Chen Zhenggao, pushed to host the 2006 International Horticultural Exposition, seeing this as an opportunity to show off his city and gain more foreign investment. In an interview pitching Shenyang as the host, he claimed 'We cannot repeat past mistakes. Economic advancement at the cost of environmental pollution cannot be allowed to continue. Neither the environment nor economic development can afford to be sacrificed' (*China Daily Business Update*, 13 January 2005, section 13).

Yet simply articulating a desire to become a National Environmental Model City is not enough. Guangzhou, for example, beginning in 2000, worked with several international think tanks in an effort to improve local air quality. One analyst involved with the project stated:

> An important driving force behind the government's desire to reduce pollution is its ambition to meet the criteria for becoming an environmental model city ... The prestige inherent in this title is expected to attract even more outside investment. Other reasons for acquiring this title include being able to continue hosting the large international trade fairs that the city is known for. (Aunan, 2000, p. 2)

Five years later, however, Guangzhou has yet to attain this status, and its air and water quality continue to deteriorate, despite articulating its desire again in 2004 to be the first 'ultra-large' city to win the title (China Council for the Promotion of International Trade Guangdong Sub-council, 2004). Some of the challenge may stem from Guangzhou residents, themselves. A bid by the Guangzhou Price Control Administration to raise water prices in September 2005 was met by a firestorm of media and public criticism amidst accusations of a lack of popular representation in the decision-making process (*South China Morning Post*, 29 September 2005: 4).

SEPA has also added value to the effort by forcing cities to be re-evaluated on a regular basis. In 2004, SEPA threatened Shantou, Guangdong province, with the loss of its model city status. According to SEPA, in its most recent evaluation, Shantou failed to achieve the necessary standards on five areas and to provide adequate information on four others. After Shantou officials complained that their city had grown from 310 sq. km to 2000 sq. km, as a result of incorporating several less environmentally proactive regions in the process, SEPA agreed to give Shantou additional time to address these new challenges (Shi, 2005).

One downside of the programme, however, is that environmental model city status may well be achieved on the back of outlying areas. For example, Zhongshan, also in Guangdong province, simply shipped the most polluting enterprises outside the city limits, thereby achieving its status at the clear expense of the outlying areas. Of perhaps even greater concern is the fact that many heavy-polluting enterprises are simply moving from the coastal to the central and western provinces. As one Xinhua editorial noted:

> Development of China's central and western regions must not come at the expense of the environment ... Local officials must balance economic development and environmental protection, and short-term interests and long-term benefits. In particular, local governments in western China must avoid lowering environmental protection standards to attract investment ... China must now face the newly emerged phenomenon of heavy-polluting enterprises moving from coastal areas to the country's hinterland. China must apply the brakes on that trend. China must act promptly. (*China Daily Business Update*, 6 April 2005)

Engaging the International Business Community

With over US$1 billion of foreign direct investment flowing into China every week and overall trade levels totalling more than US$1.5 trillion in 2004 (Hong Kong Economic Information Agency, 2005), China's opening to the global economy has the potential to be a significant factor shaping its environmental protection effort. On the trade front, China's leaders have recognised the growing pressures that higher standards place on Chinese products. Vice-Premier Wu Yi, for example, has noted that food safety issues are problematic not only for domestic public health concerns but also for foreign trade. A range of Chinese food exports have been returned to the country as a result of excessive content of heavy metals resulting from pesticides and other pollution-related contaminants (Xinhua News Agency, 22 November 2004). At the same time, Xie Zhenhua, the former head of SEPA, stated that developed countries should 'eliminate trade barriers caused by too high environmental standards' in order to advance both environmental protection and international trade (Qin, 2004).

Perhaps the more pressing issue for China's leaders is how to ensure that the extraordinary level of foreign direct investment can be channelled in environmentally constructive rather than destructive forms. As Yok-shiu Lee and Alvin So (1999: 4) argue in their study of environmental movements in Asia, many multinationals transfer 'substandard industrial plants and hazardous production processes' to Asia in order to avoid the health and pollution standards of their home countries. Yet others, such as Jose Furtado *et al.* (2000) and Arthur Mol (2001), have suggested that economic development and integration into the international economy can positively affect environmental protection by optimising efficiency of resource use, upward harmonisation of environmental product and process standards, and increasing the standard of living, thus raising the demand for environmental protection (see also Jahiel, this volume).

For the most part, domestic Chinese companies have yet to realise the economic benefits of good environmental practices. This is of course true for the large number of small and medium-sized town and village industrial enterprises (Zhang, 2002), but also for the larger Chinese companies. In a 2004 Worldwide Fund for Nature survey of 182 of China's largest companies, only 18 per cent believed there was a link between good environmental practice and saving money (Lei *et al.*, 2005). Chinese officials have therefore called explicitly for foreign multinationals to lead in environmental protection, recognising the important role they can play in setting an example of best practices for domestic enterprises and transferring environmental knowledge, technology and management schemes to China.[2] China also often rewards companies that set such an example with positive press and even significant awards. Coca Cola China Limited, for example, received an honorary 'Mother River' award from eight Chinese ministries for its contribution to the Mother River Protection Programme, environmental protection and environmental education among Chinese youth (Xinhua News Agency, 18 January 2003).

Many multinationals have risen to the challenge, setting high environmental standards, transferring technology and supporting China's environmental goals more broadly. Royal Dutch Shell, for example, dramatically raised the environmental bar by hiring ERM, an environmental consulting firm, to conduct an environmental impact assessment for a joint venture project with Petrochina to bring natural gas from Xinjiang to Shanghai (a joint venture Shell never realised). Shell's environmental impact assessment forced the pipeline to be rerouted in several places to avoid areas where rare monkeys lived and camels traversed. Based on Shell's advice, Petrochina also avoided directly intersecting with remnants of the Great Wall (Royal Dutch Shell officials, 2002).

Other companies work closely with Chinese environmental officials to try to raise standards or ensure their enforcement in an effort to make their products competitive in the Chinese or international market. The South Africa-based Manganese Metal Company has been working with Chinese officials and businesses, conducting environmental impact assessments and hosting international symposia to try to transform the highly toxic process by which China manufactures manganese metal. Their efforts sparked new activity by the Chinese NGO Green Volunteers of Chongqing to undertake field work on the local manganese metal producers' impacts on the environment and nearby residents' public health (Manganese Metal Company official, 2004). Still other multinationals have been recognised for their support of a wide range of environmentally responsible behaviour: McDonalds promotes best energy efficiency practices in its restaurants; Dow Chemical is supporting a US$720,000 cleaner production programme in conjunction with SEPA; and BP supports a US$10 million clean energies research project at Qinghua University (Hildebrandt, 2004).

Perhaps the most ambitious multinational effort to help redirect China on to a new development path is one conducted under the auspices of the China–US Center for Sustainable Development. The centre was established in 1999, when Chinese Premier Zhu Rongji visited Washington, DC for the US–China Joint Commission on Science and Technology. The centre's Chinese and US boards of councillors are chaired by Vice Minister of Science and Technology Deng Nan and well-known 'green' architect William A. McDonough, respectively. The centre's purpose is to encourage both China and the United States to 'leapfrog past limitations and accelerate sustainable development' (China–US Center for Sustainable Development, 2002) by adopting design principles for industry and living – known as cradle to cradle or the circular economy – that are found in nature. In practice, Mr McDonough and the centre's staff have made an extraordinary effort to engage a number of multinationals in the process of designing a sustainable village and several 'new towns', in which the best principles of urban planning are utilised, and renewable energy resources, water conservation techniques and habitat preservation practices are the norm.

For example, companies such as BASF, Vermeer, BP Solar and Intel have all invested human, physical and financial capital in the demonstration sustainable village, Huangbaiyu, in north-eastern Liaoning province. While clearly motivated in part by the mission of the centre, these companies also have products to sell and perceive an economic pay-off over the longer term. BASF, for example, has developed a highly energy efficient roofing and insulation material, Styropor, that can be used and reused numerous times. Its hope is that as China sets rural construction standards, its material will become a housing standard. The Iowa-based company, Vermeer Manufacturing, has a similar incentive in participating in the demonstration village, providing the equipment and technical training to manufacture a brick substitute made from compressed earth. Their efforts may well bear fruit: China's Ministry of Construction, which is in the process of setting such standards, has already signed on to support the demonstration village. BP is also betting on the long term. It has donated a 1000 W solar photovoltaic energy system for a demonstration home with the understanding that the system will be hooked up to the local power grid; BP Solar will then have the right to sell back whatever power is not consumed by the home. While in and of itself the village effort will not yield a significant financial return, BP is assuming that such a system will be adopted more widely. Intel is taking an even longer time horizon, spending three years studying life in Huangbaiyu in order to understand how technology can best be utilised in the process of rural development (Schulberg, 2005).

Each of the multinationals engaged in the demonstration village has already attempted to ensure a degree of success by identifying an opportunity within China's evolving market and governance structure to help set the rules. It remains to be seen, however, whether the lessons from the village experiment will in fact inform the development process in the rest of the country.

Impediments to 'doing the right thing' clearly remain. Some firms, such as Britain's Thames Water PLC and France's Veolia Water, have invested directly in China's clean-up process, forming joint ventures with municipal wastewater treatment facilities. In 2004, however, Thames Water PLC pulled out of one such venture, when the Shanghai government refused to honour its pledge for a guaranteed rate of return on investment (*Businessweek*, 27 October 2003). Similarly, as multinationals support Chinese laws or new initiatives, they may find that China's economy does not yet send the appropriate signals to make these new ventures viable. Dow Chemical, for example, is supporting a US$750,000 project in cleaner production.[3] Yet, in 2004, Wang Jirong, a Vice-Minister of SEPA, stated that despite the existence of a 2003 Law on Cleaner Production Promotion (see Mol and Liu, 2005), the concept has not taken hold very rapidly because the implementation of cleaner production suffers from lack of funds and technologies, a defective environmental management system, difficulty in getting information and the absence of market incentives (*Xinhua in English*, 16 June 2004).

Moreover, as Lee and So (1999) suggest, many multinationals continue to view China as an attractive investment opportunity because of its weak enforcement. Mainland officials have openly and directly criticised South Korea, Taiwan and even China's own Special Administrative Region Hong Kong for exporting their most polluting industries to China. The Chinese government has become extremely sensitive about being perceived as the repository for the world's waste or polluting industries (Wang, 2004). A report produced by the Beijing city government discusses several joint ventures with Taiwanese, Thai, and European partners that were highly detrimental to China's environment, noting that many foreign companies might be attracted to China by a 'perception that standards are lax' (Guo, 2004). To some extent, this weakness in enforcement may increasingly become the target of China's growing environmental non-governmental movement. In 2004, Greenpeace Beijing undertook an undercover investigation of the practices of Asia Pulp and Paper (APP) (the largest paper manufacturer in Asia outside Japan) in Yunnan and accused it of illegal logging, prompting an investigation by the

State Forestry Administration (Ma, 2005) that eventually found APP guilty of wrongdoing. The NGO then followed up this investigation with a 2005 investigation into the problem of computer waste in China that resulted in a campaign against Hewlett Packard and other computer companies for using unnecessarily toxic chemicals in their computers.

Using the Market: Tradable Emission Permits

The most explicit attempt by the Chinese government to use the changing nature of the Chinese economy to advance environmental protection may be the effort to promote market-based tradable permits to control SO_2 emissions. One of China's chief environmental protection goals is to curb the emission of SO_2 and acid rain, which as noted earlier, affects a significant portion of China's land and has negative impacts on agricultural production, respiratory health, and the longevity of buildings. In 1998, China established two control zones, an acid rain zone and a pollution control zone, which were designated as the 'key areas for controlling acid rain and SO_2 emissions' (Wang *et al.*, 2004). As Wang and colleagues describe, at roughly the same time, China initiated a Total Emissions Control (TEC) policy, in which the government annually set caps for the total emissions throughout the country, and divided the target among the provinces, autonomous regions and municipalities, who were then responsible for assigning their own TEC targets to local governments or emission contributors (Wang *et al.*, 2004). Within the overall policy of TEC, China also began conducting trials in emissions trading, working with a number of international partners, including Resources for the Future, the Asian Development Bank, the US Environmental Protection Agency and Environmental Defense. Emission trading is now viewed by many as a critical means of cutting SO_2 emissions (Shuwen, 2004). Advocates tout many potential advantages of this market-based mechanism, such as allowing enterprises to choose their methods of pollution abatement and achieving maximum economic efficiency as firms with lower abatement costs reduce their emissions while others buy permits or allowances (Shuwen, 2004).

As a result of much conceptual work, two full-scale pilot projects were initiated: one in Taiyuan involving 26 major polluting industries and the second in Jiangsu, between the Taicang Port Huanbao Power Co. and the Nanjing Xiaguan Power plant. The latter is in the process of expanding into a national tradable permits scheme, involving Shandong, Jiangsu, Shanxi, Henan, Shanghai, Tianjin, and Guangxi.

A great deal of positive press has surrounded these experiments. Indeed, a *China Daily* editorial (*China Daily*, 5 February 2005) trumpets the idea that the only way to protect China's environment is through such market-based policies:

> These [control] regions are required to cut their pollution by 20 per cent in 2005 from that of 2000. In 2000, the national target for the 9th Five

Year Plan had been met... but the economy again roared ahead. SO_2 emissions, as a result of the increased demand for electricity, have soared putting greater pressure on the elements of the 10th Five Year Plan to protect the environment. How can we match the problem of protecting the environment with such dynamic changes in the economy? The answer lies in the development of new market-based environmental policies such as emissions trading, that adjust automatically to changes in the underlying economy... Estimates of the economic effectiveness of this market-based environmental co-operation indicate that roughly half of the investment costs to meet the 10th Five Year Plan's emission target could be saved while still delivering the reductions... Perhaps the 46 plants recently warned could be told that they must deliver on their environmental responsibilities, but that they would also be responsible for finding the solution. Forcing these plants to add more fixed investment may not be the best use of the nation's resources. Instead, we should harness the ingenuity of Chinese companies to come up with their own approach so long as they protect the environment.

Similarly, Environmental Defense economist Dan Dudek, who in October 2004 won China's National Friendship Award for his work on tradable permits, argues:

What few outside China realise is that a real environmental revolution is occurring in the country. China has capped its sulphur dioxide emissions. New power plants have to use not only modern control technology but they must offset their remaining emissions. A permit system is being drafted and formal public participation in the policy making process has begun. (Environmental Defense, 2004)

Despite such glowing testimonials to the efficacy of this market-based solution, a number of analysts have identified significant problems in the early stages of the policy's implementation. Wang *et al.* (2004) note that there are a number of shortcomings in the current schemes: emission measurement standards and data collection are problematic because different sources use different emission methodologies that may not account, for example, for variations in the sulphur content of the coal. If a power plant uses flue-gas desulphurisation technologies, too, then information is needed about when the technology is in use and its level of efficiency (Wang *et al.*, 2004). RFF's Ruth Greenspan Bell (2003; 2005a, b), who was engaged in the Taiyuan experiment, offers a wide-ranging critique of the system and the perception by some inside and outside China that it may be a cure-all for China's acid rain problem. Bell notes that the issue of transparency goes well beyond the point of Wang and his colleagues: China only estimates the emissions whereas in the United States, continuous emission monitors transmit information directly to Environmental Protection Administration computers. In the Chinese system there is, therefore, enormous potential for both miscalculation and cheating that does not exist in the US system (Bell, 2005b). Bell has also noted a number of additional obstacles to effective implementation, such as inadequate penalties, and generally weak environmental enforcement capacity (not genuinely independent and lacking strong enforcement tools) in the Taiyuan case. Indeed, Bell argues there are no enforcement tools save inadequate fees and fines and short-term shutdowns. Bell further suggests that if China's leaders are genuinely interested in emissions reductions, they need to change their system to make it more transparent and publicly accessible (Bell, 2003). Perhaps most important, as Bell notes, trades to date are in effect 'staged trades'. They are undertaken as part of a formal government experiment, but there is no institutional infrastructure to support country-wide adoption: no real incentive to save money or energy over the long term or penalty system for doing the wrong thing that would encourage new enterprises or regions to buy into the system (Bell, 2005a). Dudek himself has expressed some concern about the larger institutional infrastructure for the trading system, noting that the plants in the Jiangsu scheme do not have emission quotas for 2006–2010: 'The government should have a plan with a longer time range, which is useful for companies to know where they should be going' (*China Daily*, 9 December 2004, section 9). But here, too, Bell goes further, suggesting that emissions trading is only one tool in the toolbox and should not be confused with the real solution, which must engage the full range of institutional, regulatory and management reforms.

Conclusion

China's extraordinary economic development has contributed to degrading and polluting the country to an extent seen only in some of the most impoverished countries in the world. Air and water pollution, land degradation, and the declining availability of resources, such as water, now top world statistics and are beginning to affect the country's economic growth, public health and social stability.

At the same time, these environmental and economic challenges, the ongoing transformation into a market economy, and the further integration into the global economy enable China's leaders to experiment with a new platform of policies. The green GDP, the National Environmental Model City programme, engaging multinationals, and tradable permits for sulphur dioxide emissions all are rooted in a belief that China's growing economy and transition to a market economy will not only permit but also need new approaches to environmental protection.

A preliminary look at these efforts suggests that while they increasingly hold attraction for Chinese officials, and most importantly for local authorities, they remain hampered by weaknesses in both technical and human capacity, as well as by the additional limitation of an economy still in market transition. In several instances, the technological, economic, or policy infrastructure appear inadequate to support the new initiatives. Each of the cases explored, if only preliminarily, brings to light a slightly different set of political and economic constraints to effective implementation.

In the case of tradable permits, for example, the physical, political and economic infrastructure lag well behind optimal conditions for effective implementation. The monitoring equipment is not adequate to the task; transparency within the system is still limited, and without a longer time frame in which expectations for SO_2 emissions levels are laid out, firms have no effective means of calculating their risk and reward for participating in the emissions trading effort and undertaking the investment in pollution control equipment or purchasing a permit to pollute.

China's effort to engage multinationals in setting a high bar for environmental protection efforts suffers from a slightly different set of political and economic constraints. Uneven enforcement of environmental protection laws means that some multinationals are able to pollute without significant penalty while others are penalised, at least in the short term, for doing the right thing because their operational costs are often higher. Appropriate pricing for natural resources, too, would even the playing field and enable multinationals with best practices to benefit.

Green GDP is still in a nascent stage; however, bureaucratic divides have emerged and concerns are already being raised – even by the policy's proponents – concerning the failings in the methodologies proposed. How to calculate green GDP, whether it accounts for all the key variables, and whether it will in reality inform decisions regarding the political futures of local leaders, are critical issues still under debate. It seems plausible that these flaws in methodology could be easily exploited by the policy's detractors to undermine its validity.

While the National Environmental Model City programme is an all-encompassing effort to incorporate economic development with effective environmental protection, it depends on achievement of a certain level of wealth that many regions in China have not yet attained. These regions then become the repository for the polluting industries from the national environmental model cities. In some respects, therefore, for much of the country, the National Environmental Model City programme perpetuates old notions of development first and then environmental protection, rather than embracing a real notion of sustainable development.

Taken together, the cases explored in this study suggest that while Chinese policy is renewing itself while moving into the 21st century, if the appropriate policy infrastructure is not present – including pricing, technology, and political capacity – the economisation of environmental governance will not succeed in a meaningful manner. As China's market enthusiasts become increasingly focused on the potential of market-based mechanisms to solve China's environmental challenges, it is worth remembering Bell's (2003) and Qu Geping's admonitions that environmental protection must also and always embrace regulatory, management, and institutional governance dimensions.

Notes

1. The calculation of green GDP has been outlined by the State Environmental Protection Administration's vice-minister for environment Pan Yue and others involved in the process. It involves three stages: determining the quantity of natural resources consumed in economic activities; evaluating the quantity of environmental loss caused by economic development; and valuing the quantity of resources and environmental loss. The National Bureau of Statistics (NBS) has begun with land, forestry, mineral and water resources as the first group of resources to be assessed. At the same time, the NBS is pursuing a separate effort to develop a valuation effort for energy resources consumed in the development process.
2. Melchert & Mol (2006) provide an interesting analysis that includes empirical data about how and to what extent multinationals with headquarters in OECD countries do and do not ecologise their premises in lesser developed nations, such as China and Brazil.
3. Cleaner production is one methodology for incorporating economics into environmental protection. By using clean technologies in the production process and recycling the waste, a company can realise profits.

References

Aunan, K. (2000) 'Blue skies ahead over Guangzhou', *Cicerone*, February.

Badawi, R., Feng, X. & Zhang, Y (2004) 'Suitable living condition within cities', *Proceedings of the Map Asia 2004 Conference*. Available at http://www.gisdevelopment.net/application/urban/overview/ma04209.htm (accessed 27 September 2005).

Bell, R. (2003) 'Choosing environmental policy instruments in the real world', *Global Forum on Sustainable Development: Emissions Trading*, Organisation for Economic Co-operation and Development, 17–18 March. Available at http://www.oecd.org/dataoecd/11/9/2957706.pdf (accessed 19 September 2005).

Bell, R. (2005a) Phone interview with author, 1 June.

Bell, R. (2005b) Email exchange with author, 21 June.

Cheung, R. (2005) 'Green GDP trials start in 10 regions', *South China Morning Post*, 1 March.

China Council for the Promotion of International Trade Guangdong Sub-council (2004) 'GZ strives for model city', 24 March. Available at http://www.getgd.net/gd_trend/english/2004/3/modelcity.htm (accessed 19 September 2005).

China–US Center for Sustainable Development (2002) 'Mission statement', Available at http://www.chinauscenter.org/purpose/mission.asp (accessed 19 September 2005).

Economy, E. (2004) *The River Runs Black: the Environmental Challenge to China's Future* (Ithaca, NY: Cornell University Press).

Environmental Defense (2004) 'Environmental Defense economist honored by Chinese government' (1 October). Available at www.environmentaldefense.org/pressrelease.cfm?ContentID=4067 (accessed 19 September 2005).

Furtado, J., Belt, T. & Jammi, R. (eds.) (2000) *Economic Development and Environmental Sustainability: Policies and Principles for a Durable Equilibrium* (Washington, DC: World Bank).

Guo, H. (2004) 'China's foreign direct investment strategy', Information Office of the Beijing Municipal Government in Business, 15 October.

Guo, P. (2005) *Corporate Environmental Reporting and Disclosure in China* (Hong Kong/Shenzhen: Corporate Social Responsibility Asia).

Hildebrandt, T. (2004) 'The greening of big oil in China', *South China Morning Post*, 1 January.

Hong Kong Economic Information Agency (2005) 'Foreign trade stands at US$1.1547 trillion in 2004', 21 February. Available at http://www.tdctrade.com/report/indprof/indprof_050202.htm (accessed 27 September 2005).

Hua, Y. (2005) 'Wrangle over green GDP', Asia Times Online Ltd.

Huang, Kevin (2005) 'Voices of the people don't speak for masses', *South China Morning Post*, 29 September.

Huber, J. (1991) *Unternehmen Umwelt. Weichenstellungen für eine ökologische Marktwirtschaft* (Frankfurt am Main: Fisher Verlag).

Jänicke, M. (1990) *State Failure. The Impotence of Politics in Industrial Society* (University Park, PA: Pennsylvania State University Press).

Japan Bank for International Co-operation (2000) 'Supporting China's environmental improvement project and inland region developments', 28 March. Available at http://www.jbic.go.jp/english/base/release/oec/1999/A06/nr99_29s.php (accessed 16 September 2005).

Kynge, J. (2004) 'Shanxi admits meagre "green GDP"', *Financial Times*, 19 August.

Lee, Y. & So, A. (1999) *Asia's Environmental Movements* (Armonk, NY: M. E. Sharpe).

Lei, P., Long, B. & Pamlin, C. (2005) 'Chinese companies in the 21st century helping or destroying the planet?', April, World Wildlife Fund survey.

Ma, J. (2005) 'Verdict due on probe into illegal logging', *South China Morning Post*, 19 January.

Mallet, V. (2004) 'Smog gives the lie to HK air quality claim', *Financial Times*, 21 August.

Manganese Metal Company official (2004) Interview with author, December.

Melchert, L. & Mol, A. (2006) 'Greening transnational buildings: in-between global flows and local places', in G. Spaargaren, A. Mol & F. Buttel (eds.) *Governing Environmental Flows. Global Challenges to Social Theory* (Cambridge, MA: MIT Press).

Mol, A. (2001) *Globalization and Environmental Reform. Ecological Modernization Theory and the Global Economy* (Cambridge, MA: MIT Press).

Mol, A. & Liu, Y. (2005) Institutionalising cleaner production in China: the Cleaner Production Promotion Law, *International Journal of Environment and Sustainable Development* 4(3): 227–45.

Mol, A. & Sonnenfeld, D. (eds.) (2000) *Ecological Modernisation around the World: Perspectives and Critical Debates* (London: Frank Cass).

Ostrom, E. (1990) *Governing the Commons* (Cambridge: Cambridge University Press).

Pan, Y. (2005) 'China's looming environmental crisis', Fortune Global Forum Panel Discussion, Beijing, 18 May.

Qin, C. (2004) 'Coordinated action needed in pollution control', *China Daily*, 27 October.

Rock, M. (2002a) *Pollution Control in East Asia* (Washington, DC: Resources for the Future).

Rock, M. (2002b) 'Integrating environmental and economic policy making in China and Taiwan', *American Behavioral Scientist* 45(9): 1435–55.

Royal Dutch Shell officials (2002) Interview with author, Beijing, July.

Schulberg, R. (2005) Phone interview with author (Executive-Director, China–US Center for Sustainable Development), 13 June.

Shi, T. (2005) 'Shantou may lose "green" distinction', *South China Morning Post*, 15 January.

Shuwen, J. (2004) 'Assessing the dragon's choice: the use of market-based instruments in Chinese environmental policy', *Georgetown International Environmental Law Review* 16(4): 617–55.

Smil, V. (1993) *China's Environmental Crisis* (Armonk, NY: M. E. Sharpe).

Tatenhove, J., Arts, B. & Leroy, P. (eds.) (2000) *Political Modernisation and the Environment. The Renewal of Environmental Policy Arrangements* (Dordrecht: Kluwer).

Wang, H., Bi, J., Wheeler, D., Wang, J., Cao, D., Lu, G. & Wang, Y. (2002) 'Environmental performance rating and disclosure. China's Green-watch Program'. Policy Research Working Paper No. 2889, World Bank, Washington DC.

Wang, I. (2004) 'We must not be the world's dumping ground', *South China Morning Post*, 28 October.

Wang, J., Yang, J., Ge, C., Cao, D. & Schreifels, J. (2004) 'Controlling sulfur dioxide in China: will emission trading work?', *Environment* 46(5): 28–39.

Zhang, L. (2002) 'Ecologizing industrialization in Chinese small towns', PhD thesis, Wageningen University.

Institutional Reform, Economic Changes, and Local Environmental Management in China: the Case of Guangdong Province

CARLOS WING-HUNG LO & SHUI-YAN TANG

Introduction

Compared with the dramatic fall of the socialist regimes in the former Soviet bloc, China's governing institutions have remained relatively unchanged in the past decade and a half, despite its dramatic economic transformation and growth. Yet it would be wrong to assume that governing institutions in China today are unchanged compared to before the start of the reforms in

1979. In fact, they have been undergoing many subtle transformations, especially in the last 15 years, partly in response to various challenges posed by the rapidly changing socio-economic landscapes (Lewis & Xue, 2003; Yang, 2004). Many of these institutional transformations, together with related economic changes, have had a significant impact on environmental management work. Yet many of these changes have never been fully documented in the literature.

In the European literature institutional transformations to improve environmental management have been brought together under the denominator of political modernisation theory (Jänicke, 1993; Mol & Buttel, 2002). Political modernisation refers to the renewal and reinvention of environmental politics and governance institutions to improve their capacity to cope with the environmental challenges of a changing modern order. Decentralisation, growing involvement of market and civil society actors and institutions, integration, and the shift to preventive politics are all elements of Western political modernisation. In this contribution we investigate the Chinese equivalent of Western political modernisation: how are environmental management institutions 'modernising' in order to make them effective in a rapidly transforming political and economic order in China?

What are the key elements of these institutional and economic transformations? One concerns efforts to reconcile the tension between local autonomy and vertical accountability. According to one interpretation, a key driving force for the rapid economic growth in the past two decades and a half has been the autonomy that has enabled local authorities to retain fiscal resources at the local level. This creates incentives for local authorities to develop pro-growth policies (Montinola *et al.*, 1995; Oi, 1999). Part of this autonomy relates to the rights of individual local agencies to retain extra-budgetary revenues. Such revenues not only create many opportunities for malfeasance and corruption (Yang, 2004), they also undermine the ability of higher-level governments to monitor local governments' fiscal conditions and to tap into local resources for supporting large-scale projects (Tsui & Wang, 2004). A key element of government reform in the past decade has been the 'two separate lines for revenues and expenses' system by which extra-budgetary funds are subject to more stringent oversight and integrated management by the local finance bureau. This new system creates a tension with a well-established principle of the Chinese environmental management system, i.e., using 'environmental protection to support environmental protection', by which agencies retain the right to spend at their discretion the pollution fees and fines they collect.

Another related reform concerns efforts by higher-level governments to regain their leverage over local officials by reforming the cadre management system. In particular, under the still evolving 'target responsibility system', leading local cadres are evaluated annually according to a set of indicators, which includes a number of economic, social, and political targets (Tsui & Wang, 2004). The system is meant to encourage local cadres to allocate fiscal resources in ways that support priorities set by higher-level governments. Environmental protection has in recent years been selected as a key evaluation indicator. In addition, higher-level governments may also set up separate responsibility contracts (*zerenshu*) with cadres at lower levels focusing on specific environmental protection targets. As argued by Rock (2002), this new system has created stronger incentives for local officials to increase their efforts in environmental protection. Yet controversies remain as to the overall impact of the new system since environmental quality is just one of the many evaluation criteria.

Although central government leaders have tried to enhance their leverage over lower-level officials, they do not want to expand the size of the state. Instead, one of their main reform priorities has been to 'downsize' the state by defining its core government functions and by shedding the non-essential ones and giving them back to society (Brodsgaard, 2002), thus the slogan 'small government, big society' (Yang, 2004). Within the environmental management system, one strategy has been to reduce the staff establishment (*bianzhi*) of the core agencies at all administrative levels that possess authority to perform key regulatory functions, and to assign non-regulatory functions to service or enterprise organisations with the ultimate aim of de-linking most of them from the core government unit.

Lastly, environmental management work has been affected not only by government reform. Changes in industrial structures have created different institutional environments in which regulatory work is carried out. One change relates to the decreasing 'embeddedness' of the regulatory agency within the socialist industrial state. In the former Soviet bloc, and in the early years of China's reform era, government agencies often found it difficult to enforce environmental regulations on state-owned or other collectively-owned enterprises, as they were all 'embedded' within the same socialist planned economy. When the institutions of governance, production, and environmental regulation are all 'embedded' with each other, there is little transparency and accountability to outside interests. As a result, many environmentally destructive activities continued unchallenged for decades (Lo & Tang, 1994; Cherp, 2001). In recent years, in many parts of China, this 'embeddedness' problem has gradually been lessened as more and more enterprises are now privately owned and are no longer part of the government system. Yet regulating private enterprises presents a different set of challenges to the local Environmental Protection Bureau.

This article examines how three institutional reforms – (1) the new system of 'two separate lines for revenues and expenses'; (2) spinning off service organisations from administrative agencies; and (3) the new environmental quality administrative leadership responsibility system – and one key economic transformation – industrial structural changes – affected the environmental management capacity in the southern province of Guangdong. With a population of 78.6 million, Guangdong Province consists of 21 cities at the county level and above, with Guangzhou and Shenzhen as the most well known. Guangdong is the forerunner in China's transformation to market economy: it has achieved an average annual growth rate of over 10 per cent since 1978, with its volume of foreign trade and gross light industrial output always staying at the top of the national statistics (Cheng, 2000). It had a GDP of 1167.4 billion yuan in 2002, and a growth rate of 10.8 per cent in 2002–03 (Guangdong Year Book Editorial Board, 2003). As a result of its vibrant economy, Guangdong is also home to tens of thousands of polluting factories. It has suffered from many major environmental problems – such as air and water pollution from both industrial and domestic sources, lack of wastewater treatment facilities, and soil contamination due to sub-standard landfills for solid waste. Trends for air pollution have been mixed – for example, the amounts of aggregated suspended particulates have been reduced compared with a decade ago, but the amounts of nitrogen dioxide and the frequency of acid rain have increased in the past decade. The same applies to water pollution. The amounts of COD discharge have decreased over the past decade, but the total amounts of industrial wastewater discharge have increased over the same period. Yet total investment in environmental protection as a percentage of GDP increased from 0.64 per cent in 1995 to 2.71 per cent in 2004.

The data for this article is drawn mainly from interviews conducted in 2004 and 2005 with high-ranking local EPB officials in the capital city, Guangzhou, and in four other cities (one at the prefectural level and three at the county level).[1] These five cities provide a good contrast because Guangzhou has a higher administrative rank, and it is more economically advanced and urbanised than the other four cities. Table 1 provides a summary of the major socio-economic characteristics and environmental conditions of the five cities. Since the main source of information for this study came from interviews with EPB officials in these five cities, our analysis is inevitably shaped to some extent by the ways issues and problems are presented to us by the officials. Yet, as will be demonstrated in our analysis, the information we obtained includes many frank assessments of key institutional and socio-economic changes, and their impacts on environmental management work in these cities.

Two Separate Lines for Revenues and Expenses (*Shouzhi liangtiao xian*)

For many years, a key characteristic of China's environmental management system was that local environmental agencies could retain a portion of the pollution fees and fines they collected from polluters. In addition, there were measures that guaranteed enterprises the refund of a portion of the pollution fees they paid. The enterprises could then use the refund, either as direct subsidies or as loans, to install and/or upgrade their pollution control facilities (National Environmental Protection Agency, 1996a). These arrangements were characterised either as 'special accounts for special purposes' (*zhuankuan zhuanyong*) or as 'using environmental protection to support environmental protection' (*yi huanbao zhi huanbao*).

Table 1. Comparison of Guangzhou and cities A–D in Guangdong Province

City (level) Dimension	Guangzhou (provincial)	City A (prefectural)	City B (county)	City C (county)	City D (county)
1. Geographical location	The largest city in the Pearl River Delta Region of southern China	A coastal city at the southeastern part of Guangdong Province	A county level city under the jurisdiction of Guangzhou, situated east of Guangzhou	A county-level city under the jurisdiction of Jiangmin, situated in the southeastern part of the PRD Region	A county-level city under the jurisdiction of Foshan, situated in the central part of the PRD Region
2. Area	7434.6 km^2	Over 7000 km^2	Over 1000 km^2	Over 1000 km^2	Less than 1000 km^2
3. Population	7.2 million	Over 1 million	Less than 1 million	Less than 1 million	Less than 1 million
4. Economic growth	Over 10 per cent/ yr over the last 2 decades	Over 10 per cent/ yr over the last decade	Over 10 per cent/yr over the last decade	Over 10 per cent/yr over the last decade	Over 10 per cent/yr over the last decade
5. Urban planning	An old city with ineffective urban planning	A lesser developed city without much urban planning	A traditional rural city with strong inspiration to economic growth but without much urban planning	A rural city striving for rapid economic growth without much urban planning	A rapidly developing city without careful urban planning where industrial and residential areas intermingle
6. Environmental conditions	1. Serious water pollution – particularly bad in the Pearl River.	1. Polluting industries including cement, steel manufacturing,	1. Serious water pollution – particularly bad in the Dongjiang	1. Serious water pollution from industries in electroplating, textile,	1. Serious air and water pollution from the manufacturing industry and the

(continued)

Local Environmental Management in China   47

Table 1. (*Continued*)

City (level) Dimension	Guangzhou (provincial)	City A (prefectural)	City B (county)	City C (county)	City D (county)
	2. Serious air pollution from vehicular emission and factories. 3. Excessive noise from a large number of construction projects running 24 hrs/day.	hardware production, and clothing. 2. The threat of water pollution in the river has been increasing.	River – caused mostly by emission from textile and circuit manufacturing plants. 2. Serious air pollution caused by a large number of cement factories.	and food production. 2. Water pollution in the Tan River is quite serious.	production of electrical appliances. 2. Excessive noise from industrial activities seriously affecting local people as residential and industrial areas intermingle.
7. EPB performance (as assessed by the Guangdong Environmental Protection Bureau)	1. Ranked 13 in 2003. 2. Achieved a pass assessment in 2005. 3. Consistently ranked last in terms of air quality.	Improving environmental performance quite visibly in the last few years.	Performance far from satisfactory in environmental protection in the 2003 assessment.	Good performance in environmental protection in the 2003 assessment.	Relatively good performance in environmental protection in the 2003 assessment.

Source: Guangdong Year Book Editorial Board (2003) and http://www.gdepb.gov.cn/SecondItem.asp?SecondID=90&ShowStyle=3.

These arrangements had mixed impacts on environmental management. On the one hand, the system helped to ensure a stable source of funding for local EPBs, making them less dependent on funding from the local finance bureau. The refund system also created a spirit in which resources generated from environmental protection were used within the system itself. On the other hand, the system might have encouraged some EPBs to focus on collecting pollution fees and fines instead of trying to decrease total pollutant emissions (Lo & Tang, 1994; Ma & Ortolano, 2000).

This revenue retention system has been changed in recent years. As part of a nationwide reform initiative, administrative units at all levels of government are required to decouple the revenue from the expense streams. The reform has been part of an attempt by higher-level governments to monitor more closely the levying and use of extra-budgetary funds by local governments (Tsui & Wang, 2004) with a view to preventing corruption and promoting account-ability. In environmental management, all pollution fees and fines now go directly to the local finance bureau, and the EPB is no longer guaranteed a portion of the revenues; similarly enterprises are no longer guaranteed a partial refund of their pollution fees (State Environmental Protection Administration, 2003). Yet local jurisdictions vary in terms of how the new system has been implemented.

Guangzhou began to implement the new system in the mid-1990s. Under the new system, all fees and fines collected become part of the general funds, with 10 per cent going to the national treasury, 5 per cent to the provincial treasury, and the remaining 85 per cent to the municipal treasury. Yet there is still a national administrative decree – Management Regulations on the Levy and Use of Pollution Discharge Fees issued in March 2003 – which stipulates that all pollution discharge fees and fines collected should be used for pollution control (State Environmental Protection Administration, 2003). The key difference between the new and old systems is that the former presumably has stronger accountability mechanisms. The EPB has to develop an annual budget each October, using the amount collected in the first nine months as the basis for estimation, to fund various pollution control projects and related works. Each expenditure item must be justified in terms of its social returns. The budget must be approved by the finance bureau and then incorporated into the municipal budget before submission for legislative approval.

In the initial years after the system was first implemented, the finance bureau tended to rubber-stamp all funding requests. As it accumulated more experience and expertise in assessing requests, the bureau began to evaluate budgetary proposals more actively, examining, for example, whether the total amounts are reasonable and whether the dispersion of funds is based on a clear accounting system. This new system contrasts with past practices in which each bureau collected its own fees and used the funds at its discretion. Under the new system, to obtain funding, each bureau has to submit detailed proposals and budgets, and the finance bureau may also monitor how the funds are allocated, dispersed, and spent.

For some officials, the new system has a negative impact on the EPB because financial power is now concentrated at the finance bureau, and it takes more time and effort for the EPB to request funding.[2] But, thanks to the mayor's emphasis on environmental protection and the city's favourable financial condition, the new system so far appears to have had no major adverse impact on the EPB's financial condition. As noted by one official, on the positive side, the EPB can now concentrate on regulation enforcement, rather than be overly concerned with the financial implications of its regulatory action.[3]

In City D, under the old system, the EPB was allowed to keep 60 per cent of the fees and fines it collected for its own expenses. Now, all the fees and fines revert directly to the finance bureau. Although the basic salaries and bonuses for the staff are still guaranteed by the municipal government, the EPB needs to submit a request for each specific project. According to the Deputy Chief of the EPB, getting approval has become more difficult.[4] For instance, the bureau was able to obtain 840,000 yuan for setting up three publicity billboards in 2003, but a request for two additional ones in 2005 was turned down. In 2004, the EPB collected a total of 15 million yuan in pollution fees and fines, but it received only 6 million yuan from the finance bureau in funding specific pollution control projects. In the view of the official, the new system did have an adverse impact on the bureau's financial condition.

Similar difficulties arose in the other three cities, with officials citing either reductions in the total amount of funds available or delays in funding for specific projects due to the need to obtain approval from multiple municipal offices. The EPB Chief in City C observed that whilst the new system has had some adverse effect on the motivation of bureau officials, it represents social progress as it is now less likely that funds will be diverted to projects that benefit individual officials rather than environmental protection.[5]

Another component of the 'two separate lines for revenues and expenses' system concerns the enterprise refund arrangement. Enterprises can no longer expect an automatic rebate of (up to 80 per cent of) their pollution fees and fines, in the form of EPB subsidies or interest-free loans to finance their pollution control operations. Pollution control is now explicitly treated as the responsibility of polluting enterprises, which must obtain financial resources by themselves. The EPB may still assist enterprises to develop or improve pollution prevention or reduction programmes, which are now treated as financial investments by the municipal government according to its own policy priorities. In addition, the EPB has to justify to the finance bureau its proposed expenditures by spelling out the anticipated social benefits.

In all five cities, pollution control has increasingly become the sole responsibility of the enterprises themselves, and there have been decreasing amounts of government subsidies and loans available. Guangzhou is the only city that still maintains substantial funding for enterprises, but those funds usually go to large state-owned enterprises. During 2003 and 2004, there were over 40 project applications, mostly from state-owned enterprises, with a great majority of them receiving funding. An annual budget of 50 million yuan has been set for this purpose. The largest amount allocated to one single project was 10 million yuan, to the Zhujiang Power Plant, which involved an investment of 600 million yuan.

This new arrangement can be considered an improvement as it creates a more accountable system by having a series of well-specified steps: individual enterprises may propose a specific pollution control project; the EPB evaluates and approves the proposal; the finance bureau endorses the EPB's recommendations and sets up an account for the project; the enterprise arranges an open bid on the project; the EPB monitors the bidding process and the project's progress; the enterprise submits quarterly reports; the finance bureau allocates funds according to quarterly progress; and the last payment will only be made by the EPB to the enterprise after the project's completion. The amount of subsidy provided by the EPB is usually not more than 20 per cent of the total investment in the pollution control project. Finally, an enterprise may be penalised if it fails to deliver on time what the project has promised to do.

The officials we interviewed, however, identified a number of specific problems with the new system. First, the new system is premised on each enterprise having good account management of its pollution control projects, but this is not true for most enterprises. Second, there have been irregularities and arbitrariness in many bidding processes that violated procedures specified in national law. Third, there are still no clear and well-developed criteria for allocating funds and for evaluating project performance.

Overall, the 'two separate lines for revenues and expenses' system appears to work well in more economically developed jurisdictions such as Guangzhou, which tend to have more financial resources available independent of pollution fees and fines, and to have a stronger leadership commitment to environmental protection. Without diminishing the overall funding available to the EPB, the new system helps to reduce the incentives for EPB officials to focus their efforts predominately on collecting pollution fees and fines. The system also contributes to improved accountability and to ensuring that funds are used for projects with higher social returns, instead of being used as regular subsidies to enterprises regardless of their commitment to pollution reduction. In the short run, however, the new system may have a negative financial impact on EPBs in some less developed areas, especially in jurisdictions in which the municipal leadership is less committed to environmental protection. In these jurisdictions, the EPB may end up having less financial resources at its disposal than before, thus undermining its enforcement capacity, a concern stated explicitly by the State Environmental Protection Administration (2003). On the positive side, however, having fewer direct subsidies to enterprises helps to free up resources for the EPB to focus on improving environmental protection infrastructure. Several officials suggested that the new system is more feasible in Guangdong Province in which local governments tend to be financially strong, but less so in provinces that are less economically developed. Indeed, while the new system has been strictly enforced in Guangdong Province, some less developed western provinces have been given a longer transition period.[6]

Spinning Off Service Organisations from Administrative Agencies

Although local EPBs in Guangdong Province fare better financially than most of their counterparts in less developed provinces, they still face the same problem that has plagued many other government agencies during the reform era: how to provide increasing amounts and varieties of services within strict financial and personnel constraints. Municipal governments in most jurisdictions have increased their funding to the EPB in the past decade, but the funding has been far below the level needed to fully support all its activities, which range from overseeing environmental impact assessment and pollution monitoring to pollutant fee collection and environmental education. Revenues derived from pollution fees and fines have helped meet the bureau's financial needs, but they are still insufficient for all its operational needs. Nationwide civil service reforms in China since the early 1990s also demanded a reduction in staff establishment (*bianzhi*) in administrative agencies. Indeed, after several rounds of bureaucratic restructuring and streamlining in the past decade (Brodsgaard, 2002; Burns, 2003), the Gaungzhou EPB, for example, had its staff establishment cut from over 70 to around 45.

Like many other administrative agencies in China, the local EPBs have responded to these financial and personnel challenges by assigning many major responsibilities to service organisations (*shiye danwei*) (Lam & Perry, 2001; Lo *et al.*, 2001). Service organisations, an organisational category that is probably unique to China, are semi-governmental organisations that perform social or public functions, partly or fully on a self-financing basis. Most service organisations are attached to a party or state administrative agency that has the power to appoint for a fixed term the director, and sometimes the deputy directors, of the organisation. A service organisation usually carries an administrative rank equivalent to one level lower than that of the parent agency.

There are three main types of service organisations in the environmental protection arena. The first has administrative duties, but without public authority. For example, monitoring stations, which exist in all the five cities in this study are entrusted by the EPB to collect pollution data, but they lack explicit public authority. The EPB usually provides a full budget to cover the monitoring stations' expenses in return for their services. To increase their discretionary resources for such things as better facilities and additional staff bonuses, monitoring stations can provide services to outside constituencies and enterprises for collecting and verifying their pollution data. All the incomes from such services must be submitted to the finance bureau, but 35 per cent (50 per cent in the past) may be kept, following budgetary guidelines of the 'two separate lines for revenues and expenses' system.

The second type possesses explicit public authority. One example is the enforcement team, which is responsible for enforcing environmental regulations, collecting pollution discharge fees and fines, and handling complaints on pollution. In Guangzhou, the enforcement team (*zhifa dadui*) (formerly the Environmental Supervision and Management Institute) was established in 1981 and has 55 staff. It functions as an administrative arm of the EPB and is responsible for enforcing environmental regulations as well as collecting discharge fees and fines from polluting enterprises. It has the authority to impose penalties on enterprises for violating related rules and regulations. This enforcement team is fully funded by the EPB and is prohibited from engaging in any income-earning activities. Its staff members were converted from non-civil servant status to that of 'managed according to the civil servant system' (*cengzhao gongwuyuan guangli*) in 1995 when the EPB was upgraded from the rank of an office to a bureau. Under this system, the staff's salary and welfare benefits are set according to civil service scales, and their employment subject to civil service terms. In general, the *bianzhi* (staff establishment) of an enforcement team is not allowed to expand beyond the limit set by the local government. All employees in the enforcement team are fully supported by the municipal budget, and thus no fee-based employees are allowed. These organisational principles also apply to the enforcement teams in the other four cities, which are smaller in size with the number of enforcement officials ranging from 33 in City A to 11 in City B.

The third type has no public authority and no formal administrative duties assigned by the EPB. One example is research institutes. The Guangzhou Research Institute of Environmental Protection Science (GRIEPS), for example, was established in 1977 to provide research support to the environmental protection agency. It has a 100 staff. The GRIEPS director is appointed by the EPB chief for a three-year term and is fully in charge of the institute. Since its establishment, GRIEPS has taken up a number of specific tasks, including preparation of environmental impact assessment reports for development projects, provision of environmental planning services for government authorities, and provision of ISO14001 certification preparation services for industrial enterprises. GRIEPS charges fees for performing these tasks, which have become its major income source. In principle, service organisations in this third category can more or less define their own work agenda, but cannot use the EPB's authority to advance their own interests. They are also supposed to compete equally with other organisations when bidding on projects overseen by the EPB. According to the officials interviewed, the long-term direction is to turn these service organisations into independent enterprise units (*qiyi danwei*).

After three consecutive years of progressive funding cuts, the GRIEPS has not received any direct financial support from the EPB since 2002 and has begun to earn its own income by operating on commercial principles. Yet, as indicated by some of our interviewees, it is unlikely that GRIEPS will be entirely autonomous from the EPB, and some informal ties will still exist in the future. In this respect, the research institute of City D EPB was a step ahead of its counterparts by converting to an independent enterprise in September 2004. In contrast, its counterpart in City A has not moved towards becoming an independent enterprise, partly due to its small establishment and lack of income generating activities.

By establishing these service organisations, local EPBs have been able to provide a larger array of services than would otherwise be possible within their financial and personnel constraints. As these service organisations have their independent means of raising revenues, they tend to provide employees with better remuneration and benefits than those provided by the EPB, particularly in the case of GRIEPS in Guangzhou. From the EPB's perspective, service organisations enable it to handle pressure to downsize the civil service, as they provide employment opportunities for its surplus staff.

In addition, one official argued that spinning off non-regulatory and profit-making activities from core administrative agencies represents political and social progress.[7] Under the old socialist system, the cadres in both government and state-owned enterprises all exercised some form of public authority, which enabled government and enterprise employees easily to create opportunities for personal gain. A key aim of administrative reform in the past decade and a half has been to define clearly who should be empowered to exercise public authority so that a clearer accountability system can be established. A series of reforms has been undertaken along this direction; for example, separating the party from the state, and the state from enterprises (Yang, 2004). Now efforts are focused on separating administrative units that exercise public authority from those that provide supportive services and those that engage in direct profit-making activities. The reform direction is to limit organisations with administrative powers to retain employees who are paid and restricted by full civil service terms – that is, developing a stable and clear compensation and bonus system that is not tied to other money making ventures. In service organisations that do not have administrative powers, employees may or may not receive basic civil service salaries and benefits, and they may seek to increase their incomes by providing paid services to clients. For those service organisations that are engaging in purely profit-making activities, such as providing expert advice on running pollution control facilities, the long-term objective is to sever their ties to any administrative agency and to operate as totally independent business enterprises.

Currently, however, many service organisations maintain strong ties to their parent administrative agency while engaging in money-making ventures, thus creating conflicts of interest. For example, although GRIEPS is only one of many organisations that are qualified to prepare environmental impact assessment (EIA) reports for development projects, it has received a majority of the contracts for the job. Indeed, it has relied on these contracts as a major source of its income. This raises doubts about the impartiality of the process since EIA reports prepared by the GRIEPS are seldom turned down by the EPB.

Overall, if successful in the long run, spinning off service organisations from administrative agencies can potentially lead to a more streamlined administrative system with clearer accountability. Yet, in the current transitional stage, most service and enterprise organisations are still connected either formally or informally to the EPB, thus creating many potential conflicts of interest.

A New Environmental Quality Administrative Leadership Responsibility System

In 1996, the State Council issued an order requiring various levels of government to adopt an environmental quality administrative leadership responsibility system. Under this new leadership responsibility system, the entire government (provincial and local), not the EPB alone, is responsible for its jurisdiction's overall environmental quality. Provincial governors, city mayors, and township heads are responsible for the overall environmental quality of their jurisdictions. All government jurisdictions must incorporate specific environmental objectives and measures into their jurisdiction's overall economic and social planning (National Environmental Protection Agency, 1996b). Under this responsibility system, key officials are evaluated annually by a higher-level government, which has the authority to appoint, reappoint, and remove the officials in question, according to a set of explicit performance indicators. These indicators, in some cases, are set by negotiation between individual governments and their superiors.

Guangdong Province was among the first to implement the new responsibility system in 1997. Every March, heads of local jurisdictions meet to discuss specific environmental targets and to sign responsibility contracts for the coming year. Higher-level authorities monitor progress in mid-year and evaluate results at year's end. A local leader failing to meet the targets for three consecutive years will not be eligible for promotion in the next five years. In 2004, there was one prefectural level city among 21 cities that failed in the evaluation exercise, mainly due to its failure to construct wastewater treatment plants (*Nanfang ribao*, 2005). The news about the evaluation result was widely reported in the media, causing considerable embarrassment to the leaders in those cities that performed poorly in the evaluation.

In Guangzhou, one official observed, the responsibility system has had positive effects on environmental protection.[8] With the signing of responsibility contracts, lower-level governments are now more motivated to accomplish environmental missions. In his opinion, the new responsibility system can help explain why wastewater treatment plants have been constructed at a much faster pace in recent years. Another high-level official indicated that other government units, such as the development, planning, and construction commissions, are now more willing to consider environmental protection issues and to support the EPB's work.[9] The same official, however, also cautioned against exaggerating the impact of the system. Although the system helps to heighten government leaders' concern for environmental protection, it remains one of the many components of an overall target responsibility system (Tsui and Wang, 2004). When higher-level officials evaluate lower-level officials, they are still likely to see economic performance as more important than environmental protection.

In City D, according to the Deputy Chief of the EPB, the administrative responsibility system has had positive impacts.[10] Under the new system, other municipal units like agriculture, water resources, industry, and commerce are more willing to cooperate with the bureau in law enforcement. It is also easier for the EPB chief to negotiate directly with other bureau chiefs.

In City A, the new system has also made a difference. Three years ago, the city was ranked the second last among 21 cities in an environmental performance evaluation exercise in the province. The dismal result triggered the municipal leadership to fire the EPB chief for having failed to undertake sufficient effort to improve the city's environmental protection infrastructure, such as wastewater treatment and solid waste disposal facilities. The newly appointed chief undertook more rigorous efforts in environmental protection, meeting with encouragement from the city leadership. As a result, City A was able to move up to seventh in the evaluation ranking in 2004.

In City B, the responsibility system has been implemented down to the township level. It is most effective at this grassroots level, because in their annual evaluation, township leaders have to go through not just the Industry and Commerce Bureau but also the EPB, thus indirectly giving the EPB more political leverage with the township leaders.

The responsibility system also appears to have heightened government leaders' concerns about negative publicity on environmental problems. In 2000, when visiting City B, a vice-governor of Guangdong Province made several public remarks about the serious air and water pollution in the city. His remark was later widely cited in the media. These events triggered considerable efforts from the mayor to tackle pollution problems in City B. After the media publicity, the mayor personally chaired a task force to coordinate anti-pollution efforts. Working with the city government, the EPB developed a number of administrative measures to address pollution problems. Efforts, for example, were undertaken to ensure that polluting enterprises had the necessary certification for their pollution control facilities. The number of enforcement officials was increased from six to 16, which began to undertake enforcement activities on a round-the-clock basis.

The administrative responsibility system has also become a useful instrument for fostering cooperation among local jurisdictions in solving region-wide problems. In an effort to clean up Tan River, the mayor of Jiangmen, a prefectural level city, developed a responsibility contract with the leaders in the other three county-level cities under his administrative supervision. Yet, as indicated by a high-ranking official in Guangzhou, the responsibility system is no magic solution.[11] In an effort to clean up the Pearl River system, the provincial government has developed a responsibility contract with 13 cities. Although different sections of the river have shown improvement, the overall progress has remained slow. Many city governments have failed to reach their assigned targets. A major problem has been a lack of the necessary funding and technologies to construct wastewater treatment plants.

Overall, the environmental quality administrative leadership responsibility system has had positive impacts by heightening local leaders' concern for environmental protection as part of social and economic planning. The system has also indirectly increased the status and negotiation power of the local EPB in relation to other municipal bureaux. In addition, the system helps to facilitate cooperation among local jurisdictions in solving regional environmental problems. Yet the overall effect of the system should not be overstated as environmental quality is after all only one of the many criteria for evaluating a local leader, who has to balance environmental protection against many competing priorities such as economic growth, health care, and social stability.

Industrial Transformations

As the economy continues to grow and transform in the province, a number of industrial structural changes have affected environmental management. First, in the late 1980s and the early 1990s state-owned enterprises and township and village enterprises (TVEs) were the most difficult for local EPBs to enforce pollution control regulations, for a number of reasons (Jahiel, 1997; Ma & Ortolano, 2000). Many state-owned enterprises and TVEs were financially strapped and relied on older, and more polluting, technology and production equipments. They tended to be reluctant to upgrade their equipments and to pay pollution fees and fines. Since they were part of the government system, paying pollution fees and fines amounted to transferring money from one arm to the other of the same person. In addition, state-owned enterprises, especially the larger ones, could easily draw on economic and construction commissions to exert political pressure on the EPB.

In all the five cities in our study, most state-owned enterprises and TVEs have either disappeared or turned into privately owned enterprises. Guangzhou is the only city among the five that is still home to some state-owned enterprises, most of which are large in scale. In the other four cities, almost all enterprises are now privately owned. These ownership changes have affected regulatory enforcement.

In Guangzhou, large state-owned enterprises, which tend to be major polluters, are still key targets of regulatory enforcement – the EPB targets around 170 major polluting enterprises for regular enforcement, of which around 70 per cent are state-owned enterprises. One official who is directly involved in enforcement work indicated that it has become easier to enforce pollution control regulations on state-owned enterprises.[12] Although EPB officials continue to have to consult/interact with related government units when carrying out their enforcement work, they can obtain their cooperation more easily than before, thanks partly to the environmental quality administrative responsibility system. But as indicated by another official, there are still cases in which the EPB has encountered difficulties in enforcing rules against some state-owned enterprises that have violated pollution control regulations.[13]

Regulating privately owned enterprises represents a different kind of challenge for the EPB. With private enterprises, the EPB avoids the trouble of negotiating with other government units, but it now carries the additional burden of collecting by itself the enterprises' pollution data. Or, if the data are provided by the enterprises themselves, they tend to be less accurate than those provided by state enterprises. As indicated by one official, private enterprises' rule conformance has improved considerably in recent years, partly due to heightened environmental awareness in society.[14] Yet enforcement has not been entirely problem-free, as enforcement officials do face various evasion tactics, and sometimes even physical resistance.[15]

In City C, as observed by the EPB Chief, compared with enforcing rules on state-owned enterprises, it is easier to deal with private enterprises.[16] But there are difficulties, too. For example, many small restaurants emit noise and smoke, which become objects of citizen complaints. EPB officials often find it difficult to act fast enough to handle those situations.

In City B, many privately owned enterprises continue to exceed pollution limits. Many still emit pollutants illegally; some, especially those that are politically connected, still refuse to pay fees and fines. One official recounted stories about how some enterprises developed elaborate schemes to evade enforcement.[17] Some enterprises, for example, jointly hired motorcyclists positioned at the town's entrance. Once they spotted any approaching EPB vehicles, the motorcyclists would trigger warning systems in the factories so that they could divert illegally emitted wastewater to the proper channels.

In City D, according to the Deputy Chief, ownership change has facilitated pollution control.[18] One notable example is that the government was finally able to close down a highly polluting, formerly state-owned, factory located in a residential area, which had been a problem case for years. Foreign enterprises, especially those from Japan and Korea, tend to be more conscientious about environmental protection. Although most industrial pollution comes from domestic enterprises, overall, they have an increased environmental awareness – especially larger ones – and have done better in environmental protection than before. Many problems, however, persist. For instance, although many enterprises have installed pollution control devices, they often choose not to run them in order to save operating costs. In 2004, in a special night-time raid, most enterprises inspected were found to have undertaken clandestine emission.

In City A, EPB officials have also found it easier to pressure privately-owned enterprises to improve on their pollution control.[19] For instance, the EPB was able to pressure the manufacturing plant of a Shenzhen-based food production group, which is one of the few major polluters in the city, to upgrade its wastewater treatment facilities despite its exemption from paying pollutant discharge fees as part of the investment incentive package granted by the City A government.

Another consequence of ownership changes concerns the new 'two separate lines for revenues and expenses' system. As there are few state-owned enterprises and TVEs in most cities except Guangzhou, it has become easier for the local jurisdictions to implement the principle that enterprises themselves are solely responsible for pollution control. Large state-owned enterprises in Guangzhou are now the main recipients of environmental protection subsidies and loans, and privately owned enterprises in the other four cities can hardly expect to receive subsidies and loans from their respective cities any more. In principle, if the leadership in the city is committed to environmental protection, more funds derived from pollution fees and fines can be made available for other basic infrastructure developments such as sewage treatment and solid waste disposal facilities.

In addition to ownership changes, another structural issue mentioned by almost all our interviewees concerns industry location. One key problem has been the mix of industrial and residential developments in older neighbourhoods, resulting in frequent citizen complaints against industrial pollution in the neighbourhood. Many cities have in recent years legislated in an attempt to correct the problem. Guangzhou, for example, has prohibited the establishment of heavily polluting industries in the city core. Another trend is for many existing highly polluting industries to move away from the city to other less developed, county-level cities. Almost all cement factories have moved outside the city. In City A, industry and commerce bureaux now must consult with the EPB before approving major enterprise and industrial projects. In City D, systematic efforts have been made to develop industrial parks with appropriate environmental impact assessment.

Mandated by various national and local legislations, many cities have also initiated industrial upgrade projects. In City B, for example, metal, glass, and cement factories that are below a certain size have been required to close down. By 1998, those cement factories with an annual production of less than 20,000 tons had to discontinue production, with the requirement raised to 60,000 tons in 2004. Cement factories have decreased from a high of around 150 in the late 1980s to 36 in 2004. With the minimum production requirement raised to 88,000 tons in 2005, it is likely that almost all cement factories will have to be closed down. In the past, many of these cement factories were family-run businesses, using low-tech burners that were highly polluting. City C has a smaller number of cement factories, but it has in recent years enforced similar size restrictions on them.

Finally, almost every official interviewed commented that regulatory enforcement is still hampered by the relatively small amount of fees and fines the EPB can levy on enterprises. In county-level cities, the maximum fine each time is 100,000 yuan, and illegal emission per ton is only 1.5 yuan. In City D, for example, around 100 enterprises were fined in 2004, and the maximum fine never exceeded 50,000 yuan. The amount is too small to have a major deterrent effect as most enterprises can easily write it off as a regular operating expense.[20]

Overall, a decrease in the number of state-owned enterprises and TVEs may have helped regulatory enforcement by reducing the need for the EPB to negotiate with other government units. In addition, the change has also helped to implement the principle that enterprises are solely responsible for their own pollution control. On the other hand, privately owned enterprises, especially the smaller ones, also create different kinds of enforcement challenges for the EPB. Most obvious is the increasing employment of legal means to protect their interests against EPB's enforcement actions. As indicated by a City D EPB official, for example, some enterprises are now more willing to challenge enforcement actions on the grounds that enforcement officials have failed to follow proper administrative procedures.

Conclusion

One cannot fully understand China's environmental management system without analysing its changing institutional and economic contexts. In this article, we have reviewed how several of these changes have affected environmental management in Guangdong Province. Overall, these institutional reforms and economic changes can be labelled a Chinese version of political modernisation, as they potentially create a more politically independent, but more accountable, administrative system for environmental management. The 'two separate lines for revenues and expenses' system can motivate officials to focus their efforts on investing in environmental projects with higher social returns rather than on collecting pollution fees and fines. De-linking service and enterprise units from the core administrative unit of the EPB contributes to the development of a more streamlined management system with clearer accountability. The environmental quality administrative leadership responsibility system can help heighten local leaders' commitment to environmental protection. With a diminishing number of state-owned enterprises and TVEs, local EPBs can potentially enforce environmental regulations more effectively because they no longer need to negotiate with other government units during the enforcement process.

Yet the same set of institutional reforms and economic changes has also created its challenges for environmental management. The 'two separate lines for revenues and expenses' system appears to work better in more economically developed jurisdictions that are financially strong and have a leadership committed to environmental protection. In jurisdictions without these conditions, the EPB may end up having less financial resources at its disposal than before, thus undermining its enforcement capacity. Although the long-term strategy is to de-link completely most service and enterprise units from the core EPB, at present, most of these units still maintain either formal or informal ties to the EPB, thus creating many potential conflicts of interest. The overall effect of the environmental quality administrative leadership responsibility system should not be overstated as environmental protection is after all only one of the many targets on which local officials are evaluated.

The mixed impacts created by these changes in the environmental management system mirror those created by other changes in the overall governing system in China. As argued by Yang (2004), many governance reforms in the past decade have helped to lessen the totalistic orientation of the Chinese state and to 'enhance the efficiency, transparency, and fairness of the administrative state, strengthen the regulatory apparatuses, remove various institutional incentives and loopholes for corrupt practices, and improve the environment for business' (p. 291). To the extent that China can develop a more streamlined, professional, accountable, and transparent regulatory apparatus, this will benefit environmental protection, since a politically autonomous and non-corrupt regulatory apparatus is a key ingredient for effective pollution control, at least in the context of the developing world (Rock, 2002). Yet, as illustrated by the structural problems identified here, and as pointed out by a number of commentators (Pearson, 2005), many difficulties continue to impair the development of a truly effective and open environmental regulatory apparatus in China.

To assess the long-term prospect of China's environmental management system, it is insufficient just to look at its regulatory apparatus. Weidner and Jänicke (2002), for example, examine a number of key ingredients for building the national capacity for environmental management. One includes the presence of a wide array of actors – notably politicians, government officials, NGOs and citizens – who can act in concert as proponents of environmental protection. In this regard, China is still at a comparative disadvantage with many other countries, as non-governmental actors, like NGOs, are yet to play a major and forceful role as advocates for environmental protection in China (Yang, 2005). In the current context, China still relies mainly on political leaders and government officials to be key proponents of environmental protection. By enhancing the accountability of local officials to environmental quality indicators and to more cost-effective deployment of organisational and financial resources, recent institutional reforms will in the long run enhance government officials' effectiveness as proponents of environmental protection. Yet, from a larger perspective, the environmental governance capacity in China will ultimately be handicapped by a lack of active involvement of the citizenry and social organisations as proponents of environmental protection.

Lastly, as argued by Weidner and Jänicke (2002), economic–technological framework conditions are important factors affecting environmental policy and management. The privatisation of industrial plants has in some respects lessened the difficulties government officials faced initially in enforcing pollution control regulations upon state-owned companies. In addition, government regulations may also help to close down gradually some highly-polluting industries and to separate industrial from residential areas. Yet these basic industrial transformations may take years, or decades, to be fully realised. In this regard, the environmental governance capacity of China will remain insufficient in the near future.

Acknowledgements

The research for this paper was partially funded by the project 'Environmental Governance in County-level Cities in the Pearl River Delta Region: Institutional Contexts, Regulatory Strategies, and Stakeholder Incentives' of the Research Grants Council of the Hong Kong Special Administrative Region (RGC no.: PolyU5231/02H). The authors would like to thank an anonymous reviewer and the editors for useful comments on an earlier version of the paper.

Notes

1. Between July 2004 and June 2005 we interviewed three high-level officials in Guangzhou, and a total of eight officials in the other four cities: two were EPB Chiefs, two Deputy Chiefs, and four leading officials. Unless otherwise stated, all information reported in the case is derived from these interviews. Specific interviews are cited only when the information relates to the personal opinion of an interviewee.
2. Interview with a high-ranking official in the Guangzhou EPB, 21 and 23 August 2004.
3. Interview with a leading official in the Enforcement Team in Guangzhou, 16 August 2004.
4. Interview with a Deputy Chief in the City D EPB, 7 June 2005.
5. The Chief recounted that a few years ago there was a scandal (in the province) when some of the pollution fees were used to construct a training centre, which triggered the People's Congress to consult with the provincial EPB to affirm the separation of revenues and expenses.
6. Interview with the Chief of the City C EPB, 7 July 2004.
7. Interview with a high-ranking official in the Gaungzhou EPB, 11 May 2005.
8. Interview with a leading official in the enforcement team in Guangzhou, 16 August 2004.
9. Interview with a high-ranking official in the Guagnzhou EPB, 11 May 2005.
10. Interview with a Deputy Chief in the City D EPB, 7 June 2005.
11. Interview with a high-ranking official in the Guangzhou EPB, 21 and 23 August 2004.
12. Interview with a leading official in the enforcement team in Guangzhou, 16 August 2004.
13. Interview with a high-ranking official in the Guangzhou EPB, 21 and 23 August 2004.
14. Interview with a high-ranking official in the Guangzhou EPB, 21 and 23 August 2004.
15. Interview with a leading official in the enforcement team in Guangzhou, 7 July 2004.
16. Interview with the Chief of the City C EPB, 7 July 2004.
17. Interview with a Deputy Chief of the City B EPB, 9 July 2004.
18. Interview with a Deputy Chief in the City D EPB, 7 June 2005.
19. Interview with the Chief and a high-ranking official of the City A EPB, 9 June 2005.
20. Some officials also complained about the complicated administrative process for penalising polluting enterprises: First identify the enterprises violating pollution control regulations. Issue a demand note to the enterprise to request compliance within a certain period of time (usually not shorter than 60 days). If the enterprise concerned fails to improve, the EPB must collect evidence of non-compliance. The EPB may then file the case to fine the enterprise. The enterprise concerned may seek administrative review and contest with the EPB regarding the accuracy of the evidence; this may take several months during which the GEPB could do nothing. Even if the enterprise concerned is fined, it has already taken advantage of this lengthy procedure to continue to pollute without doing anything.

References

Brodsgaard, K. (2002) 'Institutional reform and the *bianzhi* system in China', *China Quarterly* 170: 361–86.

Burns, J. (2003) '"Downsizing" the Chinese state: government retrenchment in the 1990s', *China Quarterly* 175: 775–802.

Cheng, J. (2000) 'Introduction', in J. Cheng (ed.) *Guangdong in the Twenty-first Century: Stagnation or Second Take-off?* (Hong Kong: City University of Hong Kong Press), pp. 1–16.

Cherp, A. (2001) 'EA legislation and practice in central and eastern Europe and the former USSR: a comparative analysis', *Environmental Impact Assessment Review* 21: 335–61.

Guangdong Year Book Editorial Board (2003) *Guangdong Year Book 2003* (Guangdong: Guangdong People's Press) (in Chinese).

Jahiel, A. (1997) 'The contradictory impact of reform on environmental protection in China', *China Quarterly* 149: 757–87.

Jänicke, M. (1993) 'Über ökologische und politieke Modernisierungen', *Zeitschrift für Umweltpolitik und Umweltrecht* 2: 159–75.

Lam, T. & Perry, J. (2001) Service organizations in China: reform and its limits, in: P. Lee & C. Lo (eds.) *Remaking China's Public Management* (Westport, CT: Quorum Books), pp. 19–40.

Lewis, J. W. & Xue, L. (2003) 'Social change and political reform in China: meeting the challenge of success', *China Quarterly* 176: 926–42.

Lo, C. & Tang, S. (1994) 'Institutional contexts of environmental management: water pollution control in Guangzhou, China', *Public Administration and Development* 14(1): 53–64.

Lo, C., Lo, J. & Cheung, K.-C. (2001) 'Service organizations in the environmental governance system of the People's Republic of China', in P. Lee & C. Lo (eds.) *Remaking China's Public Management* (Westport, CT: Quorum Books), pp. 41–66.

Ma, X. & Ortolano, L. (2000) *Environmental Regulation in China: Institutions, Enforcement, and Compliance* (New York: Rowman and Littlefield).

Mol, A. & Buttel, F. (2002) 'The environmental state under pressure: an introduction', in A. Mol & F. Buttel (eds.) *The Environmental State under Pressure* (Amsterdam: Elsevier), pp. 1–11.

Montinola, G., Qian, Y. & Weingast, B. (1995) 'Federalism, Chinese style: the political basis for economic success in China', *World Politics* 48(1): 50–81.

Nanfang ribao (2005) 'Qingyuan fails to pass in the environmental responsibility assessment', 3 June (in Chinese).

National Environmental Protection Agency (1996a) *Pollutants Discharge Fees System (Trial)* (Beijing: China Environmental Science Press) (in Chinese).

National Environmental Protection Agency (1996b) *Collection of Documents on the Fourth National Environmental Protection Conference* (Beijing: China Environmental Science Press) (in Chinese).

Oi, J. (1999) *Rural China Takes Off: Institutional Foundations of Economic Reform* (Berkeley, CA: University of California Press).

Pearson, M. (2005) 'Review on Dali Yang, "Remaking the Chinese leviathan: market transition and the politics of governance in China"', *Far Eastern Economic Review* 168(3): 64–6.

Rock, M. (2002) *Pollution Control in East Asia: Lessons from the Newly Industrializing Economies* (Washington, DC: Resources for the Future).

State Environmental Protection Administration (2003) *Pollutants Discharge Fees System (Trial)* (Beijing: China Environmental Science Press) (in Chinese).

Tsui, K.-Y. & Wang, Y. (2004) 'Between separate stoves and a single menu: fiscal decentralization in China', *China Quarterly* 177: 71–90.

Weidner, H. & Jänicke, M. (eds.) (2002) *Capacity Building in National Environmental Policy: a Comparative Study of 17 Countries* (Berlin: Springer-Verlag).

Yang, D. (2004) *Remaking the Chinese Leviathan: Market Transition and the Politics of Governance in China* (Stanford, CA: Stanford University Press).

Yang, G. (2005) 'Environmental NGOs and institutional dynamics in China', *China Quarterly* 181: 46–66.

Public Participation with Chinese Characteristics: Citizen Consumers in China's Environmental Management

SUSAN MARTENS

Introduction

Over the last two decades the Chinese government has increasingly emphasised its efforts to control depletion of the national environment, as is illustrated by the prominence of environmental issues in policy plans; the comprehensive set of national laws and regulations; and the number of environmental institutions that have been established. By boosting its capacity for environmental management and protection the People's Republic of China has made important steps on the path of environmental reform. Yet, a society's ability to identify and resolve environmental problems is not merely based on the knowledge and resources embedded in its bureaucracy and legal framework (Weidner, 2002). The presence of social actors who can act as advocates for the environment and the integration of these non-governmental forces in processes of planning and policy-making can greatly enhance the opportunities for ongoing environmental transitions (Jänicke, 1996).

Contemporary environmental challenges demand a growth of China's environmental capacity beyond the extension of the legislative and bureaucratic systems. Considering the existing implementation deficit in environmental regulation and the inability of the administrative system to monitor and guide environmental developments in all regions and sectors of this vast nation, one of the state's main concerns should be to promote and enable public participation in environmental management. The aim of this contribution is therefore to explore the currently existing, newly developing and future forms and channels for increased civil involvement in China's environmental management.

Chinese Public Participation beyond Politics

The predominance of the Chinese state in the public realm for environmental (inter)action has been stressed by various scholars (Saich, 2000; Rock, 2002). Although environmental issues have in recent years been sanctioned by the state as suitable for public debate – as opposed to, for example, China's unification policy – there remain limits to the openness of debates and to the room for societal action in this field. Especially in cases where environmental issues have close links with questions of human rights, ethnic tension or strategic economic decision-making the debates have remained under state censorship (Li, 2005).

The dividing line between those environmental topics that are and those that are not considered politically sensitive is, however, constantly shifting and contested by societal forces, as well as by voices within the huge and heterogeneous state apparatus itself (Young, 2001). Sensitive environmental issues that were previously banned from open discussion seem to become (temporarily) released to the public sphere and as a result sometimes even linked to (indirect) channels for participation. The internet also gives rise to new dynamics in this respect as it provides a forum for ongoing exchange and debate between citizens from all parts of China, which is unparalleled in terms of access and geographical scope. Moreover, the relative anonymity of the internet appears to encourage Chinese citizens to stretch the boundaries of the public debates (Yang, 2003), and political statements on environmental topics regularly pop up on Chinese web pages. Yet, it still seems safe to conclude that public participation in the field of China's environment remains heavily influenced by the power relations that are typically associated with an authoritarian regime.

Of course, other factors also contribute to the limited participation of Chinese citizens in the sphere of environmental politics. In a cultural study Lucian Pye (1985) argues that most Asians regard the political process as a competition between collective values on the one hand and the selfish desires of special interests on the other. He observed that 'In the Chinese scheme of things all legitimate power was [even in the pre-Communist era] limited to officialdom, and no significant forms of power were supposed to be at the command of any other element of the population, regardless of social station' (Pye, 1985: 57). In comparison to their Western counterparts Chinese citizens do hardly conceive of their relation to the state in terms of mutual rights and responsibilities, but rather in terms of moral obligation, incorporation and interdependence (Wakeman, 1993; Hann & Dunn, 1996). It should be noted, however, that also in Western liberal and social democracies – which are supposed to provide a better breeding ground for meaningful citizen participation – a recent decline in some forms of political participation, especially voting turnout and party membership, has occurred (Scarrow, 2002; Wattenberg, 2002).

If Chinese citizens maintain a different culturally and historically defined outlook on participation in political and social affairs we should perhaps look for different forms and shapes of public participation from those commonly found in the West. Besides, citizenship entails more than the right and responsibility to participate in the exercise of political power (Marshall, 1949). It is linked as well to participation of (groups of) individuals in all sorts of economic, cultural and social transactions. Also, from an environmental perspective, civil involvement does not have to be political in order to be significant. A focus on *political* participation – on citizens merely in their capacity as political producers and consumers – is thus too narrow. This article therefore employs a broader outlook on public participation including a wide range of positions, engagements and activities through which people contribute to environmental reform.

Public participation is not just an individual affair, but can also be the concerted effort of a group of more or less formally organised individuals. Environmental protest by groups of local citizen consumers that join forces to protect their neighbourhoods, livelihood or personal health is a common category of environmentalism to be found around the world and China is no exception in this respect. In pursuit of a liveable environment citizens all over China have been filing collective lawsuits, establishing petition movements and even turning to open demonstrations and boycotts (Jing, 2000; Wang *et al.*, 2001). Chinese local protests usually emerge as the result of a concrete conflict between parties or an acute environmental incident. Mostly the protest dissolves after the conflict has been resolved. However, recently some less localised, more broad-based and long-term voices of protest have been heard within China. The most vivid example in this respect is the protest against the planned and ongoing construction of dams in China's western provinces. Over the last two years, the anti-damming campaign has united concerned citizens from different backgrounds, regions and professions. Supported by domestic media the anti-damming campaign has challenged not only local but also national level policies (Economy, 2004; Xie & Mol, 2006).

Chinese environmental NGOs (non-governmental organisations) have played an important role in the anti-damming protest, by monitoring construction projects, appraising the related environmental and social effects and organising protest activities – a noticeable achievement, considering the relative youth of Chinese NGOs,[2] which were only established in the mid-1990s.[3] Chinese NGOs were typically set up by a committed individual, often by drawing upon personal connections to the government (*guanxi*; Xie and Mol, 2006) or international contacts (Knup, 1997). These organisations – like the well-known 'Friends of Nature' or 'Global Village of Beijing' – usually focus on education, awareness raising and hands-on protection activities. As they gradually become more professional Chinese NGOs are increasingly entering specialised fields of environmental activism. Moreover, the activities of green student groups[4] are encouraging well-trained graduates to join established social organisations in the field of the environment, or to form their own networks and organisations.

Less favourable for civil environmentalism is the dominant role that the state, particularly the Ministry of Civil Affairs (MOCA), plays by setting strict rules for the establishment of social organisations, thereby limiting the scope of NGO activities and influence (Saich, 2000; Ho, 2001). Support or recognition from the government is at present almost a prerequisite for the survival of grassroots groups (Wang, 2000). Yet, at the same time numerous groups of environmentalists aim to circumvent strict regulations and to escape state scrutiny by becoming a legal body without registration under MOCA, for example, by establishing a commercial 'facade' organisation or by avoiding registration altogether (e.g. working as a 'volunteer network'). Another outcome of the state's intervention in the development of civic organisations is the establishment of numerous 'government organised non-governmental organisations' (GONGOs). At various administrative levels government institutions established 'non-governmental organisations' for multiple reasons, such as the reallocation of government budgets and the related need for government departments to slim down; the ability of GONGOs to perform more flexibly than unwieldy bureaucratic institutions; and the desire to attract (foreign) financial resources (Wang & Sun, 2001; Wu, 2002). The actual effects of these quasi-NGOs on the development of civil environmentalism is disputed. Some observers regard the presence of GONGOs as an intermediate step towards a more mature civil society, while others consider them to be illegitimate frauds undermining the development of true social forces.

In the remainder of this article I will not explicitly discuss the organisational features of the different groups and networks that are active in China's environmental field. Yet, the particular characteristics of China's non-governmental (or semi-governmental) sector are important to keep in mind, since they influence the channels for and manifestations of citizen consumer involvement in China's environmental reform.

A Contextual Approach to Civil Environmentalism

Political and socio-cultural dynamics influence the opportunities for citizen consumers to become involved in the management of the environmental commons. The involvement of citizen consumers in environmental reform is also related to the environmental conditions in a particular locality, including the biophysical state of the environment, the level of public environmental awareness and the environmental management situation. An investigation of existing, newly developing and potential manifestations of public participation in China's environmental management should thus be thoroughly embedded in the nation's environmental and socio-political context. To allow such a contextual analysis of public participation a three-step model is proposed (Figure 1; see also Martens, 2004): first, a review of the prominent issues in China's environmental debates; secondly, an analysis of how these environmental issues are framed, in order to arrive, thirdly, at an assessment of the prospects these frames provide for concrete citizen consumer roles. I will focus especially on the latter two steps.

Environmental Frames for Theory and Action

The notion of 'frames' and the process of 'frame construction' has been much discussed in relation to social movements. David Snow and Robert Benford define frames as schemata of interpretation that allow actors to locate, perceive, identify, and label occurrences within their present, past or future life sphere and the world at large (Snow *et al.*, 1986; Snow & Benford, 1992). By presenting persuasive frames of topical debates to the public, social movement organisations aim to mobilise support for their claims and struggles. Similarly, environmental rhetoric is organised into collective action frames in order to appeal to potential supporters (Taylor, 2000).

Yet, environmental movement organisations are not exclusively active in the formulation of frames, as governments, politicians, businesses and scientists also contextualise, define, re-package and communicate their preferred frames for environmental understanding and action to third parties. And different actors might present different framings of particular environmental issues, as the construction of frames is as much a social and political process of knowledge production, as it is a straightforward reflection of biophysical reality. Environmental frames do not only refer to technical definitions of physical environmental problems; they also provide insight into the social dynamics surrounding these issues. As such, frames can be regarded as the result of the input, evaluation, selection and combination of different problem perceptions by different actors in society (Pleune, 1997). Nor is it uncommon for competing environmental frames to exist at the same time (Buttel and Taylor, 1992; Klandermans, 1992).

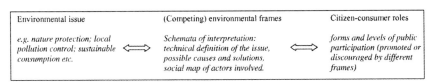

Environmental issue	(Competing) environmental frames	Citizen-consumer roles
e.g. nature protection; local pollution control; sustainable consumption etc. ⟷	*Schemata of interpretation: technical definition of the issue, possible causes and solutions, social map of actors involved.* ⟷	*forms and levels of public participation (promoted or discouraged by different frames)*

Figure 1. Conceptual model for the analysis of public participation

Yet, by means of culture, institutionalised power relations and interaction patterns within a particular society different actors are granted differential voices in the national arenas in which (environmental) frames are assembled, constructed, contested and presented (Hoffman & Ventresca, 1999; Rydin, 1999). In this respect it is important to note that societal, cultural and political arenas in the Chinese context are quite different from those common in Western settings. The environmental sociologist John Hannigan has described the construction of environmental frames as a social interaction and negotiation process between three types of actors: scientists that are dominant in discovering and assembling the basis of environmental claims; mass media that are central actors in the public presentation and legitimisation of frames; and finally political actors, including oppositional voices, who play a major role in contesting claims (Hannigan, 1995). In China, however, the state remains dominant in all stages of frame construction as well as in the different arenas in which frames are negotiated and legitimised. For example, the Chinese mass media are largely state-owned and under constant state censorship. Ongoing economic reforms have induced some changes in the management of the media sector, as state subsidies have diminished and the income from advertising has steadily increased. Newspapers are taking more and more liberties in their reporting, for instance on government malpractices (Li, 2005). However, generally speaking, the media remain careful not to take serious political risks and the frames that enter the public debate through media publications remain heavily influenced by official state policies (Lee, 2003). While Chinese NGOs are constantly exploring new roles in the field of environmental management, their limited access to political arenas for debate and decision-making adds to the state supremacy in processes of environmental framing. These limitations on the engagement of societal actors in the framing process have to be kept in mind when analysing current Chinese frames in terms of the breeding grounds they provide for increased civil involvement in environmental reform.

Understanding Citizen Consumer Roles

Different environmental frames can draw in varying degrees upon environmental capacities within civil society, thus promoting distinct forms and levels of public participation and diverse involvement of social organisations. For example, global warming can be defined as an international political affair between nations, for which the remedial strategy is to be found in the domain of global politics. Yet, a complementary or perhaps competing frame might present global warming as the result of increased domestic energy use and thus allocate the remedial strategy for this tangential problem at the domain of daily life. It is evident that the involvement of citizens in international conventions on climate change is organised along different channels from participation in the encouragement of energy-saving household practices. The dominant frames in public debates will shape the extent to which citizen consumers will label global warming as an issue that they can and should engage in personally.

Although public environmental concern is increasing in China, the actual environmental knowledge of Chinese citizen consumers is still rather low (Renmin, 1996; Lee, 2003). This relatively immature state of civil environmentalism should be taken into account in discussing citizen consumer roles, for instance by searching also for less articulated forms of civil involvement like noticing the 'abstract' discussions on environmental transformations that are going on in (inter)national arenas and networks. Yet, environmental awareness is surely not the only factor underlying the environmental involvement of Chinese citizen consumers. Public participation is only possible when enabled by an adequate socio-material foundation for ecologically sound behaviour (Spaargaren & Martens, 2005). For example, sustainable household practices can only be established when the necessary innovations and infrastructures, such as biodegradable detergents or waste recycling systems, are in place. Even well-educated West Europeans are unlikely to separate their kitchen wastes in the absence of convenient kerbside collection facilities.

Chinese Citizen Consumer Roles in Five Environmental Domains

To identify empirically different channels for public participation in China's environmental management the (future) roles for Chinese civil actors are explored in relation to the framing of five environmental issues: (1) protection of nature and bio-diversity; (2) local control of environmental pollution; (3) construction of green company images; (4) establishment of sustainable household practices; and (5) participation in international conventions and treaties.[5] By linking public participation to specific environmental frames we aim to arrive at a better understanding of the potential of Chinese citizen consumers for improved environmental management and protection.

For each of the five issues a brief description was drawn up, containing a technical definition of the biophysical environmental condition, statements related to the possible causes and solutions of the problem, and a 'social map' of the relevant actors in different realms for environmental (inter) action. These descriptions were based on information taken from widely accessible Chinese news media, to ensure similarity with the assumptions, explanations and terminology used in topical public debates. Subsequently, the descriptions were explored in 30 open interviews[6] with well-informed respondents from NGO staff and members; individual activists; officials from different government units; Chinese and international scholars; environmental student groups; members of a green residential community; managers of 'green businesses'; journalists; and staff of a communist mass organisation.[7] Respondents were especially invited to reflect on the potential for public participation in relation to the different environmental issues and subsequent frames at hand.

National Protection of Nature and Biodiversity

A main strategy for counteracting the loss and erosion of natural areas and biodiversity in China is the establishment of nature reserves and protection zones. Between 1978 and 1999 the number of nature reserves in China grew rapidly from 34 to 1227, occupying 9.85 per cent of the nation's territory (Jim and Xu, 2004). Protected areas are created at various administrative levels under the application of different rules and regulations; for instance, ecological protection zones allow limited human activity, while nature reserves are supposed to be cleared of all human presence.

The construction of natural areas and reserves can have far-reaching social and economic consequences especially in remote rural areas where nature protection is entangled with concerns about property rights, cultural heritage, ethnic minorities, and livelihoods (Harkness, 1998). For example, in the Tibet Autonomous Region the government fenced off natural areas, relocating over 900 farmers and shepherds from the upper stream of the Yangtze River to lower lying areas (*People's Daily*, 16 August 2002). Although both governmental and non-governmental experts regard such radical measures as legitimate due to the importance of the cause, they also acknowledge the top-down approach to be unsatisfactory; not only in terms of the limited involvement of local people and the absence of guaranteed use rights and adequate compensation for lost livelihoods, but also with respect to inadequate achievements in actual nature protection (Xu *et al.*, 1998). Recognising the undesirable social consequences and ineffectiveness of the traditional model, the national environmental authority SEPA has started to organise training programmes in participatory management for staff of natural reserves. However, implementation of more open styles of reserve management remains impaired due to lack of qualified staff at the local level, limited funding and corruption. Exceptions are the natural reserves that are established and managed with support from international organisations such as WWF, as these usually demand participation of local residents, for example, through the development of alternative means of living, such as eco-tourism or organic agriculture.

The inadequate achievements of, in particular, local governments in nature protection have inspired the activities of various civil environmental groups – especially urban-based NGOs. The projects that are well-received by government and public alike are those in which NGO members travel to remote parts of China to offer nature education in local schools. Much celebrated are also the cases in which non-governmental groups act as a watchdog, disclosing for example illegal logging by municipalities to the media or to higher authorities. Although volunteer groups and NGOs are involved in incidental hands-on protection and education campaigns, there exist at present no structural channels for committed citizens to become involved in nature policy and management (Jim & Xu, 2004). Moreover, in most cases even the participation of local citizens in the establishment and management of reserves is not ensured. Local residents are primarily seen as a target group in nature protection, rather than as a partner in the implementation of nature protection policies, although recently some steps have been taken towards the introduction of more participatory policy styles, for instance by SEPA.

Local Control of Environmental Pollution

Air, water and soil pollution and nuisances such as noise and stench – causing deteriorating living conditions and increased health risks – are much discussed in China (Wang, 2002). Many of the proposed and implemented solutions to local pollution problems involve traditional government regulation, such as the control of traffic emissions by banning old vehicles, the implementation of environmental production standards for local industries or regulations for the vibrant building sector. But the importance of public participation in achieving a cleaner local environment is stressed by respondents from all sectors and several concrete channels to enable civil involvement in this field have been established in recent years.

To encourage citizens to become involved in monitoring environmental quality and to increase access to environmental information the Chinese state in the mid-1990s institutionalised a system to report environmental problems and offences to the relevant authorities (Dasgupta & Wheeler, 1996; Brettel, 2004). Citizens can voice their complaints to the authorities by letter, in person or by telephone.[8] The environmental protection bureaux of many (large) cities opened environmental telephone hotlines to improve the visibility and accessibility of the reporting system. The Chongqing EPB, for instance, opened its 12369 hotline in January 2002, receiving 10,800 complaints, including 5200 on noise and 3500 on air pollution within the first six months (*China News Service*, 20 November 2002). Local officials tend to boost the success of the complaint hotlines,[9] but they are not considered as effective channels for public participation by most societal respondents in this research. To assess environmental qualities citizens are at present fully dependent on their own sensory perception, which hampers a solid foundation for their environmental complaints. According to the NGO Center for Legal Assistance to Pollution Victims citizens need access to more specific information on environmental indicators than the reports currently publicised by the authorities. Other problems relate to the inadequate handling and settlement of citizens' complaints by (local) government units and the limited opportunities for Chinese citizens to defend their environmental rights in these cases.

Improved public participation is needed at an earlier stage, when pollution and violations of citizens' environmental rights can still be prevented. The promulgation of China's Environmental Impact Assessment (EIA) Law, effective from September 2003, promotes public involvement in decision-making on projects with potentially adverse environmental impacts. EIA was officially introduced in China in 1979 through the Provisional Environmental

Protection Law. Yet the gap between the intent and actual performance of this instrument has remained large (Swanson *et al.*, 2001; Mao & Hills, 2002). Article 5 of the new Environmental Impact Assessment Law stipulates that 'the State encourages relevant units, experts and *the public* to participate in environmental impact assessments in appropriate ways'. It is further stated in articles 11 and 21 that plans and construction projects – subject to an environmental impact assessment – cannot be submitted for approval before the opinions of the public have been solicited through evidentiary meetings, testimony hearings or in other ways.

Although the EIA law can be considered a step forward in the institutionalisation of public participation several problems with respect to the inclusion of citizens remain. It is not stipulated how and when the involvement of citizens in evidentiary hearings or testimony meetings should be promoted, leaving this to the discretion of local governments. It remains difficult for citizens to attend public hearings, and even harder to join actively in the discussion. The director of the Chongqing University EIA centre explains: 'During the review of the EIA report we always set two seats for the public, but these people usually remain silent, as the EIA report is very technical and not everybody can understand it'.

From a theoretical perspective public participation in pollution control has great potential as civil involvement is easily triggered by the perception of actual environmental risks (Laurian, 2003), such as threats to health and livelihood caused by local pollution. However, reflecting on the Chinese situation we see that there are two obstacles. Firstly, the public's involvement in relevant processes of policymaking is, as noted, not yet well established at the local level. Social actors especially express the need for more transparent and effective channels for public participation in decision-making on the local environment. While current experiences with EIA procedures are not an unqualified success, it might in the future prove to be an interesting avenue for more civil involvement in local planning. SEPA at least appears to take the instrument seriously and is encouraging its staff to learn more about the facilitation of participatory processes. The second obstacle is the strong focus on solutions at the institutional level. Environmental behaviour that citizen consumers can develop independently, such as refraining from littering or cycling to work, is not recognised (yet) as an important step towards a cleaner living environment. It appears that the lower hanging and admittedly large fruits of industrial emissions and bad city planning have to be picked, before attention will turn to the potential pro-environmental actions of individual citizens.

Pushing or Pulling 'Green Company Images'?

That industries are not all indifferent towards their share in China's environmental degradation is demonstrated by China's top oil refiner Sinopec. To announce the adoption of a health, safety and environment management system it bought a full page newspaper advertisement (*Far Eastern Economic Review*, 5 July 2001). Nor is the Sinopec case an isolated example, as various Chinese companies strive to clean up their act and communicate their environmental efforts to the general public. In particular, businesses operating in the international market adopt strategies for environmental reform; in order to accommodate Western consumer preferences, to gain or maintain a good reputation and to comply with international environmental standards. Companies operating exclusively on China's domestic market are lagging behind due to less stringent national environmental standards and the absence of demand-driven incentives for improved environmental performance.

The concepts of eco-labels and green products are still relatively new to Chinese consumers and green demands from the public are only seldom heard (Chan, 2000). With respect to food, however, Chinese consumers are starting to articulate a demand for environmentally sound products, especially linked to health concerns. In practice, though, potential 'green food' consumers encounter several barriers, as prices for organic products are high, their availability limited and the certification systems confusing[10] and unreliable.

The reliability of eco-products is also in other market sectors a key concern. It remains extremely arduous for Chinese consumers to check the validity of green claims – as it would be for the individual Western consumer – and scandals surrounding fake environmental labels have had adverse effects on the interface between green provisioning and demand. Through the publication of reliable information on sustainable products several environmental groups and China's Consumer Association strive to facilitate green consumption and to support companies with an environmental profile. An interesting example is the internet publication of 'China's green pages', which provides information on a variety of companies in the environmental sector and on environmentally friendly consumer products (www.lvhoo.com). These 'green pages' are operated on a non-profit basis by the Beijing-based organisation 'GreenWeb Info'. Several environmental activist groups have also considered the publication of a black-list, naming companies as well as products with a particularly bad environmental performance. It is, however, judged too risky at present, as interests of government units and industries are often closely intertwined and action against industries could thus be 'political'.

Participation by members of the public, in their capacity as consumers of green products and services, is recognised by respondents from all environmental sectors as an important pull factor towards green company images and environmental improvements in industrial performance. Yet, a manager of the China Consumer Association states that 'a large percentage of Chinese consumers are still facing more basic concerns than questions on the environmental performance of goods and services'.[11] The global environmental discourse on green consumption and lifestyle does not fit the situation of citizen consumers in impoverished regions. Other respondents remark that individual

Chinese consumers feel powerless, experiencing little control over market forces (see Martinsons *et al.*, 1997). Several civil environmental groups are trying to fill this void by establishing platforms for exchange between consumers and suppliers of environmentally friendly goods and services.[12]

In some cases creative consumers manage to overcome the non-sustainable sameness of China's supply system by becoming co-providers or even self-providers of sustainable consumption innovations. One such example is found in a residential area in Beijing, where volunteers buy large amounts of energy-saving light-bulbs directly from a factory to sell them at attractive, wholesale prices to fellow residents. Other groups of metropolitan citizens have teamed up in order to provide their own (reliable) organic vegetables, by running a garden on the outskirts of the city.

Considering the nascent state of consumer demand for green products, the achievement of a real take-off of green supply probably requires the establishment of preferential government policies, an increase in international trade and the need to meet global environmental standards.

Establishment of Sustainable Household Practices

The sustainable households frame refers to the idea that negative environmental impacts of day-to-day practices can be reduced if household routines are shaped in more environmentally friendly ways. A 'green' turn in household practices can be realised through behavioural changes, such as taking shorter showers or via the adoption of environmental technologies, like a water-saving showerhead. Officials of the Beijing EPB are eager to point out that changing behaviour in and around the home is the first and most important stage of public participation: citizen consumers should first clean up their own act, before they can participate in environmental monitoring and decision-making.[13]

Yet, there still exist numerous impediments to the establishment of green behaviour at the household level. In China large groups of consumers remain captive in some aspects of their household decision-making through centralised systems of household provisioning. For example, heating systems in older apartment buildings do not allow individual adjustment of heating levels, while pricing and billing are floor area based (Feng, 2002). As there is no differentiation in China's public energy sector, homemakers wanting to purchase energy from sustainable sources are confronted with the absence of green energy supply.[14] Similar structures can still be found in relation to water consumption; incentives for water-saving disappeared with the introduction of communist systems for water distribution. An 80-year-old member of a 'green residential group' in Beijing explains: 'When we lived here in the *hutong* all water resources were shared. People had no idea how much water they used. But this is changing, now that the *hutong* has been replaced by apartment buildings and we all have several taps in our private apartments. People are becoming aware of their personal use and have to pay for it as well'.[15]

Public participation in reduction and re-use of household waste is also considered crucial for an improved environmental household performance by actors from diverse sectors of society. The massive disposal of paper, plastic bags, foam food packages and chemical wastes, such a batteries, represents a huge problem in China. Nearly half of the generated municipal solid waste is piled in China's suburbs, where the accumulated quantity has reached 6 billions tons, causing heavy environmental pollution (Wang & Nie, 2001). But other than intrinsic environmental awareness, there are no incentives for citizen consumers to reduce their waste volumes, or to separate different types of household wastes. On campuses and in a number of urban residential areas, student groups, NGOs and progressive neighbourhood committees have initiated programmes to educate residents about waste prevention and waste separation. Typical activities include the distribution of durable shopping bags and the separated collection of kitchen wastes and batteries. Such projects usually suffer from low participation rates. But even more discouraging is the fact that these programmes are almost symbolic since municipalities do not operate facilities for separated waste treatment.

Chongqing, the third largest city in China, is one of the municipalities working to improve waste management and is presently constructing several treatment plants, while it was formerly dumping all solid waste (4000 tons per day) directly in the Yangtze River.[16] To finance these improvements in waste treatment residents will have to pay higher treatment fees. Yet, citizens claim that waste management is a responsibility of the government – which is collecting ample taxes already – and that the costs should not be transferred to individual households.[17]

It becomes clear that a balanced effort from various actors is needed to improve public participation in the greening of households. On the one hand, consumers may well be expected to take responsibility for their personal share in collective environmental problems, shaking off traditional attitudes of passivity and indifference. Raising awareness on environmental and consumption issues is inevitable in this respect, for which increased efforts by governments and social actors are needed. On the other hand, citizen consumer involvement will remain limited, if the socio-material infrastructure for more sustainable household practices is not in place. When there is no system for separated waste treatment, it is useless and perhaps even counterproductive for NGOs to promote garbage-sorting. And it seems rather hypocritical for policymakers to push families to reduce their domestic energy use, while at the same time encouraging them to buy a private car in order to stimulate the national car industry.

Participation in International Conventions and Treaties

China's reforms have placed the country more firmly in the global environmental arena. The Chinese media regularly report on international conventions on climate change, multilateral agreements for transboundary river management, environmental trade standards and so on. However, global environmental issues clearly have a low profile, when compared with the constant stream of reports on local pollution incidents, domestic nature degradation and national environmental regulations. Yet there is no doubt that China – as the world's most populous country – is a major player in global environmental affairs. It is the second largest producer of greenhouse gas after the United States, and harbours 10 per cent of the Earth's rare species of flora and fauna. China's leaders have taken a relatively proactive and visible role in environmental policy formulation in international arenas and have signed or acceded to numerous conventions on the environment (Sims, 1999). Contrary to the state's position, the presence of Chinese non-governmental environmentalists has been far from prominent in the supranational fora, debates and institutions, which together represent the green core of a global civil society. It was not until 2002 that Chinese greens made their 'official' debut in circles of transnational environmentalism, when 12 environmental NGOs participated in the Johannesburg World Summit for Sustainable Development. Obviously, this 'late appearance' is related to the relative youth of Chinese NGOs. As the Chinese public is only slowly becoming aware of environmental issues, NGOs tend to focus on environmental issues that occur close to home, where a link to the daily life of their (potential) domestic constituency is more easily established.

Yet international networks and exchange are vital for Chinese environmentalists, as closer ties with the international environmental community can provide much-needed financial resources, information and expertise and a certain level of domestic recognition and political protection. Environmental frames, ideas and know-how from the global discourse are also gradually being adopted, interpreted and implemented by China's green groups, as demonstrated by the well-publicised NGO 'Global Village of Beijing' that strives to spread Western ideas on green consumption among Chinese citizen consumers. 'Global' environmental topics are furthermore imported by international environmental organisations that maintain offices and projects in China. Greenpeace's China office has in this respect been working on a series of human interest stories surrounding pollution in Datong, a major mining city, trying to link the domestic issue of coal-burning to the global debate on climate change.[18]

Presently there are no direct or indirect roles for individual Chinese citizen consumers in international conventions or treaties on the environment. To the extent that we can speak of *any* participation by the Chinese public in international negotiations on the environment only interest groups, such as environmental NGOs, are involved. However, this generally applies to the participation of citizen consumers in international environmental regimes, rather than to China as an isolated case: 'We cannot simply assume that the workers, the women, the peasants, or the poor of the world will make their voices heard in the global fora. They are nested in particular communities of struggle and their transnational voices are not heard without a complex process of mediation and translation' (Munck, 2002: 359). Nevertheless,

Chinese environmental activists tend to have a rather positive outlook on international regimes and treaties as they expect participation in such international networks to stimulate domestic opportunities and capacities for public participation, as well as to increase international pressure for further democratic reforms.

Chinese Channels for Civil Environmentalism

The empirical evidence above indicates that there are multiple roles, strategies and choices available for environmentally motivated citizen consumers to become involved in elements of China's environmental management. Several enabling as well as restraining factors stand out when analysing the potential for increased public participation in environmental reform.

The empirical evidence related to the 'green company' and 'sustainable household' frames illustrates that China's economic reform and development not only causes environmental problems, but at the same time provides new opportunities for the instigation and implementation of environmental improvements by multiple actors, including the public. Chinese industries, especially those with international aspirations and practices, are beginning to realise that if they want to get ahead they must go green.[19] In the food sector, for example, a growing group of producers strives to acquire organic food certificates.[20] On the demand side of the vibrant market developments, a substantial part of the Chinese population has as yet no access to contemporary consumption practices, let alone the opportunity to articulate an ecologically modernised demand for green products and services. On the other hand, however, improved economic conditions have led to the rise of a new and expanding 'consumer class' in China's urban centres. These consumers are increasingly aware of the impact environmental pollution has on their health and quality-of-life. Moreover, individual participation in environmental reform has for middle-class urbanites become – at least theoretically – more attainable through the channel of increasingly liberalised and diversified (green niche) markets. Reacting to this development several Chinese NGOs are now trying to formulate and implement ecologically sound consumer roles and behaviours, often inspired by the international environmental discourse.

Yet, environmental participation in daily life by means of green consumption and environmentally sound household practices is currently by no means the routine of the masses. Public participation in the domains of market and daily life remains hampered by the absence of a solid socio-material basis for green citizen consumer involvement. On the one hand, there is low awareness of the potential for strong consumer citizen roles, not only on the part of the public itself, but also within Chinese bureaucratic circles. On the other hand, the infrastructure for green improvements in daily life is seriously limited, ranging from the poor supply of eco-products and dubious certification systems, to outdated waste-handling at the municipal level. Evening out such barriers for the expression of green lifestyles will – in the years to come – be one of the most important tasks in the promotion of public participation in China's environmental management.

It is hard to pinpoint the exact effects of current political developments on the opportunities for environmental participation. The authorities still regard public participation first and foremost as a means to increase the effectiveness of policy measures and officials leave no doubt that the promulgation of environmental protection goals and policies should remain an exclusively state affair (Qing & Vermeer, 1999). This is for instance illustrated by the framing of nature protection as a national strategic matter, to be decided without interference from secondary local-level interests.

Nevertheless, opportunities for public participation in environmental planning and decision-making do vary with different levels of government. Environmental protection agencies at lower governmental levels, and especially those in rural areas, are institutionally weak. They therefore often welcome the support of environmental groups and concerned citizens in defending their environmental policies, as with respect to local pollution control, against other government departments such as local planning committees (see Zhang, 2003). The increased publication of data on local environmental conditions, the elaboration of environmental complaint systems and the ongoing learning process with respect to EIA procedures also point in the direction of improved channels for public participation in local environment.

Within Western societies environmental movements have played a key role in strengthening public participation: by raising environmental awareness; by mobilising public support and setting the political agenda; by acting as an intermediary level between the state and members of the public; and by formulating concrete green roles for citizen consumers. Although the Chinese state has acknowledged the need for a stronger social intermediary level between state and citizenry (Saich, 2000; Ho, 2001), the Communist Party appears to be only slightly willing to allocate the resources and power needed to enable the development of such social organisations and subsequently allow their participation in arenas for environmental policymaking. As a result it is very hard for Chinese NGOs to obtain a central role in environmental reform, although they have still managed several successes, notably with respect to the recent anti-damming campaign.

Further political liberalisation thus seems required for non-governmental capacities to develop a more independent position in processes of ecological transformation. Such political liberalisation is not necessarily or exclusively brought about by reforms that are intentionally reinforcing participation or democratisation. New policy initiatives, whether aimed at improved opportunities for civil mobilisation or not, produce new channels of communication, more organised networks of citizens, and more unified cognitive frameworks around which insurgents can mount claims and organise themselves (Tarrow, 1994). The endorsement of private property and the commercialisation of the housing market have, for example, encouraged residents in different urban neighbourhoods to mobilise against pollution, the destruction of green areas and unauthorised construction projects that threatened to decrease the value of their privately owned apartments (Zhu, 2004). The transnational dimension to China's environmental management is also likely to influence domestic opportunities for public participation in directions that might be foreseen or unforeseen, desired or not desired by the Chinese state. One illustration is China's decision to welcome international funding and assistance, which has resulted in 'show-case' nature protection projects that allow more active participation by local people in conservation and sustainable reserve management. In the foreseeable future, cautious political liberalisation might be brought to China via highly dynamic markets and transnational arrangements.

Notes

1. This research was carried out within the project 'Strengthening Environmental NGOs in China' and enabled by financial support from Senter International, The Hague.
2. Throughout Chinese history there always existed various types of formal and informal social organisations and networks, such as professional associations, friendship associations and communist mass movements (Ma, 2002).
3. Several international NGOs, also in the field of environment, were already active in China before that time.
4. A survey among Chinese universities and colleges provides evidence of more than 100 environmental student associations in 2001, located in 26 provinces (www.greensos.org).
5. The selection of the frames is based on the following criteria: (1) one frame taken from each of the five dominant domains in China's environmental debate (see also Martens, 2004); (2) regional variation in China's environmental management situation is taken into account; (3) the selection allows respondents to give an informed opinion on the related potential for public participation; (4) the selection includes – at face value – frames that encourage different forms of civil involvement.
6. Interviews conducted in December 2003.
7. Respondents have been guaranteed anonymity; therefore no references to persons will be made. The author would like to thank all respondents for their kind co-operation and their willingness to share opinions and information.
8. In China referred to as system of *Xin Fang*.
9. See also Brettel (2004).
10. The Ministry of Agriculture operates the 'green food label' classified into grade A and AA, while SEPA implemented the 'organic food label'. For information on different labels refer to China Environment and Sustainable Development Reference and Research Centre (CESDRRC) (2003).
11. Interview 12 December 2003.
12. Other NGO initiatives include seminars on green consumption by 'Friends of Nature' and a special programme for consumer and producer activities surrounding the 2008 Olympics staged by 'Global Village of Beijing'.
13. Interviews 12 April 2002, 5 and 12 December 2003.
14. The NGO 'South North Institute for Sustainable Development' conducts research into the marketing potential for green energy.
15. Interview 9 December 2003.
16. Interview Chongqing Inward Investment Project Office, 18 December 2003.
17. Survey Chongqing University Environment and Resources College, 2003
18. Interview 15 December 2003.
19. See, among others, *China Environment News*, 10 April 2003; *People's Daily*, 7 February 2001; *Far Eastern Economic Review*, 5 July 2001.

20. The Organic Food Development Center in Nanjing (a certification agency of SEPA), has since 1994 issued certificates for the production or trading of organic food to more than 100 enterprises.

References

Brettel, A. (2004) 'Nipping dissent in the bud: the institutionalisation of environmental complaint resolution in China'. Paper presented at 'Shifting Social Spaces' conference, Beijing, 22–23 April.

Buttel, F. & Taylor, P. (1992) 'Environmental sociology and global environmental change: a critical assessment', in M. Redclift & T. Benton (eds.) *Social Theory and the Global Environment* (London: Routledge), pp. 211–30.

Chan, R. (2000) 'An emerging green market in China: myth or reality', *Business Horizons*, March: 9.

China Environment and Sustainable Development Reference and Research Centre (CESDRRC) (2003) *Organic Food Consumer Guide for Beijing* (Beijing: Centre for Environmental Education and Communication).

Dasgupta, S. & Wheeler, D. (1996) *Citizen Complaints as Environmental Indicators: Evidence from China* (Washington, DC: World Bank).

Economy, E. (2004) 'China facing a flood of environmental protests over dam policy', *Taipei Times*, 17 December.

Feng, L. (2002) 'Improving energy efficiency of space heating in China: lessons learned and policy implications', *Sinosphere Journal* 4: 32–41.

Hann, C. & Dunn, E. (1996) *Civil Society, Challenging Western Models* (London: Routledge).

Hannigan, J. (1995) *Environmental Sociology. A Social Constructionist Perspective* (London: Routledge).

Harkness, J. (1998) 'Recent trends in forestry and biodiversity in China', *China Quarterly* 156: 911–34.

Ho, P. (2001) 'Greening without conflict? Environmentalism, NGOs and civil society', *Development and Change* 32: 893–921.

Hoffman, A. & Ventresca, M. (1999) 'The institutional framing of policy debates: economics versus the environment', *American Behavioral Scientist* 42(8): 1368–92.

Jänicke, M. (1996) 'Democracy as a condition for environmental policy success: the importance of non-institutional factors', in W. Lafferty & J. Meadowcroft (eds.) *Democracy and the Environment: Problems and Prospects* (Cheltenham: Edward Elgar), pp. 71–85.

Jim, C. & Xu, S. (2004) 'Recent protected-area designation in China: an evaluation of administrative and statutory procedures', *Geographical Journal* 170(1): 39–50.

Jing, J. (2000) 'Environmental protest in rural China', in E. Perry & M. Selden (eds.) *Chinese Society: Change, Conflict and Resistance* (London: Routledge), pp. 143–60.

Klandermans, B. (1992) 'The social construction of protest and multi-organizational fields', in A. Morris & C. McClurg Mueller (eds.) *Frontiers in Social Movement Theory* (New Haven, CT: Yale University Press), pp. 77–103.

Knup, E. (1997) 'Environmental NGOs in China: an overview', *China Environment Series* 1(3): 9–15.

Laurian, L. (2003) 'A prerequisite for participation. environmental knowledge and what residents know about local toxic sites', *Journal of Planning Education and Research* 22: 257–69.

Lee, Y. (2003) *Public Environmental Attitudes in China: Some Early Empirical Evidence* (Hong Kong: Centre for China Urban and Rural Studies).

Li, J. (2005) 'The position of Chinese newspapers in the framing of environmental issues', MSc thesis, Wageningen University.

Ma, Q. (2002) 'Defining Chinese nongovernmental organisations', *Voluntas* 13(2): 113–30.

Mao, W. & Hills, P. (2002) 'Impacts of the economic–political reform on environmental impact assessment implementation in China', *Impact Assessment and Project Appraisal* 20(2): 101–11.

Marshall, T. H. (1949) *Citizenship and Social Class* (Cambridge: Cambridge University Press).

Martens, S. (2004) 'Civil involvement in China's environmental reform: exploring frameworks for theory and action'. Paper presented at 'Strengthening Environmental NGOs in China' conference, Beijing, April.

Martinsons, M., So, S., Tin, C. & Wong, D. (1997) 'Hong Kong and China: emerging markets for environmental products and technologies', *Long Range Planning* 30(2): 277–90.

Munck, R. (2002) 'Global civil society: myths and prospects', *Voluntas* 13(4): 349–61.

Pleune, R. (1997) 'The importance of contexts in strategies of environmental organisations with regard to climate change', *Environmental Management* 21(5): 733–45.

Pye, L. (1985) *Asian Power and Politics. The Cultural Dimensions of Authority* (Cambridge, MA: Harvard University Press).

Qing, D. & Vermeer, E. (1999) 'Do good work, but do not offend the "old communists"', in W. Draguhn & R. Ash (eds.) *China's Economic Security* (Richmond, VA: Curzon Press), pp. 142–62.

Renmin, D. (1996) *Survey of People's Environmental Awareness* (Beijing: China Environmental Protection Fund).

Rock, M. (2002) 'Integrating environmental and economic policymaking in China and Taiwan', *American Behavioral Scientist* 45(9): 1435–55.

Rydin, Y. (1999) 'Can we talk ourselves into sustainability? The role of discourse in the environmental policy process', *Environmental Values* 8: 467–84.

Saich, T. (2000) 'Negotiating the state: the development of social organisations in China', *China Quarterly* 161: 125–41.

Scarrow, S. (2002) 'Parties without members? Party organisation in a changing electoral environment', in R. Dalton & M. Wattenberg (eds.) *Parties without Partisans* (Oxford: Oxford University Press), pp. 79–101.

Sims, H. (1999) 'One-fifth of the sky: China's environmental stewardship', *World Development* 27(7): 1227–45.

Snow, D. & Benford, R. (1992) 'Master frames and cycles of protest', in A. Morris & C. McClurg Mueller (eds.) *Frontiers in Social Movement Theory* (New Haven, CT: Yale University Press), pp. 133–155.

Snow, D., Burke Rochford, E., Worden, S. & Benford, R. (1986) 'Frame alignment processes, micro-mobilisation and movement participation', *American Sociological Review* 51(4): 464–81.

Spaargaren, G. & Martens, S. (2005) 'Globalisation and the role of citizen-consumers in environmental politics', in: F. Wijen, K. Zoeteman & J. Pieters (eds.) *A Handbook of Globalisation and Environmental Policy. National Government Interventions in a Global Arena* (Cheltenham: Edward Elgar), pp. 211–45.

Swanson, K., Kuhn, R. & Xu, W. (2001) 'Environmental policy implementation in rural China: a case study of Yuhang, Zhejiang', *Environmental Management* 27(4): 481–91.

Tarrow, S. (1994) *Power in Movement: Social Movements, Collective Action and Mass Politics in the Modern State* (Cambridge: Cambridge University Press).

Taylor, D. (2000) 'The rise of the environmental justice paradigm. Injustice framing and the social construction of environmental discourse', *American Behavioral Scientist* 43(4): 508–80.

Wakeman, F. (1993) 'The civil society and public sphere debate: western reflections on Chinese political culture', *Modern China* 19(2): 108–38.

Wang, M. (ed.) (2000) *Zhongguo NGO Yanjiu* (Research on NGOs in China), no. 38 (Beijing: United Nations Centre for Regional Development).

Wang, Y. (2002) 'Environmental degradation and environmental threats in China', *Environmental Monitoring and Assessment* 90: 161–69.

Wang, H. & Nie, Y. (2001) 'Remedial strategies for municipal solid waste management in China', *Journal of the Air and Waste Management Association* 51: 264–72.

Wang, Y. & Sun, B. (2001) *Introduction to the Development of Civil Organisation in China* (Beijing: Institute of Development Studies).

Wang, C., Xu, X., Hu, J., Liu, M., Terao, T. & Otsuka, K. (eds.) (2001) *Studies on Environmental Pollution Disputes in East Asia: Cases from Mainland China and Taiwan* (Tokyo: Institute of Developing Economies).

Wattenberg, M. (2002) 'The decline of party mobilization', in R. Dalton & M. Wattenberg (eds.) *Parties without Partisans* (Oxford: Oxford University Press), pp. 64–76.

Weidner, H. (2002) 'Capacity building for ecological modernization: lessons from cross-national research', *American Behavioural Scientist* 45(9): 1340–68.

Wu, F. (2002) 'Environmental GONGO autonomy; unintended consequences of state-strategies in China', *China Environment Series* 5: 45–58.

Xie, L. & Mol, A. (2006) 'The role of *guanxi* in the emerging environmental movement in China', in A. McCright & T. Clark (eds.) *Community and Ecology* (Oxford: Elsevier) (in press).

Xu, H., Wang, S. & Xue, D. (1998) 'Biodiversity conservation in China: legislation, plans and measures', *Biodiversity and Conservation* 8: 819–37.

Yang, G. (2003) 'Mingling politics with play. The virtual Chinese public sphere', *IIAS Newsletter* 33: 7.

Young, N. (2001) 'Green groups explore the boundaries of advocacy', *China Development Brief* 4(1).

Zhang, L. (2003) 'Ecologizing industrialization in Chinese small towns', PhD thesis, Wageningen University.

Zhu, J. (2004) 'Not against the state, just protecting the residents' interests: a resident's movement in Shanghai'. Paper presented at 'Strengthening Environmental NGOs in China' conference, Beijing, April.

Same Longitude, Different Latitudes: Institutional Change in Urban Water in China, North and South

JAMES E. NICKUM & YOK-SHIU F. LEE

Growth in Urban Regions During the Reform Period

Accompanying China's phenomenal economic growth over the past two decades has been an equally astounding growth in its cities that is not expected to abate for decades. Infrastructure has expanded commensurately, but often more for development than to meet environmental needs. In particular, as the cities have grown, the problem of supplying them with water, and disposing of wastewater, has expanded as well, both geographically and across sectors. Stresses are most pronounced in the north, where an event such as the 2008 Beijing Olympics can pose difficult problems for water planners. Yet, increasingly, conflicts over water are becoming salient as well in the boom megalopolises of the Pearl River delta, especially in the face of recent prolonged droughts (Luo & Liu, 1997; Li, 1999; Lin, 2001; Gu, 2002). As this article demonstrates, integration of environmental considerations into water policy-making and, to a lesser degree, implementation, is firmly established, at least in principle and in rhetoric. Given the lingering influence of centralised uniform policy making, it is no surprise that institutional responses have often been similar. At the same time, there is little wonder that they exhibit important differences in practice, reflecting in part differences in water scarcity. Institutional change, while critical to China's economic success, is often slowed or stopped altogether by the inertia of the larger administrative and political framework. After providing an overview of the two areas under investigation, we examine three examples of institutional change and the problems seen in their implementation in practice.

Beyond Infrastructure

As in many countries, the conventional approach to urban water supply in China has been project-oriented and largely built and operated by 'the state', an imagined entity that in effect unbundles into ill-coordinated congeries of territorial bureaucracies and vertically- and horizontally-segmented administrative boundaries. Environmental problems, which almost by definition are 'external' to conventional decision-making, have posed a fundamental challenge to this system, as their solution requires both coordination across boundaries and internalisation (or integration) of environmental factors into each decision-maker's calculus. Yet the achievement of greater policy coordination and integration, widely recognised as a key principle of sustainable development, informs the contemporary debates about Environmental Policy Integration both internationally (Lenschow, 2001; Lafferty & Hovden, 2003) and in China.

Reliance on a project culture that frames the problem as one of increasing supply to meet existing shortages or 'needs' has become increasingly untenable as the costs of adding new supplies and rehabilitating aging structures have escalated while different uses or users, including the environment, have come to compete for the existing sources. Conflicts, especially those over quality, watershed management, and maintaining environmental flows, have made imperative the need to find new mechanisms that facilitate negotiation across bureaucratic and administrative borders, including between private and public parties (Nickum, 1999).

For example, there is an enduring complaint, especially from the Ministry of Water Resources, that 'too many dragons manage the water' (*duolong guanshui*) (Luo & Liu, 1997). In the context of the urban water cycle, 'The water source does not manage water supply, water supply does not manage discharge, discharge does not manage pollution control, pollution control does not manage reuse' (Beijing Shi Renmin Zhengfu, 2001: 10). Thus, water, understood in its most generic form and measured in terms of its volume, is managed by the Ministry of Water Resources (through the river basin commissions) in association with local governments. Problems of water pollution, most of which could be traced to land-based sources, fall largely but not entirely under the ambit of the State Environmental Protection Administration (SEPA).[1] Soil erosion is a separate matter of concern to the

Ministry of Agriculture and the State Forest Administration. The administration of hydropower stations is shared between the State Power Company and regional authorities (Gu, 2002). Urban water supply and sewerage have been the traditional domain of the Ministry of Construction. Water prices are set by separate pricing bureaux that are usually more concerned about social stability than cost recovery. In a nutshell, the current institutional arrangement does not map well onto either the hydrological cycle or the ecosystem and is overly complex and prone to rivalries and inefficiencies. China's policy makers appear to be in an active search for a better set of institutions.

Significant changes are being made in transforming the rights regimes and permissible transactions across administrative barriers. Most dramatically, there has been a major policy shift to market-oriented urban water enterprises (*chengshi shiye*) since 2003. At the same time, urban areas are engaged in establishing water services bureaus that, it is hoped, may serve better to integrate many functions of water management than the former sector-bound approach. By 2004, 52 per cent of China's local-level jurisdictions (including county-level governments) and a somewhat smaller 31.4 per cent of its 663 designated cities had reportedly established water services bureaus (Shuilibu Shuiziyuansi, 2004; Wu, 2004). Nonetheless, because of the expanding complexity of water and the degree to which its management is complementary to other activities, it may not be realistic to expect one agency to be able to handle everything (Biswas, 2004). Even when bureaux are merged, they may only internalise conflict, not solve it. Negotiation across bureaucratic and administrative borders is unavoidable.

The Dry and the Wet: Same Longitude, Different Latitudes

Our interest here is to explore the degree to which institutional reform in China's urban growth engines appears to be coping with pressures on their water resources. Our focus is on two quite different parts of China's high-growth coastal areas – Beijing Municipality in the Hai river basin and the Pearl River Delta. We begin with an overview of the two sites, at roughly the same geographical longitude but at quite different latitudes. Then we explore the course of institutional reform in three problem areas.

Beijing

China's capital region is located in the middle reaches of the Hai river basin, the most water-stressed in the country, with 1.5 per cent of China's water resources (on a highly variable average) but with 10.1 per cent of its population, 11.2 per cent of its farmland, and 11.3 per cent of its GDP. Per capita water resources average 350 cubic metres per annum (Wang *et al.*, 2005), one-eighth of the national average and about the same as the desert country of Jordan. Administratively, Beijing Municipality consists of a core urban area of about 8 million people and a large, still mainly rural periphery of roughly

6 million. The municipality lies in the midstream of the Hai basin, so its surface water is affected by what happens in the poor but relatively sparsely populated upper watershed, while its own use affects the more developed downstream areas of Hebei Province and, especially, coastal Tianjin Municipality, which has even less water per capita than Beijing for its over 10 million people. The province of Shanxi to the west, one of the most water-short in China, also includes some of the upper reaches of the Hai, and has recently become a source of occasional interbasin water transfers to Beijing.

Because of its location at the northeastern edge of the alluvial North China Plain, Beijing has relatively favourable groundwater conditions and some of the best sites in the Hai basin for water storage. According to the Beijing Municipal Water Resource Bureau (*Beijing Shi*, 2002), in a median (P = 50 per cent) year, Beijing receives 2.2 billion cubic metres in surface water and 2.5 billion cubic metres of groundwater inflow. Since much of the ground water comes from the surface, there is some double counting, and the net average annual water resource is 3.5 billion cubic metres.[2] Thus in a normal year, the municipality should have roughly comparable magnitudes of surface and groundwater available. Since surface water is more variable, however, and does not linger, there has been a tendency to draw down the aquifers, in drought years by as much as an average of 1 metre.

Two large reservoirs have dominated Beijing's surface water supply. The Guanting Reservoir, visible from the popular Badaling section of the Great Wall, was built in 1954 primarily for flood control, and secondarily to provide supplementary surface water to Beijing, which relied at the time on ground-water and springs for its supply. The dam and most of the reservoir are in Hebei Province, while the catchment area is located in Hebei, Shanxi and Inner Mongolia as well as Beijing. Subsequent upstream construction of dams in these provinces to meet their own water demands led to a dramatic drop in the inflow of water to the Guanting. They did not halt the silt, however, that has progressively reduced the storage capacity of the reservoir, while urban, industrial and agricultural wastes eventually degraded the stored water in places to the lowest level, sub-grade V (*lie V lei*), rendering it unusable for any purpose. In 1997, the Beijing municipal government stopped drawing water from the Guanting for urban supply (*Beijing Shi shuihan zaihai*, 1999; Peisert & Sternfeld, 2005).

The Leading Group for the Protection of Guanting Reservoir was set up in 1972, in what was considered to be the beginning of Chinese environmental politics. A regulation drafted by this group to create zones in the catchment and regulate pollutant discharge was ratified by Beijing, Hebei and Shanxi in 1985, but was not well implemented because of disagreements among the parties over who would be financially responsible for the cleanup (Sternfeld, 1997; Peisert & Sternfeld, 2005).

The Miyun Reservoir to the north, built shortly after the Guanting during the Great Leap Forward, originally provided water to agricultural areas downstream, including Tianjin and Langfang County in Hebei, and was not directly connected with the municipal area of Beijing. The State Council gave Beijing exclusive rights over this water in the early 1980s, and provided more limited alternative supplies to Tianjin. Miyun now provides most of Beijing's surface water, and has become the primary source of drinking water as the city switched away from its overdrawn aquifer for this purpose in the 1980s and 1990s. Unlike Guanting, the Miyun and its immediate catchment lie within Beijing Municipality, which has relied on zoning to control (with mixed success) tourism and economic development, including agriculture and fishery, in critical areas. Nonetheless, over two-thirds of the water flowing into the Miyun comes from upstream in Hebei. Inflow has dropped precipitously during recent drought years (including 1999, 2001 and 2003), due both to low rainfall and to the development of reservoirs in the upper catchment. A few wet years would help relieve some of the pressure, as will a large-scale diversion of water from the middle Yangtze, due to begin in 2010. If all goes according to plan, this diversion will increase Beijing's annual water supply by 1.0 billion cubic metres, or almost 30 per cent in an average year (and much more in drought), but at a high economic cost that is expected to result in a considerable increase in end-user charges.

In the meantime, the 2008 Olympics have given greater urgency to addressing problems of both quantity and quality before the arrival of this source of relief. On the hardware side, with central government legitimisation and financial support and coordination by the Ministry of Water Resources, up to 410 million cubic metres of water per year are to be diverted to Beijing from neighbouring provinces, notably Shanxi and Hebei, until the Yangtze water arrives. The central government and Beijing municipal government have allocated 22 billion yuan for the projects, including compensation (*China Daily*, 3 Oct. 2003)[3]. Also, Beijing has turned back to groundwater, opening up large well fields in the suburban areas.

At the same time, there is widespread recognition that the Yangtze water will not be a panacea, and that a more long-run and less crisis-driven solution will require significant changes in the ways water resources are developed, used, paid for, managed, and disposed of. Addressing pollution and ecological concerns is imperative. A number of new sewage treatment facilities are expected to increase the treatment capacity from 22 per cent in 1999 to 58 per cent in 2004 and 90 per cent in 2008. On the quantity side, the focus is on various forms of demand management and on allocating water to its highest value uses. Changes in the structure of production, cutting back on water-using agriculture and relocating heavy industrial users such the Shougang Iron and Steel Plant, are on the table. There is talk of capping the population of Beijing, but it is difficult to see that as a politically realistic option. Of greatest interest for present purposes, however, are the efforts in Beijing, as elsewhere in urban China, to deal with increasingly knotty institutional coordination problems between functional bureaucracies and across administrative boundaries.

The history of the development of Beijing's water economy until the past decade has been covered in authoritative detail in Sternfeld (1997) and, to a lesser degree, in Nickum (1994). Each decade after the water-rich 1950s has brought a crisis. The *Beijing Sustainable Use Plan (2001–2005)* (Beijing Shi Renmin Zhengfu, 2001) sums up the responses as follows:

> We made it through the urban water supply crisis of the mid-1960s by digging the Jing-Mi diversion that brought in Miyun Reservoir water [to the urban area]; we made it through the water supply crisis of the 1970s by drawing down the aquifer; and we made it through the water supply crisis of the early 1980s by relying on a Central Government policy shift to reserve the water of the Miyun exclusively for Beijing, cutting off Tianjin and Hebei, as well as on developing planned water use and water saving.

More recent information may be found in Peisert and Sternfeld (2005). We refer the reader to those sources for details, especially about the earlier years, and limit ourselves to a brief overview of three key institutional and political issues of the past decade that, as we will show in the Pearl River Delta (PRD), reflect a more general situation of urban water politics in China than just the politically pampered capital. These issues, discussed after an overview of our southern case study, are transboundary problems, retail water pricing, and integration of functions in a cross-sectoral water bureau.

Pearl River Delta Region

Nowhere else in China is urban growth more spectacular than that observed in the Pearl River Delta region in the past two decades (Lee, 2002). Administratively, the PRD region consists of the cities of Guangzhou, Shenzhen, Dongguan, Foshan, Jiangmen, Zhongshan, Zhuhai and the urban areas of Huizhou and Zhaoqing – home to a total population of 42.88 million in 2000,[4] more than doubling the corresponding figure of 20.57 million recorded in 1982.[5] Not counting the Hong Kong and Macau Special Administrative Regions (SARs), the PRD houses 45 per cent of the total population in Guangdong Province but accounts for 75 per cent of the province's total GDP, 87 per cent of its FDI, and manufactures 94 per cent of its exports (*South China Morning Post* (*SCMP*), 14 October 2002).

   With some rather substantial variations in absolute terms, all the cities in the PRD region have recorded phenomenal economic growth figures since the early 1980s (Enright *et al.*, 2005). These economic gains have come with a price: a commensurately high rate of growth of the volume of wastewater generated from agricultural, industrial and domestic sources (Luo & Liu, 1996; Lin, 2001). Although the water quality of the Pearl River Basin as a whole is still considered the best among the seven major river basins in China, rapid population and industrial growth have led to a sharp decline in overall surface water quality in the delta region since the early 1990s (Zhu *et al.*, 2001; Liu, 2002). Moreover, even though the annual costs of economic losses attributed to water pollution in the Pearl River Basin were estimated to reach RMB 3 billion in the late 1990s (Xue, 1998), this is well below 1 per cent of total gross domestic production and therefore it has had a minimal economic impact.

Only a very small proportion of the domestic wastewater in most PRD cities, including Guangzhou, Shenzhen, Dongguan, Foshan, and Zhuhai, was treated before discharge. For instance, in 2000 only about 14 per cent of Guangzhou's domestic wastewater was treated prior to disposal. Cities such as Jiangmen, Huizhou and Zhaoqing did not operate any domestic wastewater treatment facilities at all. With the provision of municipal wastewater treatment facilities lagging far behind the expansion of water supply networks in the PRD region's rapidly growing cities – a phenomenon commonly found throughout the rest of urban China – the rapid deterioration in water quality has become an increasingly salient issue, particularly among populations residing in downstream jurisdictions (Jin *et al.*, 2001; Zhu *et al.*, 2001). The rapid increase in the total volume of wastewater discharged into the delta's midstream waterways – those of the Dongjiang in particular – has led to a noticeable decline in the overall quality of surface water bodies, effectively reducing the amount of clean water supply for downstream jurisdictions (Ye, 1998; Yuan, 1999; Jin *et al.*, 2001; Liu, 2002).

Between 2002–2005, the problem of declining water quality in the PRD region was compounded by drought – a perennial problem in the north but an extremely rare phenomenon in the relatively water abundant coastal provinces in southern China (*SCMP*, 14 December 2004). Three consecutive years of drought in the upper reaches of the tributaries of the Pearl river basin led to serious saline tides in early 2005 that threatened urban water supply systems in several coastal cities, prompting jurisdictions in southern China to look into a bundle of policy strategies that have long been pursued by cities in the north – such as water price reform, water conservation measures, and long-distance water diversion projects (*SCMP*, 8 February 2005).

Hong Kong and the Dongjiang

Contributing around 80 per cent of the total flow, the Xijiang is the main tributary of the Pearl River basin, with a catchment that covers an area of 45,500 square kilometres extending through the provinces of Yunnan, Guangxi, Guangdong, and Jiangxi (Zhao & Kuang, 2003). The much smaller Dongjiang is, however, the focal point of recent controversies over water resources management in the PRD region since it provides at least 80 per cent of water supplied to the downstream megacities of Hong Kong and Shenzhen (Lee, 2006; *Renmin Ribao*, 25 January 2005).

About 80–85 per cent of the water demand in the Hong Kong Special Administrative Region (SAR) is met by the Dongjiang, with the remainder provided by rainwater collected by local catchments and stored in reservoirs (Works Bureau, 1998). The Dongjiang water has been delivered to Hong Kong at a cost of more than HK$2 billion a year (Lung, 2001) via a transfer system of pumping stations and open aqueducts from Dongjiang to Shenzhen Reservoir and then transmitted to a reception point at the Muk Wu Pumping Station in Hong Kong. This arrangement was made under the 1965 Dongshen (Dongjiang–Shenzhen) Water Supply Scheme, a formal agreement instituted between the then colonial government and the Guangdong government to secure a steady and stable source of fresh water for Hong Kong to counter the periodic droughts that had plagued the city in the early 1960s (*SCMP*, 15 March 2001).

The first signs of public concern in Hong Kong over the water quality of the Dongjiang were brought on by a 1993 Hong Kong Water Supplies Department finding that the quality of the Dongjiang's water did not meet Class 2 of China's 1983 national surface water quality standards – in other words, it was considered degraded but potable, barely (*SCMP*, 15 March 2001).[6] From then on, and increasingly so for the remainder of the 1990s, Hong Kong's mass media dwelt on the continuing deterioration of the Dongjiang's water quality.

As a reaction to repeated requests made by the Hong Kong government, Guangdong authorities reportedly undertook several engineering works towards the end of the decade to assure the quality of the Dongjiang's water. First, the water intake point on the Dongjiang was relocated in September 1998 to another point a few hundred metres upstream where the water quality was considered better and where the contamination from an inflowing tributary could be avoided. Secondly, a bio-nitrification plant was installed in the Shenzhen Reservoir in December 1998 to lower the ammonia content and to increase the dissolved oxygen content of the raw water (Works Bureau, 1999a). Finally, the Guangdong authorities also proposed enclosing the existing open aqueduct to protect the water from being polluted by domestic and industrial wastewater in transit (Works Bureau, 1999b).

In a major effort to allay public concerns, the post-1997 Hong Kong government responded by providing an interest-free loan of HK$2.36 billion to the Guangdong government to pay for about half of the HK$5 billion total cost of constructing an 83-kilometre concealed aqueduct from the Dongjiang to the Shenzhen Reservoir (*SCMP*, 4 April 1998). This scheme was hailed by some observers as 'a new chapter of co-operation' between Hong Kong and the Guangdong authorities that could serve as a forerunner of many other cross-border and trans-border infrastructure projects (*SCMP*, 31 March 1998).

The Hong Kong SAR government and the Guangdong provincial government, the two principal proponents of this engineering solution, which was completed in 2003, argued that it would help improve the quality of untreated water delivered to Hong Kong (*SCMP*, 20 November 1998). Critics, mostly Hong Kong-based environmental NGOs and academics, argued that this scheme shied away from the need to confront the fundamental problem of preventing and reducing pollution in the Pearl River Delta region in the first place (*SCMP*, 21 September 1999). They claimed that the proposed aqueduct would not only fail to improve the water quality but could exacerbate the problem because the enclosed aqueduct would lead local officials to downplay the seriousness of addressing pollution. Worse yet is the possibility that pollutants will continue to wash back into the aqueduct at high tide (Lung, 2001). They thus insisted that a more sensible way for Hong Kong and Guangdong to spend their money on an engineering solution would be on a comprehensive waste-water treatment system along the Dongjiang (*SCMP*, 11 May 2000).

Recent Trends

It goes almost without saying that institutional reform has driven the Chinese economy in recent decades, but that abiding rigidities continue to work against the success of many innovations. In the urban water sector, the pace of institutional change has stepped up recently in response to the growth of the market economy and mounting resource pressures. Here we focus on three domains: transboundary problems; intersectoral coordination; and the use of end-user water charges to promote water saving. This is, of course, not an exhaustive list of relevant institutional reforms.

Dealing across Boundaries

Since the nation's leaders rely on its water, Beijing is well situated both politically and geographically to deal with many of its transboundary problems. The reallocation of the water of the Miyun was followed in 2001 with a municipal sustainable water plan for Beijing that obligated upstream provinces to protect the water supply of the capital (Beijing Shi Renmin Zhengfu, 2001). In both cases, the Central Government smoothed the way with financial allocations to the affected neighbours. The short-term diversions mentioned above, beginning with a 20-day shot of 50 million cubic metres from the Cetian Reservoir in Shanxi in September 2003,[7] would appear to have been enabled by the plan.

Nonetheless, the water disputes between provinces and municipalities sharing the most water-short river basin in China are notorious for their frequency, especially during the recent drought. Recently reported instances include a 2003 quarrel between Hebei and Beijing over the latter's plan to intercept additional water from the midstream of the shared Juma River, and between Beijing and Tianjin over the latter's construction of a dam on the upper reaches of the Juhe River, which is the principal source for the Haizi Reservoir in Beijing. Underlying the disputes, as in the case of the failure of the 1985 Guanting regulation, are different views over the allocation of costs and compensatory payments. The Water Resources Committee of the Hai River, affiliated with the Ministry of Water Resources, has been given the responsibility for 'coordinating' water management between administrative units, but it has been criticised on the one hand for lacking authority and on the other for its lack of 'democratic consultation' (*China Daily*, 26 February 2004, 27 July 2004).

In the Pearl River Delta, transboundary disputes have centred mostly on quality, not quantity. In 1999, in an attempt to allay public concern – primarily, if not exclusively, as expressed in Hong Kong – over the quality of water supplied by Dongjiang, the Guangdong provincial authorities said that they had closed down more than 130 polluting industries up to 1996 and had since then barred new factories from locating along the Dongjiang and Dongshen channels (*SCMP*, 11 May 2000). Furthermore, about 1.2 million pigs had been removed from pig farms located on the banks of a section of the Dongjiang to help curb a major agricultural source of water pollution (*SCMP*, 31 August 2000).

Despite all these efforts, however, by mid 2000, 70 per cent of the effluent discharged into Dongjiang was still untreated (*SCMP*, 11 May 2000). As we saw in the case of Beijing and its neighbours, underlying this problem has been a failure of the financing institutional mechanisms. While the Guangdong provincial government has long said it would improve water treatment facilities along the Dongjiang where it draws water to supply Hong Kong, local officials are reluctant to act because they claim that they do not benefit from the water sales and cannot finance the treatment plants on their own (*SCMP*, 7 August 2000). Moreover, local jurisdictions addicted to the project culture have consistently turned to the engineering approach to resolve their water supply problem. For instance, Shenzhen has recently completed a pipeline to tap a cleaner supply of fresh water at a point 50 km further upstream from Hong Kong's source (*SCMP*, 19 June 2000). Several vocal environmental NGOs based in the SAR argued that Shenzhen's pipeline would further degrade the quality of water supplied to Hong Kong because the reduction in water volume would diminish the ability of the Dongjiang to dilute pollutants. They continued to point out that, in response to the rapidly deteriorating water quality in the Pearl River region, many cities were trying to obtain water from new intake points located as far upstream as possible. All of these billion-dollar water delivery infrastructure projects, however, were planned and conducted without any co-ordination among local jurisdictions in the region, much less any thorough evaluation of the aggregate impacts of the projects.

Water Pricing

The need for economic pricing of water and wastewater treatment has long been recognised in principle and in law in China as a means of promoting water saving and recovering costs. Indeed, on paper, Beijing's policy makers are very much exponents of neoclassical economic principles. For example, the *Beijing Sustainable Use Plan (2001–2005)* (Beijing Shi Renmin Zhengfu, 2001) notes that the excessively low water and sewerage prices have discouraged water saving, source protection, and the optimal allocation of water resources and forced the respective utilities to rely on limited government subsidies for operations. One consequence is that funds for investment are extremely limited, water is wasted, and shortages are aggravated. In addition, it forces the government to rely on a quota-based allocation system, at least for industry, but this is only feasible where measurement is possible, and until recently the quotas have been too lenient to provide an effective constraint. The Sustainable Use Plan provided for a significant increase in water fees by the year 2005, to 6 yuan/cu.m. on average and 4.5 yuan/cu.m. for household users, including sewerage as well as water supply. However, despite the efforts by the government to push through water price reform measures in recent years, the water fees in Beijing were only raised to an average level of 3.7 yuan/cu.m. in late 2004 (*Xinhua she*, 23 December 2004). Yet even the target level remains too low (1–2 per cent of disposable income) to have a significant impact on household water use behaviour or to make operations attractive to private investors. The sewerage charge, initially levied in 1996, is far from adequate to cover operations and maintenance, much less the large number of new facilities that will be required to bring sewerage coverage over 90 per cent by the time the Olympic torch is lit in 2008 (Han, 2004).

In order to balance efficiency and fairness, Beijing proposed instituting block pricing in 2005, where higher uses are charged at increasing rates, but action on this has been postponed, perhaps because of continuing incompleteness of metering in residential areas. Prepayment systems using IC (integrated circuit) cards have not been extended from other utilities to water yet, again possibly because of metering complexities.

The idea of block pricing has also been floated in major cities in the Pearl River Delta in 2004 but, as in Beijing, it has yet not to be implemented because of resistance coming from both the water producers and consumers. In Guangzhou, for instance, water supply plants complained that it was unreasonable for them to be asked to pay for the entire costs of installing water meters in the city's residential buildings – reportedly reaching 5 billion yuan – and argued that the users should also be asked to bear half of these expenses (*Jinyang wan*, 17 December 2004). In Dongguan, an early 2005 government proposal to increase the water fees from 1.0 yuan to 1.2 yuan/cu.m. met strong objections from resident representatives in a public hearing (*Dongguan Daily*, 30 March 2005). In an effort to help dampen Guangzhou's inflationary pressures in early 2005, the city government decreed a freeze, for a period of three months, on the fee levels of public utilities including water charges (*Xinkuai Bao*, 26 March 2005), even though residents in Guangzhou were consuming on a per capita basis one of the largest volumes of water among the country's major cities but were paying the lowest water fees level – at 0.9 yuan/cu.m. (excluding wastewater treatment fees), as compared with the highest level of 1.9 yuan paid by residents in Shenzhen – in the entire Delta region. Yet, even in Shenzhen, where water supply is charged at the highest level in Southern China, water fees still account for only 0.22 per cent of an urban household's disposable income on a per capita basis (*Nanfang Ribao*, 24 March 2005).

Even though water price reform measures have been introduced by the central authorities since the early 1990s and the water fees in half of the country's cities have since been increased, implementation at the local level is extremely uneven in terms of the extent of price increases (*Xinhua she*, 23 December 2004). Generally speaking, cities in northern China have imposed the highest levels of water fee increases whereas residents in cities in the south have mostly been spared the pain of paying higher fees. For example, whereas the water prices in Beijing were raised nine times during the 1990–2004 period (*Xinhua she*, 17 December 2004), water prices in the city of Dongguan in the PRD have remained unchanged since 1999 (*Dongguan Ribao*, 30 March 2005). To some extent this reflects differences in the relative scarcity of water.

Thus, due mostly to institutional constraints and political considerations, water prices in urban China, despite repeated increases, are still being held down at levels that are financially unviable for water supply plants. Water fees, on average, still account for not more than 1 per cent of urban households' disposable income. As a consequence, the average urban resident has remained non-receptive to the message that water is a scarce commodity and water utilities, including wastewater treatment facilities, remain under-financed and continue to rely on public finance to subsidise their operations.

Water Services Bureaux

As in north China, engineering solutions continue to be seen in the PRD as central features of water strategy, in part because they are simpler from a transactional point of view – and they have large economies of scale. At the same time, also as in north China, it is increasingly recognised that engineering solutions alone, such as ever longer diversions, are not by themselves adequate for addressing medium-term water supply issues. Demand (including the use of public waters for discharge) has to be brought under control, and the water bureaucracies need to be coordinated better. Pricing is an important part of demand management. Water services bureaux (WSBs) are efforts to improve the bureaucratic end of things.

Although coordination is severely lacking among jurisdictions, some cities in the Pearl River Delta have led the way in seeking a functional coordination of water management. Reportedly modelled after the water services department in Hong Kong, China's first city-level water services bureau was established by the Shenzhen government in July 1993 to help fight the twin problems of drought and flooding that have hit the city particularly hard since the early 1990s. In 1991, the volume of daily water supply was sharply reduced by 30 per cent as a consequence of a partial shutdown of the city's water supply plants for maintenance purposes, causing major disruptions to economic and social lives and resulting in an estimated total economic loss of RMB 1.2 billion. In 1993, Shenzhen lost another RMB 1.4 billion to damages caused by two major rain storm-fed floods. In order to avert similar and further economic damages, the Shenzhen city government then decided in 1993 to transform the city's water resources bureau (WRB) into the country's first water services bureau (Wu, 2003). The latter differs from the former in two major ways. First, the

WSB was accorded a higher level of bureaucratic status in the city's hierarchical structure than the WRB, with a commensurately higher level of authority to re-distribute and manage water resources effectively across the urban–rural divide thorough the city's entire jurisdiction. Secondly, unlike the rural-oriented WRB, the WSB was asked to focus on accomplishing two urban-centred tasks: establishing a modern, reliable urban-based water supply system and building an effective urban flood-control mechanism (Wu, 2000). Of these two objectives, the articulation of the urban and rural water supply systems into one single network was billed as the first step toward building an integrated water management structure for the rapidly burgeoning city-region (Wu, 2004). In practice, however, WSBs have made their presence felt more in flood control, a more southern concern.

Shenzhen's urban-based integrated water management structure was gradually replicated elsewhere and effectively instituted, by the end of 2003, in 50 per cent of country's city and county-level jurisdictions (Wu, 2004). There were, however, substantial variations in the level of services provided by these newly created WSBs: while 96 per cent of them have assumed the flood control function, only 68 per cent were running the water supply networks, with 37 per cent managing the drainage facilities and an even smaller portion – 28 per cent – overseeing the wastewater treatment plants (Wu, 2003). It is also interesting to note that the majority of the jurisdictions in the Pearl River Delta have not yet opted for the WSB model (Kong & Bian, 2000).

Accomplishments in terms of major financial gains in scale economies in constructing city-wide integrated water supply projects, improved efficiency in water allocation as well as reduced tensions between territorial and functional sectors competing for water have been claimed by cities – such as Shenzhen and Shanghai – that have established the WSBs (Wu, 2003). These urban-based offices have also been credited with the strengthening of the institutional basis for the introduction of price reform measures and commercialisation schemes in the water sector, at least in areas such as water supply and sewerage, where, as noted, the WSBs are least likely to exercise direct control, although they have responsibility for integrated water resource management (Zhang, 2004).

Despite such initial claims of success, some researchers are quick to point out that the effectiveness of the WSBs is severely constrained by the lack of consistency and urgency in the implementation of this institutional form at a nationwide level. Beijing did not establish a WSB until March 2004. With only a minority of the country's designated cities embracing the integrated water management structure, old and new systems continue to coexist, and the nation's vertical hierarchy and horizontal bureaucracy relating to water resources management are plagued by confusion and sometimes contradictions in administrative 'property rights' (*guanli zhineng*), organisational goals and project objectives. These problems are aggravated by the ineffectual design and half-hearted implementation of politically sensitive reform measures such as price hikes in water fees and wastewater treatment charges (Wang *et al.*, 2004). Hence, almost without exception, water supply and wastewater treatment enterprises throughout urban China have remained money-losing entities and continue to rely on substantial subsidies paid for from municipal budgets (Jin, 2003; Hu, 2004). As it has become increasingly imperative to turn to external, largely international, sources of funds and management such as the World Bank or international water companies, pressure has been building for a continuing progressive increase in water charges until they reach economic levels.

Concluding Observations

As our title indicates, the Hai and Pearl river basins share much of the same geographical longitude, and both are coastal areas with rapidly growing urban economies. At the same time, they are at quite different geographical latitudes, resulting in quite different hydrological 'latitudes' for action. In many ways this leads to clear differences – in the north, there is a lot more emphasis on policies that elicit water saving, including changes in industrial structure, and perhaps more emphasis on economic instruments such as block pricing or water markets between administrative units, Hong Kong's purchase of Dongjiang water, initiated in colonial times, being a notable exception. In the PRD, Shenzhen is quite water-short, but in most cases, the problem is one of quality.

In both north and south, rapid urbanisation has seen rapid construction of urban infrastructure. In most cases, water shortages are due to infrastructure lags, but these have not apparently increased in relative magnitude over time. What may have increased is deterioration in the quality of existing supplies, often necessitating a reach across basins for supplemental sources, or the construction of expensive treatment plants or, in the case of Hong Kong, the enclosure of the delivery system. Wastewater treatment has lagged behind needs, but in part because there was so little before. Serious problems remain in funding both water supply and sewerage facilities, in part because prices remain too low to attract private investors or to provide adequate recurrent funds for operations and maintenance.

Major water conflicts in the north tend to be between administrative jurisdictions, although there are serious problems of coordination among functional units as well. In the south, the large cities are scrambling for clean and adequate water from the same upstream source, but conflicts between bureaux are more salient. The river basin commissions affiliated with the Ministry of Water Resources have responsibility for coordination and conflict resolution, but usually have inadequate competence or resources to be effective. Metropolitan Water Services Bureaux, which began in the south, are a more urban-based approach to integration that sometimes operate in multiple basins but only in a part of any one basin. These bureaux have had some reported successes, but are rarely given authority over the full water cycle in cities, and, being less than universal, lead to a lot of bureaucratic confusion in China's centralised system.

There does appear to be a serious commitment to administrative reform to meet growing environmental challenges to urban water, in the context of an increasingly marketising economy. Nonetheless, there is little evidence of a commitment to widening stakeholder participation to include non-governmental organisations. China's administrative system, in water as elsewhere, still operates with a weak level of social capital, which is kept frail. The consequent lack of trust leads to serious problems of enforcement, and, together with inadequate funding mechanisms (themselves due in part to a lack of trust), may explain in part the continuing lags in the application of economic instruments and more market-based institutional forms when most seem to agree on their utility. Enduring and often worsening water quality and watershed problems will ensure that at least those parts of the environment will force their way into policy making and implementation. So far, China's major urban areas appear to have muddled or muscled their way through, but not necessarily by means of institutional reform.

Notes

1. The Water Resources Bureau's basin commissions monitor water quality in the river but are not responsible for its control. SEPA monitors point-source discharges from urban land sources, but does not have the capacity to monitor non-point sources, for example, fish ponds. Basically, there is no monitoring of water quality in agricultural areas. Interview with Wang Jin, Zhujiang Commission, 17 March 2005.
2. This works out to 250 cu.m./capita in an average year, a much lower figure than that given more recently by Wang *et al.* (2005), despite a continuing string of drought years that should if anything have lowered the median. Hydrological statistics are like that. According to the 2004 *Zhongguo Shuili Nianjian* (Yearbook of China Water Resources, 2004), the year 2003 brought only half the average amount of water to Beijing, putting per capita water availability at Bedouin levels.
3. At http://www2.chinadaily.com.cn/en/doc/2003-10/03/content_269165.htm (viewed 2 August 2005).
4. This figure is the actual population as measured by the Fifth Population Census in 2000. Subsequent population figures, such as those reported in the annual statistical yearbooks, are based upon official residence, and are not comparable.
5. These figures were published in the 1991 and 2001 *Guangdong Statistical Yearbooks*, the results of the 3rd and the 5th population censuses conducted in 1982 and 2000.
6. Surface water quality in China is graded into 6 classes, with Class 1 denoting the best quality and sub-Class 5 being the worst, unusable for any human activity and often incapable of supporting any form of life. Water classified from Class 1 to Class 3 is considered as potable water; Class 4 water is used for industrial purposes, and Class 5 water is only good for agricultural use.
7. It was estimated that only about half of the water would actually make it the full 157 kilometres. http://www2.chinadaily.com.cn/en/doc/2003-10/03/content_269165.htm (viewed August 1, 2005).

References

Beijing Shi Renmin Zhengfu & Zhonghua Renmin Gongheguo Shuilibu (2001) *21 shiji chuchi (2001–2005 nian) shoudu shui ziyuan kechixu liyong guihua zong baogao* (Beijing: Shuili Shuidian Chubanshe).
Beijing Shi shui ziyuan gongbao (Beijing Water Resources Bulletin) *2001* (2002) (Beijing: Beijing Shi Shuiliju).

Beijing Shi shuihan zaihai (1999) (Beijing: Shuili Shuidian Chubanshe).

Biswas, A. (2004) 'Integrated water resources management: a reassessment', *Water International* 29(2): 248–56.

China Daily (various dates). Available at http://www2.chinadaily.com.cn/en/doc.

Enright, M., Scott, E. & Chang, K. (2005) *Regional Powerhouse: the Greater Pearl River Delta and the Rise of China* (Chichester: Wiley).

Gu Junhai (2002) 'Guangdong Sheng shui ziyuan gongxu maodun tuchu de yuanyin ji duice' (Causes of and strategies to resolve the intensification of contradictions between supply and demand of water resources in Guangdong Province), *Renmin Zhujiang* (*People's Pearl River*) 1: 17–20.

Han Xiangyun (2004) 'Beijing Shi shuijia gaige yuanyin ji xiaoying fenxi', *Zhongguo Shuili* 20: 48–9.

Hu Wenxiang (ed.) (2004) *Chengshi wushui chuli sheshi jiance jiankong de shijian yu tansuo* (The practice and research on the monitoring of urban wastewater treatment facilities) (Beijing: Zhongguo Huanjing Kexue Chubanshe).

Jin Hui, Li Liufen & Zhu Jianmin (2001) 'Dongjiang zhongyou shui wuran zhuangkuang ji qi bianhua qushi' (The state of water pollution and its changing trends in Dongjiang's mid-stream section), *Guangxi Shiyuan Xuebao: ziran kexue ban* (*Journal of Guangxi Normal University: Natural Sciences Edition*) 18(2): 60–2.

Jin Zhaofeng (ed.) (2003) *21 shiji de shui chuli* (The management of water in the 21st century) (Beijing: Huaxue Gongye Chubanshe).

Kong Qingyu & Bian Yijie (2000) 'Guangdong shui ziyuan kechixu fazhan yanjiu' (Research on sustainable development of water resources in Guangdong), *Guangdong Shuili Shuidian* (*Guangdong Water Resources and Hydropower*) 6: 33–6.

Lafferty, W. & Hovden, E. (2003) 'Environmental policy integration: towards an analytical framework', *Environmental Politics* 12(3): 1–22.

Lee, Y. (2002) 'Tackling cross-border environmental problems in Hong Kong: initial responses and institutional constraints', *China Quarterly* 172: 986–1009.

Lee, Y. (2006) 'Managing Water Resources in the Delta Border Zone: Challenges and Opportunities', in A. Yeh, V. Sit, G. Chen & Y. Zhou (eds.) *Developing a Competitive Pearl River Delta in Southern China* (Hong Kong: University of Hong Kong Press), pp. 357–82.

Lenschow, A. (2001) *Environmental Policy Integration: Greening Sectoral Policies in Europe* (London: Earthscan).

Li Zhihua (1999) 'Zhujiang liuyu shui ziyuan baohu gongzuo de huigu yu qianzhan' (Efforts in protecting the water resources in the Pearl River basin: retrospect and prospect), *Renmin Zhujiang* (*People's Pearl River*) 5: 12–14.

Lin Xudian (2001) 'Guangdong Sheng shui ziyuan liyong cunzai de wenti yu duice tantao' (A discussion on the problems in and strategies for the utilisation of water resources in Guangdong Province), *Guangdong shuili shuidian* (*Guangdong Water Resources and Hydropower*) 4: 6–7.

Liu Wan'gen (2002) 'Zhujiang liuyu shui ziyuan wenti ji tongyi guanli qianxi' (An analysis of the problem and integrated management of water resources in the Pearl River basin), *Renmin Zhujiang* (*People's Pearl River*), supplementary issue.

Lung, V. (2001) 'Troubled water', *Post Magazine*, 18 February: 10.

Luo Chengping and Liu Xinyuan (1997) 'Zhujiang sanjiaozhou jingjiqu shui huanjing guihua' (The planning of water issues in the Pearl River delta economic region), *Shuili Xuebao* (*Journal of Water Resources*) 6: 71–6.

Nickum, J. (1994) 'Beijing's maturing socialist water economy', in James E. Nickum and K. William Easter (eds.) *Metropolitan Water Use Conflicts in Asia and the Pacific* (Boulder, CO: Westview Press), pp. 37–60.

Nickum, J. (1999) 'After the dam age is done: social capital and eco-partnerships in urban watersheds: with focus on the Lake Biwa–Yodo River basin', in Takashi Inoguchi, Edward Newman and Glen Paoletto (eds.) *Cities and the Environment: New Approaches for Eco-societies* (Tokyo: UNU Press), pp. 140–160.

Peisert, C. & Sternfeld, E. (2005) 'The need for integrated management for the endangered Miyun Reservoir', *China Environmental Series* 7: 33–46.

Shuilibu Shuiziyuansi (2004) 'Chengshi shuiwu shichanghua gaige diaoyan', *Zhongguo Shuili* 15: 6–12.

Sternfeld, E. (1997) *Beijing: Stadtentwicklung und Wasserwirtschaft* (Berlin: Technische Universität Berlin).

Wang Hao, Luo Raozeng, Ma Jing & Chen Yiming (2005) 'China's water resources: crisis and sustainable utilization – challenge and opportunity'. Paper presented at the Second Regional Orientation Workshop of the World Business Council for Sustainable Development Water Scenarios Project: Navigating a Sustainable Course in Water, Beijing, 1–3 June.

Wang Jinnan, Tian Rensheng & Hong Yaxiong (eds.) (2004) *Zhongguo huanjing zhengce* (China's environmental policies), Vol. 1 (Beijing: Zhongguo Huanjing Kexue Chubanshe).

Works Bureau, Hong Kong Special Administrative Region Government (1998) 'Information paper for Provisional Legislative Council, Panel on Planning, Lands and Works and Panel on Environmental Affairs; joint meeting on 27 March 1998', 20 March.

Works Bureau, Hong Kong Special Administrative Region Government (1999a) 'Paper prepared for Legislative Council; Panel on Environmental Affairs and Panel on Planning, Lands and Works; quality of Dongjiang water', January.

Works Bureau, Hong Kong Special Administrative Region Government (1999b) 'Supplementary information paper for LegCo Panel on Environmental Affairs; quality of Dongjiang water', June.

Wu Jisong (2000) 'Yingzhan 21 shiji mianlin de di er pinkun – shui pinkun' (Water poverty: facing the second type of poverty in the 21st century), extracted from *Shui ziyuan ji qi guanli de yanjiu yu yingyong* (Research on and practice of water resources management) (Beijing: Zhongguo Shuili Shuidian Chubanshe).

Wu Jisong (2003) *Shuiwu zhishi duben* (A reader on water services knowledge) (Beijing: Zhongguo Shuili Shuidian Chubanshe).

Wu Jisong (2004) 'Zhongguo shuiwu guanli xianzhuang yu zhanwang' (The current state of water services management and its prospect), in Jing Zhengshu (ed.) *Zhongguo shuili fazhan baogao* (Report on China's water resources development) (Beijing: Zhongguo Shuili Shuidian Chubanshe), pp. 271–84.

Xue Jianfeng (1998) 'Zhujiang liuyu shui ziyuan baohu wenti de tiaozhan yu duice' (Problems of protecting water resources in the Pearl River basin: challenges and strategies), *Renmin Zhujiang* (People's Pearl River) 1: 3–6.

Ye Linyi (1998) 'Dongjiang gongshui shuiyuan yu xi shui dong diao' (The sources of water supply in Dongjiang and the transfer of water from the west to the east), *Shuili Jingji* (*Economics of Water Resources*) 5: 24–7.

Yuan Jisen (1999) 'Dongjiang liuyu shuizhi wuran yu shui huanjing baohu duice yanjiu' (Water pollution in the Pearl River basin and research on strategies for the protection of water quality), *Huizhou Daxue Xuebao* (*Journal of Huizhou University*) 19(4): 101–4.

Zhang Yue (2004) 'Beijing chengli shuiwuju shi baowei shoudu anquan de zhanlue jucuo', in *Zhongguo shuili fazhan zhanlue wenji (1996–2004)* (Beijing: Zhongguo Shuili Shuidian Chubanshe) (reprint of document dated May 2004), pp. 417–18.

Zhao Zhenhua & Kuang Yaoqiu (eds.) (2003) *Zhujiang sanjiaozhou ziyuan huanjing yu kechixu fazhan* (Resources, environment and sustainable development in the Pearl River delta) (Guangzhou: Guangdong Science and Technology Press).

Zhongguo Shuili Nianjian (Yearbook of China water resources) (2004) (Beijing: Shuili Shuidian Chubanshe).

Zhu Zhaoyu, Deng Qinglu, Zhou Houyun, Ouyang Tingping, Kuang Yaoqiu, Huang Ningsheng & Qiao Yulou (2001) 'Zhujiang sanjiaozhou jingjiqu kechixu fazhan zhong de shui huang wenti' (The issue of water in promoting sustainable development in the Pearl River delta region), *Huanjng Kexue Xuebao* (*Journal of Environmental Science*) 21(4): 405–410.

Environmental Implications of Energy Policy in China

NATHANIEL T. ADEN & JONATHAN E. SINTON

Energy, Governance, and Environment in China

Acquiring and using energy damages the environment more than almost any other set of human activities. However, as Deng Xiaoping stated in 1980, 'Energy is the priority issue in the economy'. Given the strong positive correlation between energy consumption and income, the environmental Kuznets curve (EKC) provides a useful theoretical framework for evaluating the relationship between energy and environment in China. Simon Kuznets unveiled his eponymous, inverted U-shaped curve in 1955 to conceptualise the relationship between income inequality and development. In 1993, Grossman and Krueger adapted the original Kuznets curve to describe pollution trends at various stages of economic development.[1] The substitution of energy consumption for per-capita income generates an energy–environmental Kuznets curve (EEKC), which illustrates the range of relationships between energy, governance and environmental outcomes in China.

At the initial stages of development, energy consumption increases at the cost of environmental degradation. The EEKC model predicts that environmental degradation will subside as the economy reaches higher per capita energy consumption (and income) levels. However, the optimistic logic of the EEKC (represented by the solid line in Figure 1) is disputed by 'race to the bottom' proponents, who foresee an ongoing positive relationship (along the dotted line) (Dasgupta *et al.*, 2002). For the purpose of environmental analysis, the EEKC model is path dependent and dynamic: energy systems vary by region according to local economic, demographic, and geographic conditions, and the shape of each region's EEKC is mutable according to government policies, implementation, and institutions. In light of recent economic growth trends and the environment's already parlous condition, the positive or negative slope of China's aggregate energy–environmental Kuznets curve will have important implications for future generations.

As with many economic theories, the causal logic of the EEKC is largely contingent on full information and low transaction costs. For example, increasingly energy-consuming, wealthy citizens' ability to perceive the costs of environmental degradation, organise collective action, and address pollution problems provides an essential mechanism for abatement. While local citizen action is limited by political restrictions, lack of full information and high transaction costs do not necessarily relegate China to a future of environmental calamity. Rather, the Chinese Communist Party's ongoing restrictions on information and collective action increase the importance of government policy, implementation, and institutions in determining the shape of China's EEKC. For evaluation of the environmental effects of energy usage, the utility of the EEKC model is derived from its aggregation of driving factors, including exogenous economic, demographic, and geographic variables, as well as local usage factors including available technology, consumer behaviour, and

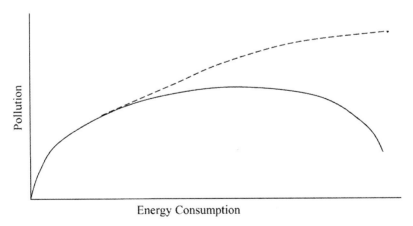

Figure 1. The energy-environmental Kuznets curve (EEKC)

prevailing fuel structures. Within the context of China's gradual move towards liberalised energy markets, decentralised administration, internationalised energy politics, and ongoing urban growth, government policy, implementation, and institutions play an important role in determining the EEKC slope.

Figure 2 illustrates the interconnected range of factors involved in the formation of the energy system as well as intervening variables that influence the environmental impacts of energy usage. The energy system is primarily shaped by China's economy, demography, and geography. Among these key variables, availability of energy inputs is perhaps the most obvious foundational factor. China has extensive domestic energy reserves, particularly in coal and hydropower. The precise extent of China's energy endowments varies according to the system of calculation. Table 1 illustrates the range of reserve estimates between internationally standardised 'economically recoverable reserve' estimates and Soviet-derived 'proven technologically-recoverable reserves'. Regardless of the system of measurement, the data in Table 1 clearly show that hydropower, of which China has the world's largest electricity generation potential, and coal make up the vast majority of domestic energy resource endowments.

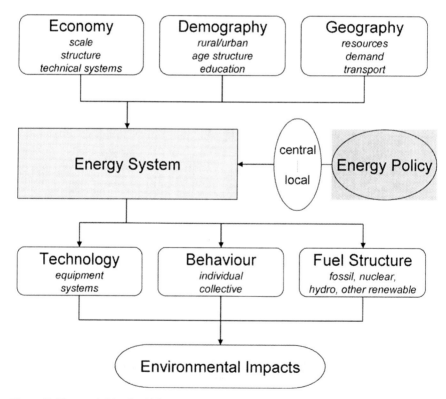

Figure 2. Key variables in China's energy–environment system

Table 1. Estimates of China's energy resource endowments

Source	Coal	Oil	Gas	Hydro	Biomass
1999 estimates of the World Energy Council (2004)	114.5 billion tons (12 per cent global reserves)	4.8 billion tons (3 per cent global reserves)	1368 billion m³ (0.9 per cent)	1260 billion kWh (17 per cent)	28 million tons (not including 130 Mt firewood)
China Energy Development Report (2003)	724 billion tons	13.7 billion tons	2250 billion m³	1923 billion kWh	N/A

Beyond domestic endowments, access to secure, internationally-traded resources further defines China's energy and environmental choice set. Openness to trade, security of supply, and access to technology inform domestic energy strategy. For example, the leadership's strategic ability to shift to cleaner, more efficient fuels such as natural gas is delimited by the internationalisation of China's energy politics. Within these resource parameters, China has formulated energy policies and organised institutions to maximise low-cost production, and thereby fuel economic growth.

Since the initiation of economic and political reforms in 1978, institutional restructuring has generated increased energy supply. New institutions reflected the state's gradual withdrawal from the economy and its prioritisation of economic growth as the chief source of legitimacy. Property rights reform in particular served to emphasise individual-level production incentives over ideology. Within the energy sector, production was stimulated by the clarification of mineral exploration rights, the diversification of management structures, the increase of investment sources, the development of transport infrastructure, and the liberalisation of energy markets, including pricing, taxes, environmental and safety regulation, opening to trade, and the abandonment of full employment. Figure 3 illustrates the growth of national energy consumption and per-capita GDP since the initiation of China's extensive reforms.

Between 1980 and 2004, China's aggregate energy consumption grew by 166 per cent, from 25.2 EJ to 67 EJ, and per-capita GDP rose from $172 (2000 RMB) in 1980, to $1161 in 2004. While shares of hydropower, nuclear, and natural gas have grown, coal remains China's dominant source of energy. In

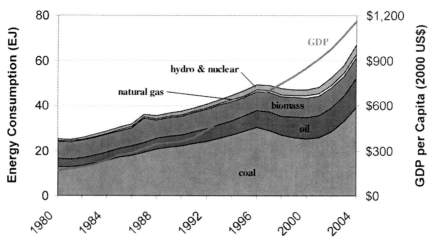

Figure 3. China's energy consumption by fuel, 1980–2004. *Source: China Statistical Yearbook* (various years); *China Statistical Abstract* (2005)

fact, the proportion of coal in China's energy mix increased from 51 per cent in 1980 to 62 per cent in 1996 – a year when the economy was expanding particularly quickly. Institutional reforms account for the aggregate growth of energy production, as well as the ongoing dominance of coal in China's energy portfolio.

Energy intensity (EI), and particularly energy elasticity of GDP, provides a metric for understanding the nature of China's expanding energy usage. During the early reform period, institutional restructuring facilitated remarkably energy efficient economic growth. GDP grew more quickly than energy usage during the 1980s and 1990s, as augmented property rights provided incentives for increased productivity and competition-driven efficiency. However, energy consumption began to grow more quickly than GDP in 2001 as a result of changing leadership priorities and macroeconomic shifts to more heavy industry. The data in Figure 4 illustrate the low energy elasticity of GDP from 1980 through 2000, at which point economic growth became more energy intensive. Energy usage, and particularly coal consumption, is likely to have been under-reported in the late 1990s; however, recent shifts towards increasingly energy intensive economic growth underscore the importance of effective governance for internalising the costs of environmental degradation.

The environmental implications of ongoing energy sector growth have been mediated by a series of regulatory oscillations between state and market-based

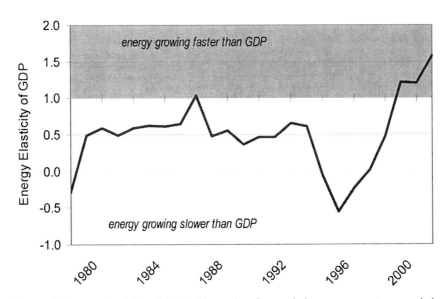

Figure 4. Energy elasticity of GDP (the ratio of growth in energy use to growth in GDP), 1980–2003. *Source*: National Bureau of Statistics (various years); *China Statistical Yearbook* (Beijing: China Statistics Press); NBS (2005) 'China statistical communique of the People's Republic of China on the 2004 National Economic and Social Development' (www.stats.gov.cn)

approaches. The juxtaposition of these diverse regulatory mechanisms with energy and environmental outcomes provides data for evaluating some components of China's EEKC. These relationships are most clearly illustrated in an historical review of China's energy strategy and institutions. In the next sections we examine developments in the coal sector in detail, and survey rural energy and hydropower as well. After evaluating recent changes in the organisation of government organs of energy administration, we offer some thoughts on key institutional factors likely to influence how energy policy will affect environmental quality in the coming years.

Coal Sector Reform: Decentralisation and Market Liberalisation

Institutional restructuring in the initial reform period was driven by fiscal decentralisation and the gradual expansion of rural property rights. In 1983, 'township and village enterprises' began to replace 'commune and brigade enterprises', thereby increasing local fiscal autonomy and introducing incentives for growth. Within the coal industry, these reforms stimulated the expansion of small collective and private mines from 18 per cent of total production in 1980 to more than 48 per cent in 1996 (Figure 5).

During the 1980s the central government enacted a series of laws, measures, and plans to stimulate coal production, thereby compensating for disappointing returns in the domestic petroleum sector (Levine & Sinton, 2004). In 1983,

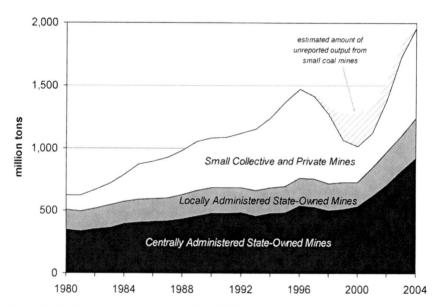

Figure 5. Coal production by ownership, 1980–2004. *Source: China Energy Databook* (2004); *Coal Industry Yearbook* (various years); *Interfax China Energy Report Weekly* (4(4), p. 14)

the Ministry of Coal Industry issued a 'Report on Eight Measures to Accelerate the Development of Small Coal Mines', as well as a 'Notice of Further Relaxation of Policies and Development of Local Coal Mines' the same year. Gradual price liberalisation and regulatory 'relaxation' encouraged local and small scale coal production. A three-tier system of 'plan', 'indicative', and 'negotiated' (market) prices was established, and in 1984 state-owned coal mines were permitted to sell 5 per cent of their output at negotiated prices. Small coal mines, on the other hand, were free to determine amount of production and level of product pricing. Regulatory decentralisation further benefited small and local producers insofar as the local governments that supervised small mines were also dependent on them to generate scarce tax revenue – a situation that persists in many localities.

Beyond the structural implications of fiscal and regulatory decentralisation, coal industry production was stimulated by central government investment and industry subsidies. For example, the Sixth Five Year Plan, which was adopted in 1982, articulated investment and production goals for the expansion of a Shanxi Energy Base for national coal production. Industry-wide production incentives were provided by low taxes and subsidies, including the central government's 'coal replacement of oil' programme. According to government budget statistics, these coal subsidies grew from 940 million RMB in 1983 to 2.3 billion RMB in 1990.[2]

While industry subsidies grew, the passage of the Mineral Resource Law in 1986, and the coal industry corporatisation in 1988, extended the central government's withdrawal from energy sector management. The Mineral Resource Law constituted an ex-post-facto reassignment of coal exploration rights from central to local governments and local entrepreneurs. Rather than defining a strong institutional framework, this law codified central government non-intervention – the Rules for the Implementation of the Mineral Resources Law were not published until eight years later, in 1994. In 1988 the Ministry of Coal Industry (MOCI) was transformed into the China National Coal Corporation, the Northeast Inner Mongolia United Coal Industry Corporation, and the China National Local Coal Mine Development Corporation, thereby echoing the transfer of property rights to small collective and private mines on a national level. The regulatory functions of MOCI were transferred to a newly created Ministry of Energy under the State Planning Commission. Given the dearth of rural capital, coal corporatisation encouraged the establishment of small, low technology/investment mines with minimal overhead.

During the initial reforms and into the 1990s, a rough balance was achieved between the costs and benefits of small coal mine proliferation. Aside from dramatically increasing aggregate low-cost energy production, small mines stimulated rural employment and economic growth while reducing bottleneck pressure on limited rail and water transport capacity. However, the environmental, human safety, and market distortion costs of local mining became more evident as the coal sector continued to boom in the 1990s. In raw cost-of-life terms, the perilous nature of small, local coal mining is reflected in its average death rate of 10.33 miners per million tons of coal produced between 1995 and 2003, compared to 1.27 for miners in large, centrally-administered state-owned mines during the same period.[3] Coal consumption is also associated with a range of health problems, primarily caused by combustion of mineralised coal, which can lead to arsenic, fluorine, selenium, and mercury poisoning (Finkelman *et al.*, 1999). Anecdotal evidence also abounds on the deleterious impacts of mines on land and water resources, which have been the cause of numerous environmentally-motivated disputes. Moreover, local governments' dependence on small mines for revenue resulted in lax regulation. An exclusive focus on production and revenue led to sub-optimal levels of investment and poor environmental, health, and safety performance, thereby undermining the market for coal produced by larger, properly regulated mines.

When export demand began to wane with the 1997 Asian financial crisis, the central government initiated a spate of structural reforms intended to improve government cost-effectiveness and state-owned enterprise (SOE) competitiveness. Within the energy sector, the 1998 reforms were oriented around bureaucratic restructuring and industry consolidation, including an extensive campaign to close down small unregistered coal mines. Flagging demand and more rigorous government regulation combined to steeply reduce coal production, particularly from small collective and private mines, between 1996 and 2000. Changes in the coal sector were reflected in structural reform of the central government bureaucracy. China's energy bureaucracy had been marked by periodic decentralisation and reconsolidation: in 1993 the Ministry of Energy was dissolved in favour of more specialised oversight by the Ministry of Coal Industry, only to be taken over the by State Administration of Coal Industry (SACI), an office of the State Economic and Trade Commission (SETC), in 1998 (Levine & Sinton, 2004). In addition to cutting government costs, the 1998 reforms were intended to separate economic regulation (SETC), strategy (State Development Planning Commission (SDPC)), and management (local govern-ments and the Ministry of Land and Natural Resources (MLNR)) of the energy sector, and particularly the coal industry. As such, the reforms included the transfer of large SOE coal mines from SACI to provincial authorities. Although the 1998 reforms served to reduce central government costs rather than introduce effective local regulation per se, they did provide impetus for subsequent measures to increase competitiveness and level the producer playing field.

The principal thrust of the 1998 reform process was an enforced consolidation of mining enterprises into larger conglomerates. Agglomeration complemented the transfer of large mining assets to provincial governments and the hardening of budgetary constraints. The 1998 reforms, as well as more recent central government enforcement of mine safety regulations, have facilitated the gradual internalisation of health and environmental externalities into China's coal pricing system. By increasing producer competition and strengthening local regulatory mechanisms, these reforms presented an opportunity to improve the environmental performance of China's coal sector, provided that local state ownership, policy-making, regulation, and management functions were kept separate (Andrews-Speed, 2004).

The Environmental Consequences of Coal Industry Growth

Coal mining and combustion are associated with a range of environmental costs including land subsidence, degeneration of water quality, air pollutant emissions, and acid rain. Three key measures of environmental air quality are the concentration of total suspended particulates (TSP), carbon dioxide emissions, and sulphur dioxide emissions. Within China, TSP levels are measured by city environmental bureaux. Figure 6 illustrates the annual decline of average urban TSP levels as a function of rising per capita energy consumption between 1980 and 2003. According to Chinese government data, average urban TSP levels declined from their peak of 729 $\mu g/m^3$, at 0.61 tons of standard coal equivalent (SCE) per capita energy consumption (in 1982), to 256 $\mu g/m^3$ at 1.3 tons SCE in 2003. The data in Figure 6 also illustrate the reported decline of annual per-capita energy consumption between 1996 and 2000 as a result of the central government's mine closure campaign and a decline in economic demand that was exacerbated by the 1997 Asian financial crisis. TSP abatement represents one downward-sloping China air-pollution EEKC. Market competition functioned as a central driver for the downward slope of China's coal-TSP EEKC by increasing demand for more efficient, higher-quality coal. Other drivers included coal substitution of less-efficient biomass energy sources, increasingly effective end-user regulation, and availability of new combustion technologies.

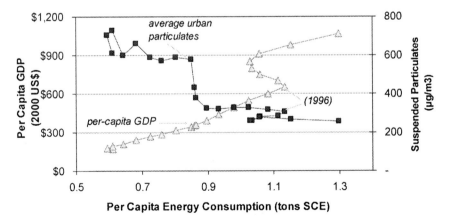

Figure 6. Per capita GDP and suspended particulates as a function of energy consumption, 1980–2003. *Source*: National Bureau of Statistics (various years); *China Statistical Yearbook* (Beijing: China Statistics Press); *China Environment Yearbook* (various years)

The downward slope of China's coal–TSP EEKC (Figure 6) has been offset by increased carbon dioxide and nitrogen oxides emissions. China is currently the second largest contributor of anthropogenic carbon dioxide emissions, accounting for 12 per cent of worldwide emissions in 2001 (IEA, 2004; Figure 7). With continued growth of coal combustion, China may become the world's largest emitter of carbon dioxide before the middle of this century, contributing one of the largest increments to global greenhouse gas emissions. Meanwhile, increased motor vehicle usage has driven an increase in NO_x levels in ambient air from 65 to 90 Mg/m^3 (Chen *et al.*, 2004).

Sulphur dioxide and particulates are considered by many environmental experts in China to be the air pollutants of gravest concern, and efforts at controlling air pollution have focused on them (Figure 8). Since the 1980s, the fraction of China's coal that has been washed has been stable, and flue gas desulphurisation is only now becoming widespread. However, sulphur content in delivered coal has declined as efficiencies have improved, and better particulate removal has captured some sulphur dioxide, so overall emissions have fallen. A growing fraction of coal is used in power plants with tall stacks, and less in residential and small industrial applications, and much coal-using industry has been relocated outside cities. Ambient concentrations of sulphur dioxide in cities have consequently fallen; although in many places levels exceed China's air quality standards. Simultaneously, the regional problem of acid precipitation had become more serious. Acid precipitation affects over 40 per cent of the country's land area and causes damages of US$1 to 2 billion annually.

As more becomes known about the health impacts of airborne particulates, especially very small particulates that are drawn deep into the lungs, they are

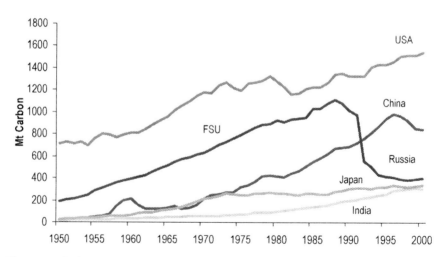

Figure 7. Carbon dioxide emissions of six major economies, 1950–2002. *Source*: International Energy Agency (2004)

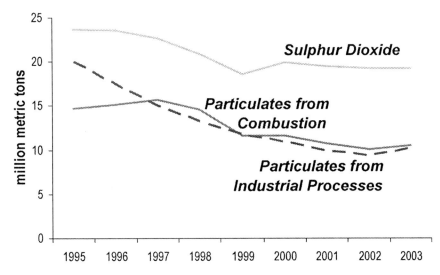

Figure 8. Sulphur dioxide emissions and particulate emissions, 1995–2003. *Source*: Editorial Board of the China Electricity Yearbook (various years); NBS (2004)

considered responsible for a greater share of the world's ill health than was previously thought (WHO, 2004). Particulate emissions from combustion and physical processes (like industrial grinding) fell rapidly in China in the 1990s as relatively inexpensive particulate controls were installed on a larger share of industrial facilities. In recent years, however, rising coal use and industrial activity have led to an upturn in particulate emissions. Ambient particulate levels show very similar trends, especially since particulates from motor vehicles and construction activities have replaced falling industrial emissions in many cities. Most residents of China's northern cities live with annual average particulate levels about twice as high as national standards, and some cities experience much higher averages.

The impacts of a coal-dominated energy economy are felt all along the fuel chain. About 6000 miners die each year in accidents in China's coal mines, according to official statistics, though the actual number may be substantially higher. An unknown number die from occupational diseases. Coal gas and coking plants are also associated with high incidences of cancer. While new combustion technologies and improved regulation will help to abate some of the most egregious health impacts, the ongoing dominance of coal portends continued environmental costs associated with expanded energy usage.

Rural Energy

The pattern of energy use in rural households reflects several decades of industrialisation and vigorously pursued rural energy and economic policies overlaid on traditional patterns established over millennia. Even with rapid urbanisation, nearly 60 per cent of China's population still lives in rural areas, where they rely on biomass for 80 per cent of their energy needs and coal for a further 10 per cent (NBS, 2005a, b). Per capita energy demand is smaller than in urban areas, but the average rural dweller still uses the equivalent of 600 kg of coal each year, mainly in the form of crop wastes, wood, and coal. Typically, these are burned indoors in a bewildering variety of hand-built stoves, often with inadequate ventilation.

Agricultural activities currently produce about 705 million tons (Mt) of biomass by-products in the form of crop stalks, straw, and hulls each year (Sinton *et al.*, 2005). In 2000, about 194 Mt of this was used as livestock fodder, 106 Mt as fertiliser, and 19 Mt for industrial materials. Rural households are the largest consumers, and directly burned about 288 Mt (41 per cent) of agricultural biomass in 2000. Farmers often burn the remaining agricultural biomass directly during the harvest seasons, which not only causes local air pollution but also affects air and road transportation. The forestry sector contributes approximately 170 Mt of biomass annually in the form of firewood each year. About 20 Mt is consumed by rural industry and 150 million tons by rural households for cooking and space heating. There is widespread concern that this level of use represents overharvesting of China's wood resources, leading to soil erosion, degraded water quality, and increased flooding.

The solutions to persistent rural energy problems include providing greater access to higher quality fuels and to electricity, and improving the ways that available solid fuels are used. China has pursued many initiatives aimed at implementing these solutions in different ways. Perhaps the ultimate method of dealing with such issues is to raise rural incomes to a level approaching urban wealth. Other things being equal, greater wealth leads to a lower reliance on biomass (and other solid fuels), as is especially evident in China's wealthiest provincial-level cities (Figure 9). In areas where biomass resource endowments are scarce, such as the dry northwest, reliance on biomass is also lower than average. But in those areas people do without rather than switch fuels. Until the distant goal of making everyone wealthy is realised, rural energy policies will remain in the government's tool kit.

Concern about rural energy came to the fore in the early 1980s, when serious and chronic energy shortages emerged. By the early 1980s, China already had substantial experience with rural energy programmes, including fuel wood plantations and promotion of household- and village-scale biogas systems (Taylor, 1981). These had already established a pattern by which a national programme was used to mobilise mainly local resources through local branches of the agricultural bureaucracy, with a focus on training locally based technical personnel who had responsibility for implementing programmes in accordance with specific regional conditions. This experience was used in carrying out a large-scale programme to introduce more-efficient stoves, with the aim of reducing pressures on biomass resources (Smith *et al.*, 1993). At the same time, local mines were allowed to flourish, as discussed in the previous section, supplying households as well as the growing rural segment of industry. In the

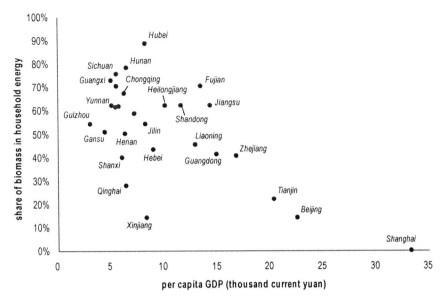

Figure 9. Per capita GDP and share of biomass in rural household fuels by province, 2002. *Source*: NBS (2004); *China Energy Statistical Yearbook* (Beijing: China Statistics Press)

1990s, rural energy programmes, still run mainly by the Ministry of Agriculture, but also through other lines of authority, began to focus more on incorporating technical solutions, like improved stoves and household- and village-scale biogas equipment, into integrated programmes for improving the well being of rural dwellers. Such schemes often included financial components, like access to small-scale loans, to allow investment in better dwellings, improved sanitation, and equipment for agricultural production and small-scale industry. Programmes have exhibited great regional variation, since county-level authorities have considerable autonomy in details of implementation, as well as responsibility for fund raising.

In parallel with these activities, the various incarnations of the electricity ministry ran programmes to extend the grid to as many villages as possible. Heavily subsidised by the central government, construction of power transmission and distribution systems and, in some parts of the country, small hydropower stations, gave at least minimal access to electricity to over 98 per cent of China's households by 2002 – a significant achievement for a developing country (Editorial Board of the China Electricity Yearbook, 2004). Where grid extensions have not been possible, wind and solar systems, often supported by international assistance projects, and with contributions from recipient households as well as various levels of government, have brought electricity to many communities.

Unlike electricity, however, household access to modern fuels has been left mainly to the market. While diesel for agricultural applications – tractors and irrigation pumping, mainly – remains subsidised, households that wish to buy LPG must often go to great trouble and expense. Most rural households with access to LPG use both gas and solid fuels at different times, depending on circumstances. Since LPG is expensive and cash incomes are relatively low, households tend to use significant amounts of 'free' biofuels and relatively cheap coal, balancing expensive convenience with cheaper inconvenience.

After the failures of the biogas programmes of the 1970s, biogas began to receive renewed policy attention in the 1990s (Dai, 1998), garnering the high-level support and enthusiasm once accorded to improved stoves. High-profile successes in R&D and pilot applications have led to efforts at replication across the country, accompanied by sometimes extravagant claims for its potential to transform rural energy systems. The benefits of well-run biogas digesters can indeed be significant, and are epitomised by the recently developed 'four-in-one' systems, in which greenhouses are constructed to house crops in one part, and a livestock pen in a smaller part, underneath which is installed a biogas digester that provides gas to the greenhouse or nearby homes and fertiliser (digester waste) to the greenhouse. Such systems are complicated and expensive to build and run, however, and their long-term viability on a large scale has yet to be demonstrated. By 2003, biogas accounted for nearly 1 per cent of rural household energy, about the same as LPG, but still far from offering a comprehensive solution (NBS, 2005a).

In general, the political salience of rural energy issues *per se* is not high. Since coal became widely available in most places by the early 1990s, sufficiency of supply has not been considered a problem. It is the relationship of energy to more pressing issues, such as distributional inequality, social stability, and, to a certain extent, urgent environmental issues, that brings it to the attention of political leaders.

Some of the most urgent issues are nearly invisible, in a political sense. For instance, if ambient air pollution is a serious matter, then air quality indoors, where people spend most of their time, is even graver. Even after two decades of gradually rising availability of cleaner fuels and the spread of improved stoves, most rural residents are exposed to even higher levels of suspended particulates, carbon monoxide, and other pollutants than in the country's most polluted cities (Sinton *et al.*, 2004a). Ambient air pollution in villages, due to low heights of household flues and the persistence of solid fuels, is also a growing issue.

The link between biomass energy use and land and water quality remains a potentially significant issue. In fact, the link between the household use of wood and charcoal and the over-harvesting of forests is probably of much less concern in most areas than the burgeoning demand for wood products for construction. Moreover, coal has replaced crop wastes to such an extent in many areas that there is a surfeit of biofuels. Nevertheless, there are some communities where poverty and geography make obtaining fossil fuels difficult, and do put household demand in conflict with environmental quality. The former State Development Planning Commission (SDPC), in response to destructive flooding along the Yangtze River in 1998, initiated the Yangtze River Valley Environmental Protection Project to reduce soil erosion by instituting logging bans and afforestation projects. In some areas, the programme included promotion of improved stoves to reduce demand for fuelwood. In some areas, this led to greater use of other biomass (mainly crop wastes) and coal (widely available in these areas), and reliance on purchases from woodlots permitted to harvest and sell wood for fuel (Sinton *et al.,* 2004b). Elsewhere, however, there appeared to be little impact on fuel structure.

After decades of rural energy policy activity that has aimed to reduce biomass use and to increase the availability of modern fuels, the share of biofuels had fallen to about 15 per cent of total primary energy consumption in 2003 – slightly more than half its share in the late 1970s. However, after declining slightly in the 1990s, the total amount of biomass used began to grow again in 2000. This may be in part a response to the long-running campaign to close the small, polluting, and unsafe rural mines that supply farming households with coal, forcing families to turn back to biomass. If so, this increase would exemplify how initiatives to improve environment and safety can have unintended environmental consequences in other arenas. With the demand for biomass resources from China's long-stressed rural environment once again on the rise, and few large-scale alternatives within the geographic and economic reach of most rural residents, meeting rural China's energy needs in an environmentally sustainable manner remains a significant challenge for China's policy makers.

Hydropower

China's ability to harness its superlatively large hydro-electricity generating potential has been limited by institutional, financial, and environmental obstacles. Whereas fiscal decentralisation and augmented rural property rights stimulated the proliferation of small, local coal mines, the number of small hydropower stations continuously declined from its 1979 peak of 90,000 projects.[4] Fiscal decentralisation, a dearth of rural capital, and a general shift from political to economic investment criteria served to undermine hydro development. Large up-front investment requirements combined with low, government-controlled retail electricity prices and technical transmission difficulties to give hydropower a low rate of return on investment (ROI), especially compared with small scale coal mining (Li, 2002). Over the course of the reform period, these institutional and financial obstacles shifted hydro expansion from small to large, centrally-administered projects – in 2002, for example, the government announced plans to invest $35 billion to double national generating capacity by 2010 (Andrews-Speed, 2004).

In spite of its high investment cost and low ROI, hydropower continues to be promoted by the government on the basis of energy security and environmental considerations. According to China's National Energy Strategy and Policy

(NESP), the country aims to install 200 to 240 GW of hydro-electricity by 2020, which means adding 7 to 9 GW of capacity per year – the equivalent of one Three Gorges Dam every two years (Sinton *et al.*, 2005). An annual addition of 7 to 9 GW hydropower is estimated to require $13 to $23 billion of capital investment per year.[5] Investment costs are further complicated by the need for inter-provincial cooperation on large-scale hydro projects. The promotion of Chongqing municipality to provincial status, for example, served to streamline the financing and administration of the Three Gorges Dam.

Hydropower development has also been limited by environmental complications and electricity transmission limitations. Whereas the environmental costs of coal based power are often externalised, as with widely dispersed air pollutant emissions, hydropower efficiency is directly contingent on environmental quality. Droughts and severe silting of watercourses diminish hydro effectiveness and make hydropower less dependable than coal burning power plants (Thomson, 2005). China's hydro potential is also disproportionately dispersed around the south of the country – the four provinces of Sichuan, Guangdong, Fujian, and Yunnan account for nearly 60 per cent of overall capacity. The geographic distribution is compounded by the difficulty of storing and transmitting hydro-electric power.

Although its efficiency is contingent on water and ecological quality, hydro development is associated with a range of social and environmental costs. Water and land environmental quality are directly affected by the flooding, erosion, silting, and accumulation of toxic waste generated by new hydro development. However, environmental degradation caused by hydro development is often eclipsed by the social and economic impacts of relocation and downstream displacement effects. Recent development of the Lancang (Mekong) and Nu (Salween) Rivers in Yunnan, for example, have become international disputes between Chinese power companies and rural communities in Vietnam, Laos, Cambodia, Burma, and Thailand (Stanway, 2005). The involvement of local stakeholders in these disputes and the contingency of hydropower on local environmental quality are two factors that can help to generate a downward slope for China's hydro-EEKC.

Despite the barriers, regional authorities and the country's large, nominally independent power generators are scrambling to claim a share of the remaining sites suitable for large dam projects. Environmental rules have been invoked by the newly vocal State Environmental Protection Agency (SEPA) to halt development projects, including many hydropower projects, but the stoppages have been only temporary, and the fines levied on projects out of compliance have been vanishingly small compared to total investment costs. Even if China takes maximum advantage of opportunities to improve the efficiency of its transmission and distribution system and the potential to raise efficiency in end uses, large increments to generating capacity will be needed. The large, but focused environmental impacts of hydropower projects may come to be seen by China's policy makers as less dire than the consequences of the main alternative: coal-fired power generation.

Recent Developments in China's Energy and Environmental Politics

Starting in the summer of 2004, China has experienced sustained electricity, petrol, and coal shortages – 24 provinces and municipalities have been ordered to reduce consumption to assuage the ongoing crisis (Thomson, 2005). Rapid growth in energy demand, driven by a boom in manufacturing of materials needed for buildings, infrastructure, and consumer products for domestic and overseas markets, has collided with high international energy prices. The roots of the current energy crisis, however, are primarily institutional. The partial liberalisation of China's energy pricing system – coal prices are largely market-oriented while electricity rates remain subject to strict controls – has created price differentials between suppliers and retailers that generate inter-sector conflict (Thomson, 2005). The same problem has arisen between oil producers and domestic refiners; while crude prices have risen, retail prices for oil products remain tightly controlled, squeezing refiners and marketers. Wholesale, retail, domestic and international price disparities have also created problems for coal transport as railroad operators are not able to determine prices freely, thereby limiting rates of return to levels too low to attract necessary investment for capacity expansion.

The ersatz liberalisation of China's energy pricing system can be traced to lack of strategic coordination within the energy bureaucracy. In 2005, the central government moved to address energy bureaucracy dysfunction by restructuring its policy-making and regulatory structure. The Energy Bureau (EB) of the National Development and Reform Commission (NDRC) had done an ineffectual job coordinating energy sector development and regulating powerful state-owned energy companies. The first problem was the EB's lack of sufficient resources or authority to override vested supplier interests. This problem was addressed by creating a National Energy Leadership Group composed of Premier Wen Jiabao, and Vice Premiers Huang Ju and Zeng Peiyan, as well as high-level representatives from the State Environmental Protection Agency (SEPA) and the People's Liberation Army (PLA) (Qiu, 2005). The inclusion of Xie Zhenhua, the director of the SEPA (at that time) in the cabinet's energy coordination task force signalled the importance of environmental considerations in China's energy politics. Directly under the Leadership Group, a State Energy Office (SEO) was created in order to provide bureaucratic coordination, formulate strategy and policy, and enforce existing policies. Meanwhile, the EB remained under the NDRC, but was also placed under the purview of the SEO. The SEO has a broad decision-making mandate, while the EB is charged with policy administration and enforcement. Figure 10 illustrates the current structure of China's energy bureaucracy.

The 2005 reorganisation was a domestic iteration of the leadership's larger focus on issues of energy supply. This focus has also been reflected in the compilation of a National Energy Strategy and Policy (NESP) document with domestic supply targets through 2020 (Development Research Centre, 2004). Within China's foreign policy, this orientation has manifested itself in the

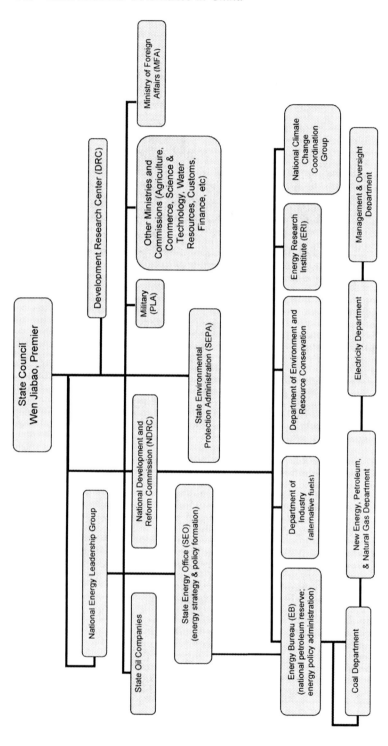

Figure 10. Bureaucratic structure of China's national energy policy apparatus, 2005. *Source:* NEDO (2005); Downs (2004); Asia Times Online (http://www.atimes.com/atimes/China/GF03Ad01.html)

'going out' strategy of seeking energy resources abroad. In the summer of 2005, this policy stirred up a hullabaloo in the US Congress as politicians scrambled to block the attempted takeover of Unocal by CNOOC, a partially state-owned Chinese oil company. Perceptions of scarcity and zero-sum competition serve to sharpen the leadership's focus on energy security and efficiency. However, these ongoing discussions have yet to produce clear, effective mechanisms for reducing the environmental costs of increased energy consumption.

The disappointing returns of China's 'going out' strategy have reinvigorated government investment in innovative domestic supply sources such as coal liquefaction, nuclear power, and renewable energy. Coal liquefaction (CL) is a process whereby high-quality coal is either directly or indirectly converted into liquid fuel that can be used as a gasoline product. The largest and most advanced CL project in China is run by the Shenhua Group in Shanxi province. The Shenhua Group was planning to float an IPO on the Hong Kong Stock Exchange in 2005, but the company was already estimated to have raised more than $9 billion of aggregate investment, compared to total construction investment in the coal industry in 2002 of $1.3 billion (Nolan *et al.*, 2004). By substituting for oil imports and domestic coal combustion, CL is attractive on security and environmental grounds. However, current CL technology is not a long term solution because the conversion process has negative energy return on energy investment, is highly water intensive, and currently requires 3–5 tons of coal input to produce one ton of oil (Nolan *et al.*, 2004). In spite of its energy inefficiency, CL investment and research are advancing in China, with more than a dozen pending project proposals.

Intersecting goals of energy supply security and environmental improvement have also advanced government promotion of nuclear power and renewable energy. According to the NESP, China is planning to build six to eight nuclear reactors per year over the next twenty years with the goal of quadrupling nuclear capacity by 2020. In the same vein, the government has articulated ambitious goals for renewable energy growth of 90 to 100 GW by 2020, to eventually comprise 10 per cent of national energy supply. A lack of transparency makes official claims of an excellent safety record for China's nuclear power plants impossible to evaluate. In any case, plans to raise the capacity of nuclear generators to 40 GW by 2020 add urgency to the need to implement a publicly credible system to protect safety through the entire fuel cycle (Sinton *et al.*, 2005). In spite of its large environmental safety risks and high costs for waste disposal, nuclear power may be seen by the government as a cleaner alternative to coal combustion.

In 2005 Chinese policy makers restructured the energy bureaucracy and released a spate of policy incentive programmes and future targets designed to address national energy needs. However, ongoing fuel and electricity shortages, an increase in deadly mining accidents, and sustained environmental degradation reveal fundamental energy problems yet to be solved. Within the larger milieu of China's energy system, the publication of the Chinese Communist Party's 'suggestions' for the Eleventh Five Year Plan (2006–2010) indicate that the central government is embracing the optimistic logic of the EEKC. In contrast to earlier plans, the Eleventh FYP thus far only articulates two quantitative targets: the doubling of year 2000 per capita GDP by 2010, and the reduction of aggregate energy intensity (EI) of GDP by 20 per cent between 2005 and 2010. While diminished EI is conducive to economic competitiveness and efficiency, it is not clear that the Eleventh FYP's gestalt approach to energy governance will generate a downward curve for China's EEKC.

Future Determinants of China's EEKC

Since the initiation of reform in 1978, three major themes in China's energy sector have been decentralisation, the shift to liberalised markets, and internationalisation. According to specific energy sector dynamics and local characteristics, these processes have had positive and negative effects on the slope of China's EEKC. Decentralisation, for example, stimulated the proliferation of dirty, unsafe, and inefficient local coal mines, thereby pushing up the coal EEKC. On the other hand, decentralisation combined with gradual liberalisation to increase economic competition, energy efficiency, and substitution towards cleaner, more efficient fuels. Within national narratives of decentralisation and liberalisation, the central role of the state in China's EEKC is illustrated by the importance of regulatory effectiveness. Two examples of strong state regulation pushing down China's EEKC are the government-mandated transition from leaded to unleaded vehicle fuels and the replacement of cfc-using refrigerators. The importance of governance effectiveness is further illustrated by the structural and systemic discontinuities (e.g., pricing) arising from the lack of a powerful, coordinated Ministry of Energy.

Neither a strong state apparatus nor a fully liberalised market economy will necessarily facilitate the achievement of a downward sloping EEKC. Rather, an effective regulatory mechanism is necessary to override vested interests and prevent free-rider problems. Between the false dichotomy of command-and-control economies and liberalised markets, community-based environmental monitoring is likely to provide the most cost-effective method for improving China's environmental quality with increased energy consumption. Gradual adoption of more liberalised energy markets can influence China's EEKC in combination with local political reform: increased economic liberalisation without expanded rights or accountability is likely to augment supply-side dominance and an upward-sloping EEKC.

The reported absolute decline of China's aggregate energy consumption from 1997 to 1999 serves as a reminder that governance is but one among several variables determining the environmental impact of energy usage. Energy system structure is also dependent on exogenous economic, demographic, and geographic factors, and environmental outcomes are also conditioned by usage factors including technology, behaviour, and fuel structure. Within this array of variables, the leadership's recent moves toward energy market liberalisation have further empowered vested interests to ignore environmental costs and push up China's EEKC. Nonetheless, energy market liberalisation provides central and local governments with timely opportunities to avoid some deleterious environmental consequences of unregulated growth.

Notes

1. The environmental Kuznets curve (EKC) was developed in Grossman and Krueger's analysis of the environmental effects of NAFTA.
2. All RMB values are in deflated year 2000 RMB unless otherwise noted; source: *China Energy Industry Yearbook* (1991).
3. Mortality data are derived from *Coal Economic Research*, 2005 edition, p. 24, chart 23.
4. This decline of micro-hydro is masked by constant upward revisions of the statistical parameters of 'small hydro' (Smil, 2004).
5. This range is based on an average capital cost of $1900 to $2600 per kW; IEA (2004).

References

Andrews-Speed, P. (2004) *Energy Policy and Regulation in the People's Republic of China* (The Hague: Kluwer Law International).

Chen, B., Hong, C. & Kan, H. (2004) 'Exposures and health outcomes from outdoor air pollutants in China', *Toxicology* 198: 291–300.

China Energy Development Report (2003) (Beijing: China Computation Press).

Dai Lin (1998) 'The development and prospective of bioenergy technology in China', *Biomass and Bioenergy* 15(2): 181–6.

Dasgupta, S., Laplante, B., Wang, H. & Wheeler, D. (2002) 'Confronting the environmental Kuznets curve', *Journal of Economic Perspectives* 16(1): 147–68.

Development Research Center (2004) 'National energy strategies and policies report'. Available at http://www.efchina.org/documents/Draft_Natl_E_Plan0311.pdf (accessed March 2005).

Downs, E. (2004) 'The Chinese energy security debate', *China Quarterly* 177: 21–41.

Editorial Board of the China Electricity Yearbook (2004) *China Electricity Yearbook 2003* (Beijing: Electricity Press).

Editorial Board of the China Environment Yearbook (all years 1996 to 2004) *China Environment Yearbook*, all editions 1996 to 2004 (Beijing: China Environmental Science Press).

Finkelman, R., Beklin, H. & Zheng, B. (1999) 'Health impacts of domestic coal use in China', *Proceedings of the National Academy of Science* 96: 3427–31.

Grossman, G. & Krueger, A. (1993) 'Environmental impacts of the North American Free Trade Agreement', in P. Garber (ed.) *The US–Mexico Free Trade Agreement* (Cambridge, MA: MIT Press), pp. 13–56.

International Energy Agency (IEA) (2004) *World Energy Outlook 2004* (Paris: Organization for Economic Cooperation and Development/ International Energy Agency).

Kuznets, S. (1955) 'Economic growth and income inequality', *American Economic Review* 45(1): 1–28.

Levine, M. & Sinton, J. (2004) 'China: national energy policy', in C. Cleveland (ed. in chief) *Encyclopedia of Energy* (Boston, MA: Elsevier Academic Press).

Li, F. (2002) 'Hydropower in China', *Energy Policy* 30: 1241–49.

National Bureau of Statistics (NBS) (2004) *China Statistical Yearbook 2004* (Beijing: China Statistics Press).

National Bureau of Statistics (2005a) *China Energy Statistical Yearbook 2004* (Beijing: China Statistics Press).

National Bureau of Statistics (2005b) *China Statistical Abstract 2005* (Beijing: China Statistics Press).

NEDO (2005) *NEDO Overseas Briefing* 957: 20–23.

Nolan, P., Shipman, A. & Rui, H. (2004) 'Coal liquefaction, Shenhua Group, and China's energy security', *European Management Journal* 22(2): 150–64.

Qiu, X. (2005) 'China overhauls energy bureaucracy', *Asia Times Online*. Available at http://www.atimes.com/atimes/China/GF03Ad01.html (accessed 17 August 2005).

Sinton, J., Smith, K., Peabody, J., Liu, Y., Edwards, R. & Gan, Q. (2004a) 'An assessment of programs to promote improved household stoves in China', *Energy for Sustainable Development*, 8(3): 33–52.

Sinton, J., Smith, K., Peabody, J., Liu, Y., Edwards, R., Milet, M., Gan, Q. & Yin, Z. (2004b) *Improved Household Stoves in China: an Assessment of the National Improved Stove Program (NISP)*, revised edition (San Francisco, CA: Institute for Global Health, University of California, San Francisco and School of Public Health, University of California, Berkeley).

Sinton, J., Stern, R., Aden, N. & Levine, M. (eds.) (2005) *Evaluation of China's Energy Strategy Options* (Berkeley, CA: Lawrence Berkeley National Laboratory).

Smil, V. (2004) *China's Past, China's Future: Energy, Food, Environment* (New York: Routledge Curzon).

Smith, K., Shuhua, G., Kun, H. & Daxiong, Q. (1993) '100 million improved cookstoves in China: how was it done?', *World Development* 21(6): 941–61.

Stanway, D. (2005) China's hydropower development is an issue for all of Southeast Asia, *Interfax China Energy Report Weekly* 4(25): 25–9.

Taylor, R. (1981) *Rural Energy Development in China* (Washington, DC: Resources for the Future).

Thomson, E. (1996) 'Reforming China's coal industry', *China Quarterly* 147: 726–50.

Thomson, E. (2005) 'Power shortages in China: why?', *China: an International Journal* 3(1): 155–71.

World Health Organization (WHO) (2004) *Global Burden of Disease* (Geneva: World Health Organization).

China's Environmental Governance of Rapid Industrialisation

HAN SHI & LEI ZHANG

Introduction

China's industrial output has been growing at an average annual rate of over 11.4 per cent since the start of the economic reforms in 1978 (NBS, 2004). This unprecedented pace and scale of industrial growth has not only greatly improved the quality of life of 1.3 billion Chinese people, but also caused significant environmental risks for public and ecological health at the local, regional, and global levels (World Bank, 2001; SEI and UNDP, 2002). Despite China's increasingly vigorous efforts in curbing industrial pollution over the last two decades (see below), industry remains the principal culprit of environmental deterioration in China. For example, industry accounts for 83 per cent of total SO_2 emissions and over 80 per cent of total particulate emissions in 2003. Exceptionally, industrial COD discharges have undergone a drastic decline from 6.92 million metric tons in 1999 to 5.12 million tons in 2003 due to a consistent and effective industrial wastewater treatment programme since 1996. The total industrial solid waste generation added up to 1004 million tons while the domestic garbage collection volume amounted to 148.57 million tons in 2003 (NBS, 2004). Industrial energy consumption accounts for more than 68 per cent of total energy consumption in China from 1990 through 2002, and industry consumed 90 per cent of total coal consumption in China (NBS, 2004). China is the world's largest consumer of coal, the second largest consumer of oil, and the second largest emitter of the greenhouse gas carbon dioxide in 2002 (IEA, 2004).

China began to develop a system of environmental institutions, regulations, and programmes in the wake of growing pollution in the 1970s (Jahiel, 1998; Ma & Ortolano, 2000). The relatively comprehensive environmental state apparatus has played a key role in stabilising the industrial pollution emissions over a period of rapid industrialisation in the 1980s and 1990s, but has not prevented the overall deterioration of environmental quality in China (World Bank, 2001). Xie Zhenhua, then administrator of the National Environmental Protection Agency (NEPA), acknowledged that the nation's efforts to abate pollution has slowed, but not stopped, the deterioration of environment quality (as quoted in Ma and Ortolano, 2000). The national campaign from 1996 onwards to mandate all industrial enterprises to comply with pollutant discharge standards by the end of 2000 achieved limited results (SEI and UNDP, 2002; Shi, 2003). In 2003 about 1.3 million business entities paid pollution levies, most of which were industrial enterprises violating the national pollution discharge standards (SEPA, 2004).

On the other hand, an increasing number of Chinese companies have started to pursue environmental performance beyond government regulations. The growing number of ISO 14001 certified Chinese companies is an example. As of October 2005, the State Environmental Protection Administration (SEPA) had designated 32 companies as 'Environmentally Friendly Enterprises', as they fulfil the criteria of the voluntary programme launched by SEPA. Moreover, civil society and environmental non-governmental organisations (NGOs) become increasingly active in putting pressures on polluting companies and lax governments.

These developments raise a number of questions. Are we witnessing a major change in the roles of state and non-state actors in environmental policy-making and decision-making related to industrial environmental management, not unlike that which has been interpreted in Western countries under the label of environmental governance? What are the characteristics of and drivers behind these changes in what was until recently a state-monopolised environmental reform? How will these transitions influence and shape the future environmental performance of China's industrialisation?

Building upon results of earlier studies (Sinkule & Ortolano, 1995; World Bank, 1997, 2001; Jahiel, 1998; Ma & Ortolano, 2000; SEI & UNDP, 2002), this article further explores these questions by focussing on the transition of China's industrial environmental governance since 2002. Several reasons make a concentration on recent transitions interesting. First, since President Hu Jintao and Premier Wen Jiabao took office in March 2003, China has embarked on a new pathway of industrialisation, giving higher priority to social justice and environmental sustainability (in addition to economic growth; Wen, 2004; Hu, 2005). Second, China's accession to the World Trade Organisation (WTO) in November 2001 codified existing openness to the global economy but also further accelerated integration into the global economic system, making China increasingly susceptible to international rules, norms and practices in the economic, social and even environmental arenas. Third, the domestic (next to international) environmental NGOs have expanded in China, parallel to an increasingly active civil society and public media. These trends have profound implications for environmental governance, making a fresh review of China's industrial environmental management both timely and useful.

The remainder of this article is structured as follows. The next section briefly reviews China's industrialisation path and some relevant industrial transformations that affect pollution control. Subsequently, a new analytical model is suggested to understand better industrial environmental governance over the last decade. The following sections apply this framework to the analysis of the innovating roles of the state, market and civil society in pollution control.

Industrialisation and Industrial Transformation

China's initial industrialisation between 1953 and 1978 was almost exclusively based on the Soviet industrial development model and technological system. The sector was dominated by state-owned, heavy industry. The R&D capacity was situated outside the industry itself. The industrial development during this period was solely output driven, rather than efficiency and profit oriented. This formed a root cause of serious energy and material inefficiencies and the high pollution intensities of industrial production in China.

The contribution of industry to China's GDP rose from 17.6 per cent in 1952 to 44.4 per cent in 2002 (NBS, 2003). Among the primary (agriculture), secondary (industry and construction) and tertiary (service) sectors, industry tends to be most polluting, especially heavy industry. Within the industrial sector, the added value of the heavy industry (especially the raw materials industry) rose from 57 per cent in 1996 to 65.8 per cent in 2003 (NBS, 2004).

During the same period, China's industry also witnessed a consolidation process in the face of increasingly fierce domestic and international competition. Large-scale enterprises accounted for 51.14 per cent of the total industrial value added in 2001, compared to only 43.4 per cent in 1996. The scale of industry also affects the economies of scale of both pollution prevention and abatement activities, and in turn has implications for the pollution intensity of industrial production.

Since 1979, but especially during the last decade, three parallel industrial restructuring themes can be identified that are relevant for our analysis, i.e. the reform of state-owned enterprises (SOEs), the proliferation and privatisation of township and village enterprises (TVEs), and the considerable expansion of foreign direct investment (FDI) and international trade.

Reform and Privatisation of SOEs and TVEs

In the early 1980s, China started a gradual and lasting process to reform its SOEs and develop a private sector to improve its overall industrial competitiveness, create adequate jobs for its ever-expanding workforce and accommodate escalating urbanisation. Another key component of China's economic reform has been the rapid growth of the TVEs, referring to non-agricultural businesses owned and run at the township and village levels (UNIDO, 2005). During the 1980s and 1990s, TVEs grew at an average annual rate above 20 per cent (Zhang, 2002). In the peak year of 1997, TVEs generated almost one third of the national GDP, and about half of the national industrial added value (Zhu, 1998).

A World Bank research report (Dasgupta *et al.*, 1997) suggests that SOEs in China are significantly more pollution-intensive than heavy manufacturing companies in the US and Europe. Among the direct reasons for this are their use of old equipment and technology, which lead to lower operating efficiency, the absence of a profit motive to encourage more efficient operating practices, low prices for natural resources, and limited environmental pressures from outside the industrial sector.

In the long run, the reform of industrial ownership is expected to contribute to more effective management and more efficient operations pursuing cost saving and profit making, more responsive to price and other market signals, and in turn to increase the resource utilisation efficiency and environmental performance. It may also be easier for environmental regulators to get tough on the non-compliance of private firms compared to SOEs. In China, a government office of lesser rank has no bureaucratic authority to compel compliance from one of a senior rank; nor can government units of equal rank issue binding orders to each other (Ma & Ortolano, 2000). As many managers of SOEs also have an implicit government ranking, they are in many ways senior in rank to directors of Environmental Protection Bureaux (EPBs) that are supposed to regulate the enterprises. This has constituted a major barrier to stringent enforcement of environmental regulations. Gradually many small and medium-sized SOEs and TVEs have been privatised and an increasing number of large- and medium-scaled SOEs have been restructured into shareholding or joint stock companies. This makes it easier for environmental regulators to monitor and enforce the compliance by these enterprises.

However, in the short term, there are several negative environmental impacts associated with industrial privatisation. First, environmental management personnel are among the auxiliary workers typically fired first to cut the overhead costs under conditions of fierce competition. Second, some environmental protection programmes, such as programmes for industrial energy conservation and recycling of secondary resources, which the state had been running successfully in a planned economy context in the 1980s, have become dysfunctional after the industrial restructuring towards a market economy. Third, the initial industrial environmental regulation, which was principally designed to regulate SOEs, has gradually become less effective, while a new regime, better adapted to the new situation, is still in development. For instance, it was common for SOEs to access public financing to construct their pollution treatment facilities, but public financing has become no longer available after privatisation. In the mean time no alternative financing mechanism is yet in place.

Expansion of FDI Inflow and International Trade

After the late 1980s, FDI started to soar in China, and since 1992 China has been the developing country that has attracted the largest amount of FDI. In assessing the impact of the growing FDI flows on China's environment we can witness both pessimists and optimists. Pessimists stress the 'pollution haven' and 'race-to-the-bottom' hypothesis, while optimists tend to put a premium on Multinational Corporations (MNCs) as a vehicle for introducing and disseminating environmentally sound technologies and management systems. There is empirical evidence that over the last decade, MNCs have played an increasing role in disseminating environmental management best practices to their Chinese counterparts, transferring clean technologies, and striving for more regulatory transparency and consistency in China (UNCTAD, 2004). But at the same time, examples of FDI in polluting industries are not too difficult to find, for instance in used computer 'recycling' and heavy industries. Many polluting industries were also relocated to the Pearl River Delta and Yangtze River Delta from Hong Kong, Taiwan, and some Southeast Asian Countries.

China's international trade has been growing at an extraordinary rate and in 2004 China became the third largest international trading nation. The immense growth in trade, following the opening of China to the global economy, had a variety of (environment related) effects. On the one hand, China became increasingly aware of standards in international markets and the need to conform to them. China's WTO accession in 2001 has played a special role in encouraging China's development of sound and transparent environmental regulations. WTO obligations promote clear and effective notice of environmental regulations and greater public participation in policy making, standard setting, and implementation of environmental legislation and standards in China. It also implies that environmental legislation will be implemented more uniformly and coherently across the country and that China's environmental standards will be more likely to reflect international environmental standards (Shi, 2003). On the other hand, not all exports go to OECD markets and not all imports come from OECD countries, enabling polluting enterprises still to find ways to route their products out of or into China.

From Environmental Regulation to Environmental Governance: a Framework

China's Initial Industrial Environmental Regime

Industrial pollution regulation is at the origin and remains the cornerstone of China's environmental management system. As a follow-up to China's participation at the Stockholm Conference on the Human Environment in 1972, the State Council convened the First National Conference on Environmental Protection in August 1973. Consequently, the State Council decided to make the first work plan for environmental protection and created the first environmental institution – the Office of State Council Leading Group on Environmental Protection in 1974. This is seen as the first step in developing Chinese environmental policy and environmental institutions (Jahiel, 1998).

The government promulgated China's Environmental Protection Law for trial implementation in 1979. Since then, the central government has introduced more than 100 environmental laws and regulations, a range of environmental regulatory schemes such as Environmental Impact Assessment (EIA), Three Synchronisations, and Pollution Levy System, and over 500 environmental standards to regulate industrial pollution. To implement these regulations and programmes, China established a national environmental authority (i.e. SEPA) and more than two thousand EPBs at the provincial, municipal, county, and even township levels.

The initial industrial environmental regime in China is illustrated in Figure 1. The state played a dominant role, while industry and community had little influence in affecting this regime. The state primarily consisted of administrative agencies, including environmental departments and economic agencies, with little, if any, participation from the legislative and judicial institutions. The industrial sectors were only passive subjects regulated by the state, without any interest in compliance beyond state environmental regulations.

Before the mid-1990s, there existed no truly environmental NGOs in China. China lacked a strong civil society articulating environmental interests and pressing environmental policy implementation (Ho, 2001). Civil society

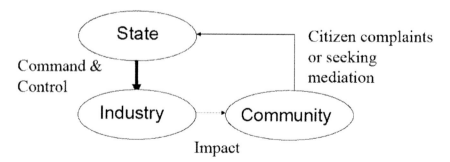

Figure 1. China's initial industrial environmental regulation: actors and influences

and victims of industrial pollution could only resort to three means to safeguard their interests in environmental conflicts. First, citizens could complain about damages caused by industrial pollution at EPBs at various levels. Second, deputies to the people's congresses and representatives of people's political consultative conferences at the national, provincial, municipal, and country levels could put forward motions and proposals to suspend industrial pollution or compensate victims. Third, individual victims could plea for mediation by environmental authorities in cases of environmental conflicts with industrial polluters, which, in rare instances, resulted in compensation.

Failures of the State-dominated Environmental Regime

By the mid of 1990s, it became clear that the relatively comprehensive environmental regulatory framework established since the late 1970s had failed to prevent the overall deterioration of environmental quality. There are a number of reasons underlying the unsatisfactory performance of China's early industrial environmental regulation.

First, when China started to develop its environmental regulation in the 1970s, there was little experience and virtually no institutional capacity. China had to model its initial environmental regulations on those of Western countries, but China's international isolation in the 1970s and early 1980s made the learning process difficult and deficient.

Second, for the initial regime of industrial environmental pollution control to function properly, a strong environmental state, with large and effective monitoring and enforcement capacity, is indispensable. Due to EPBs' lack of authority, capacity, and resources to monitor and enforce industrial environmental compliance, this regime proved ineffective in addressing industrial pollution. This is especially true at the town level. By 2004, there were no environmental monitoring stations and environmental supervision and inspection agencies at the town level. Table 1 is illustrative of the monitoring incapacities of the environmental state. The table compares the number and gross industrial output values of industrial enterprises under the EPB monitoring schemes with the number and output value of all industrial enterprises included in the statistical system of the National Bureau of Statistics (NBS). What is worrisome is that nearly 50 per cent of industrial economic activities remain outside the monitoring of EPBs at various levels.

Third, the regime was principally designed to target large SOEs within a centrally planned economy via direct command-and-control interventions. The most important basis of the regulation was the concentration-based pollutant discharge standards. As a result, all the regulatory programmes were biased in favour of end-of-pipe pollution abatement, which proved technologically unreliable and economically costly in China. Moreover, the system was

Table 1. Industrial enterprises under environmental monitoring as part of all industrial enterprises in the national statistical system

Year	No. of enterprises included in the NBS statistics	Gross Industrial Output Value (GIOV) (billion RMB)	No. of enterprises included in environmental statistics	GIOV under environmental statistics (billion RMB)	Ratio of GIOV of environmental statistics to that of national statistics
2002	181,557	11,077.6	70,831	6075.7	54.8
2001	171,256	9544.9	71,425	5382	56.4
2000	162,885	8567.3	70,944	4979.8	58.1
1999	162,033	7270.7	70,997	4146.8	57.0
1998	165,080	6773.7	74,101	4259.1	62.9
1997	468,506	6835.2	54,909	3669.7	53.7
1996	506,445	6274	62,867	3597.1	57.3
1995	510,381	5494.7	70,177	2732.1	49.7

Source: China Statistics Yearbooks (1996–2003) and China Environment Yearbooks (1996–2003).

ineffective and costly in dealing with the large quantity of emerging small-scale industrial entities, especially the TVEs in rural areas (Zhang, 2002; Zhang & Chen, 2003).

Finally, industry experienced constant and rapid change in the 1990s, both in scale (quantitatively) and in structure (qualitatively). The industrial transformation formed a moving target and it proved difficult to develop a corresponding environmental regulatory system.

A New Industrial Environmental Governance Regime-in-the-making

Industrial environmental management in many OECD countries has shifted during the last two decades, and different authors have used different concepts to characterise these changes. Tietenberg (1998) and Khanna (2001) have emphasised the use of new market-based and voluntary instruments in addition to, and sometimes instead of, command and control regulation. Others have framed the changes in term of a transition from government to governance (e.g. Jordan *et al.*, 2005), emphasising the role of non-state actors in environmental politics.

We claim that similar tendencies can be witnessed in China, albeit with the specific national characteristics that mark China's historical background. In order to understand and explain the transition of China's industrial environmental regime we have to replace the analytical scheme of Figure 1 with a multi-actor environmental governance model. The environmental performance of factories is then determined by the interactions of multiple agents, with multiple incentives via multiple institutional arrangements. Although the state continues to have a major role in regulating pollution externalities, one can no longer understand China's industrial pollution control regime when civil society and markets are ignored or made solely dependent upon the state. The new analytical framework is illustrated in Figure 2, where three main actors and institutions take more balanced positions, i.e., the state, economic actors and institutions, and civil society. Although the state remains the primary player, now economic actors and civil society start to play significant and ever-increasing roles. The state represents all the government bodies affecting industrial environmental management, including administrative, legislative, and judicial branches at different levels. Economic actors include industry, investors, customers and financial institutions, which have become increasingly independent from the state. In this article, we define civil society as a self-organising and coordinating network of societal actors that are relatively independent of control by the state and private sector.

Following this analytical framework, we first examine the changes with respect to the environmental state, and subsequently analyse what innovations emerge in the roles non-state actors and institutions play in improving industrial environmental performance.

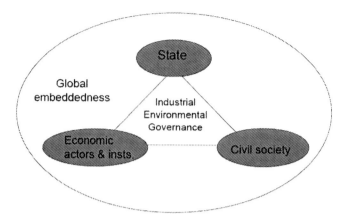

Figure 2. Actors and interactions involved in industrial environmental governance

Transition of China's Environmental State: the Reorganisation of Environmental State Institutions

Over the past decade, new trends in environmental state institutions include the continuous empowerment of environmental agencies, the gradual greening of economic departments, as well as the growing role of legislative institutions in shaping industrial environmental governance. Even the judiciary, which was previously insignificant, has recently started to play a more visible role.

Local Environmental Regulators

Local EPBs have been under constant attack due to their incompetence in effectively monitoring and enforcing industrial environmental regulations. But despite some occasional setbacks, EPBs as a whole have been empowered over the last decade. Recently, a decentralisation tendency has provided lower level EPBs with more industrial regulatory responsibility, although these lower level EPBs still have a weak institutional capacity and are more likely to surrender to the economic growth priorities of the local governments with whom they are affiliated. At the same time, local EPBs have started to experiment with innovative environmental management approaches and instruments, such as SO_2 emission trading and information disclosure programmes regarding industrial pollution.

The long-standing underfinancing of EPB operations has driven EPBs towards additional fundraising to subsidise their operations, for instance via establishing affiliated services institutions, such as environmental research institutes, environmental monitoring stations, and environmental engineering companies (see Lo and Tang, this issue). These semi-autonomous organisations carry out activities for a variety of clients, both governmental and private.

While it does improve the financial situation, it has also greatly undermined the credibility and neutrality of EPBs in performing their responsibilities and has resulted in some corruption (Zhang, 2002; van Rooij, 2004). What seems important is to provide EPBs with full funding to enable them to monitor and enforce environmental compliance independently, and to decouple their affiliations with the services institutions.

Greening of Economic Agencies

As environmental agencies to some extent remain incompetent and short of authority in China, the greening of powerful economic state institutions is a parallel track for effective industrial pollution control. In China, it seems impossible to empower environmental agencies without a minimum environmental management capacity and alliance within the dominant economic departments. Key economic agencies, such as SDPC and the State Economic and Trade Commission (SETC) – now both part of the National Development and Reform Commission (NDRC) – are increasingly playing a leading role in greening China's industry. Table 2 lists the major Chinese initiatives in greening industry and their respective lead agencies.

This takes place against the background of an institutional restructuring of the economic state agencies. The 1998 reform of the State Council reorganised all nine industrial ministries into bureaus, subordinate to the SETC. In autumn 2000, the State Council took another step forward in overhauling the state's management of the economy by eliminating those bureaus. During the central government restructuring in 2002, the SETC was merged into the NDRC. These changes are related to China's abandonment of direct state management of the economy in favour of more macro-economic regulation. The loss of competences of a major state apparatus may have contributed to its increasing activities in new fields, such as the environment.

The inter-departmental coordination and cooperation between NDRC (and previously SETC) and SEPA in the field of industrial environmental management has also brought improvements and strengthening of industrial pollution control. For instance, in January 2005 SEPA launched a so-called 'Environmental Storm' to suspend the construction of 30 major power and infrastructure development projects due to their violation of the Environmental Impact Assessment Law. NDRC offered critical support to SEPA in this, which ultimately ensured that a few powerful SOEs, like the China Three Gorges Project Corporation, abided by the SEPA's requirements in fulfilling all the EIA procedures.

Rising Role of Legislative and Judicial Institutions

Environmental state institutions at the national level have all been confined within the administrative sector, from the Environmental Protection Leading Group created under the State Council in 1974, to the Environmental

Table 2. Major greening of industrialisation programmes carried out in China

Programme	Starting year	Leading government agencies
Industrial pollution control ('Three Waste' treatment)	1974	Initiated by Environmental Protection Office and later SEPA and SETC jointly took the lead
Industrial energy conservation	1980	SETC and SPC; and led by NDRC since 2002
Comprehensive utilisation of resources	1983	SETC and State Planning Commission (SPC)
Cleaner production	1993	First promoted by NEPA; SETC resumed the leadership in 1998; and led by NDRC since 2002
Environmental industry	1993	First promoted by NEPA; SETC became the lead agency in 1998; NDRC took the lead in 2002
Closure of polluting TVIEs	1996	SEPA
ISO 14001	1997	SEPA and General Administration of Quality and Quarantine
Eco-industrial parks	2001	Initiated by SEPA; NDRC overtook the leadership in 2004
Circular economy	2001	Initiated by SEPA; NDRC overtook the leadership in 2004

Protection Bureau formed within the Ministry of Urban and Rural Construction and Environmental Protection in 1982, to the National (and later State) Environmental Protection Agency established directly under the State Council in 1987. Currently, hot discussion is underway on whether to convert SEPA into a full environmental ministry. But arguably a more interesting development in environmental institutions has been the activities of state institutions outside the administrative branch, in the legislative and judicial domains.

In 1993, the Environmental Protection and Resource Conservation Committee (EPRCC) was created under the Standing Committee of the National People's Congress (NPC), China's top legislative body, to take charge of formulating and supervising environmental protection and natural resources management legislation. Since then, EPRCC has been playing an increasing role in expediting the environmental legislative process, as well as supervising the implementation of environmental laws.

The judiciary used to play a very limited role in China's environmental governance, but the strengthening of the rule of law resulted in a more active role for judicial institutions in environmental protection. The amendment of the Criminal Law in 1997 explicitly imposes criminal penalty on serious environmental damage. Consequently, China imposes administrative, civil, and criminal sanctions on the violation of environmental laws and regulations. Although punishments remain rather low on violations (Mol & Liu, 2005), the tendency is in the right direction. Victims of industrial pollution activities infrequently resort to courts for safeguarding their own interests, but also here interesting developments are emerging, in part through NGO support. In addition, there is a growing debate about forming special environmental courts, like special intellectual property courts, to handle better the ever-increasing environmental lawsuits in China.

The inadequate environmental law expertise among Chinese judges and lawyers and the low consciousness of environmental laws and resultant litigation on the part of the public, is increasingly being addressed. In 1999, an environmental and resource law group was established with the China Law Society. In 2001, the All China Lawyers Association set up an environmental and resource law committee and NGOs in the field of environmental law (such as the Beijing-based Center for Legal Assistance to Pollution Victims), which play an active role in advancing research, promoting professional training on environmental law and assisting pollution victims in courts.

Innovative Environmental Policy Instruments and Processes

Except for the Pollution Levy System, before the 1990s China's environmental policy consisted basically of command and control instruments. Since the 1990s, however, China has started to experiment with and employ other instruments and programmes, including economic incentives, voluntary programmes, and information disclosure approaches. Table 3 lists the major industrial environmental policy instruments and programmes in China throughout the years.

Under the initial environmental regulatory regime, the relationship between environmental regulators and regulated industries was rather confrontational with a lack of mutual confidence. In recent years, EPBs have started to promote voluntary approaches within industries and have tried to develop partnerships with industries. SEPA launched a voluntary programme for environmentally friendly enterprises in 2003. Some MNCs also demonstrate their willingness and interest in sharing their advanced in-house environmental management tools and experiences with EPBs. But of course, many polluting enterprises continue to play a game of cat and mouse with EPBs, where the financial dependencies of local EPBs on pollution levies provide polluters with a favourable negotiating position on the amount of pollution levy payments.

Major Drivers of the Transformation of the Environment State

Three main drivers can be identified behind these institutional innovations of the Chinese environmental state.

First, the overall development in China's institutional reform/modernisation process forms a key driver behind the transformation of the environmental state. In that sense, what is happening in the field of the environment reflects wider transformations. For instance, the State Council adopted a milestone policy, entitled 'An Outline on All-round Promotion of Administration in Conformity with the Law' in March 2004. The policy is aimed at changing the 'omnipresent government' into a 'government with limited-power' as well as a law-abiding government in 10 years. This is clearly reflected in the environmental institutions of the state.

Second, there was a clear perception of the need to address some of the inherent weaknesses associated with the initial environmental regulatory regime, for example the high costs associated with command and control measures and end-of-pipe approaches, the incompetence of environmental regulators in basic environmental monitoring and enforcement, the confrontational relationship between state and industry, and a regulatory approach that was geared towards a centrally planned economy, but ill-fitted for a more market-oriented system.

Third, China's increased orientation to the outside world and improved international relations have triggered environmental state transformations. China has been very successful in attracting international support for its environmental protection endeavours. It is estimated that nearly 15 per cent of the total environmental protection budget around the turn of the millennium came from international assistance (Economy, 2004). Multilateral development agencies, such as the World Bank, Asian Development Bank (ADB), and UN agencies, have had a substantial impact on China's environmental and energy policies (World Bank, 1997; SEI & UNDP, 2002). International

Table 3. Major industrial environmental regulatory instruments/programmes in China

Year	Title of programme/instrument	C&C	EI	VI	ID
1979	Concentration-based pollution discharge limits	X			
1979	Environmental Impact Assessment	X			
1979	Three Synchronisations policy	X			
1979	Pollution Levy System		X		
1988	Total pollutant mass load control	X			
1989	Ecological damage compensation system		X		
1989	Centralised pollution control		X		
1989	Pollution control within deadlines	X			
1991	Environmental labelling			X	
1992	Sulphur dioxide emissions fee (pilot programme)		X		
1993	Cleaner Production			X	
1996	Two Compliance Policy	X			
1997	ISO 14001			X	
1999	Commercialised industrial pollution treatment			X	
1999	Emission trading		X		
2003	Environmental information disclosure of selected enterprises	X			X
2003	Award of national environmentally friendly enterprises			X	
2003	Environmental performance verification of applications for public listing or refinancing in the stock market				X
2003	Eco-industrial park pilot programme			X	

Note: C&C = command & control; EI = economic instrument; VI = voluntary instrument; ID = information disclosure.

organisations have also been actively diffusing international practices and lessons by means of high-level policy advocacy, technical assistance for institutional building among government and industry, technical support for environmental legislation development, and direct financial support for demonstrating advanced technology and equipment (Mol & Liu, 2005).

Bringing in the Economic Actors

Industries are adapting their environmental management approaches, both internally and externally, following not only state requirements but also a number of other (institutional) pressures, leading to new governance arrangements.

First, driven by the prohibitive economic costs associated with conventional end-of-pipe abatement approaches, from the early 1990s China and Chinese industries started the arduous search for more affordable pathways towards sustainable industrial development. China's experiments with prevention and cleaner production approaches are perhaps the most visible. There have been a number of success stories in this connection (as reported for instance through the various Cleaner Production websites, especially http://www.chinacp.com/), but the situation at large remains unsatisfactory (Shi, 2003).

Second, following an export-oriented development strategy and wider processes of globalisation, international oriented companies are more susceptible to reputation risks, foreign green consumerism and global standards. Chinese industries increasingly have to adhere to international environmental standards and respond to other market pressures that focus on the environmental implications of products and services. Companies are responding in many ways (e.g., claiming to offer 'green' products, improving relations with regulators, beautifying their facilities), but one of the most popular and visible demonstrations of environmental responsiveness is by obtaining a third-party certification of products or environmental management systems. In China, ISO 14001 certification (of company environmental management systems) expanded rapidly in recent years and increasingly includes domestic firms (Table 4).

Third, as more stringent environmental enforcement affects not only the business bottom lines but also their primary processes, such as the Extended Producer Responsibility requirements included in the newly amended Solid Waste Pollution Prevention and Control Law, so industries have started to become more sensitive towards and involved in government policies. Initially, foreign invested enterprises, but now also domestic ones, have sought more active involvement in governmental policy-making processes, either individually or collaboratively. It is now common practice that SEPA consults industries on new policies and regulations and actively publicise all new policy developments. It has also led to new institutions. For instance, as a result of cooperation between the China Enterprise Confederation (CEC) and the World Business Council for Sustainable Development (WBCSD), the China

Table 4. Survey on global ISO 14001 certificates (at 31 December 2003)

Year	World total	Number of countries/economies	China	% of China to world total
2003	66,070	113	5064	7.66
2002	49,449	117	2803	5.67
2001	36,765	112	1085	2.95
2000	22,897	98	510	2.23
1999	14,106	84	222	1.57
1998	7887	72	94	1.19
1997	4433	55	4	0.1
1996	1491	45	0	–

Source: ISO (2004).

Business Council for Sustainable Development (CBCSD) was officially launched in October 2003. CBCSD provides a platform for exchange and cooperation among Chinese and foreign enterprises, government and social organisations. By sharing information, experiences and best practices in the field of sustainable development this platform not only helps companies to improve their performance in environmental management, but also coordinate the business stances with regard to critical environmental issues and policies.

Fourth, in response to increasing environment-related pressures or market signals such as sustainable investment, green consumerisms, environmental campaigns organised by NGOs, some pioneer companies in China take new steps, including advocating corporate social responsibility, supporting external environmental activities, and unilateral reporting and disclosure of environmental and sustainability information. As in most of the new developments, the frontrunners tend to be subsidiaries of MNCs and most local enterprises are significantly lagging behind in awareness and practice.

Finally, there are some early signals that financial and capital markets are starting to respond to the environmental performances or risks of industry. For instance, the Agriculture Bank of China incurred substantial bad debts that were brought about by the crackdown on rural polluting industries, which in turn could not repay their loans to the Agriculture Bank. China's stock exchanges have required an environmental review by SEPA on those pollution-intensive corporations that seek to list shares or apply for refinancing at the stock market since 2003. With a growing number of Chinese firms listing shares in the overseas stock markets and more MNCs operating in China, socially responsible investments will start to exert an increasing influence on those Chinese and MNCs seeking Socially Responsible Investments (SRIs).

Pollution Control beyond State and Market: Civil Society

In general, the retreat of the state in the recent reform era in China has been paralleled by the emergence of a civil society. While the retreat of the state has been less obvious in the field of environment, the emergence of an environment-oriented civil society has been increasingly visible. The founding of Friends of Nature (FON) in 1994 inaugurated a decade of vibrant growth of environmental NGOs in China, articulating and lobbying for environmental interests against specific political and economic decisions (Yang, 2005). Recently, new trends can be identified regarding the role of civil society in shaping the industrial environmental governance in China.

First, with the rapid growth of public environmental awareness and the rise of environmental NGOs in China over the past decade, the use of three traditional ways of public participation, i.e. citizen complaints, proposals to People's Congresses and Political Consultative Conferences, and administrative mediations by EPBs, have increased. The number of citizen complaints by letter soared from 67,268 in 1996 to 595,852 in 2004, nearly a tenfold increase. Meanwhile, the number of proposals raised by delegates of People's Congresses and People's Political Consultative Conferences at all levels doubled from 6177 in 1996 to 12,532 in 2004 (SEPA, 2005).

Second, new ways of public participation emerged in China, including public hearings in the Environmental Impact Assessment processes on significant investment projects, information dissemination via mass media and the Internet, administrative lawsuits against environmental agencies concerning administrative inaction or injustice, civil lawsuits against polluting enterprises to seek legal redress through courts, and the inputs of environmental NGOs and experts in governmental policies and decisions (OECD, 2005). Despite the strict oversight of NGOs by the Chinese government in terms of their activities and financial situation, SEPA as the central environmental watchdog, has sought strong collaborative relationships with environmental NGOs (Pan, 2005). Another innovation is the involvement of the public in environmental monitoring and enforcement, as happens in the so-called bounty programme, initiated in Fuyang City, Zhejiang Province in June 2000. This successful programme stimulates the public to report environmental non-compliance incidents and has been replicated by many other cities and provinces, including SEPA.

Third, violent mass incidents triggered by residents directly affected by industrial pollution have occurred with rising frequency, driven by better information through the media, more pollution and accidents and a larger self-consciousness of citizens (*New York Times*, 19 July 2005). The incidents have drawn the attention of senior national government officials, who are concerned about social unrest. Therefore, these pollution-related protests have imposed great pressure on local EPBs, as they may affect the career development prospects of the respective EPB leaders.

Fourth, SEPA and EPBs have become proactive in involving civil society (next to industry) in environmental policy-making. SEPA has been working towards more transparency in environmental policy making. One example of its efforts is a nationwide survey to understand better public environmental opinions and priorities in preparing the 11th Five Year Plan for National Environmental Protection.

The mass media, particularly television, newspapers, and the Internet, pay increasing attention to environmental problems, and with economic development the general public now has substantially improved access to these media. New technical means such as electronic publications and new forms of Internet-based actions such as online discussions, online mailing lists and Internet petitions have greatly enhanced the communication, coordination, and organisation capability of environmental NGOs as well as individuals.

Finally, the national government has also made a big effort to strengthen environmental awareness, public participation and disclosures as part of a deliberate strategy to encourage citizens to monitor and put pressure on local governments to enforce environmental regulations (Pan, 2005). The disclosure of the information on pollution emissions of enterprises remains strongly controlled, except for a few cases where provincial or municipal EPBs publicised blacklists of top polluters in their jurisdictions. However, a few recent developments show some openness: (1) SEPA and the World Bank implemented a joint pilot programme 'Green-Watch' to disclose information on the environmental emissions of the firms that cannot comply with pollution emission standards or pollutant discharge permits (see Wang *et al.*, 2002); (2) any polluting industrial company that apply for a public offering or refinancing at China's stock exchanges have to seek EPBs to appraise and disclose their environmental performance; (3) in accordance with the Cleaner Production Promotion Law, local development and reform commissions and EPBs have started to experiment with disclosing information about polluting enterprises that cannot comply with either pollutant discharge limits or total pollutant discharge loads; and (4) voluntary disclosure of environmental performance by domestic environmentally friendly companies.

These developments indicate that there is an attempt to shift accountability mechanisms to civil society to operate alongside the conventional vertical state lines.

Conclusion

In this contribution, we have adopted a multi-actor environmental governance model to examine the ongoing transformation of industrial pollution control in China. This approach is probably common sense for understanding current pollution control in OECD countries, but rather radical for China, where traditionally environmental protection – among many other sectors – has been strongly monopolised by the state. A multi-actor environmental governance framework points us towards the recent – and arguably ongoing – transition to a more horizontal and participatory system of industrial pollution control in China.

In general, the Chinese environmental state has been changing along three parallel lines: modernising the existing environmental regulatory networks;

decentralising environmental policy and strengthening the environmental capacity at all levels; and involving non-state actors and institutions in pollution control. The first strategy enables the central regulatory agencies and institutions to adapt better to the new circumstances of a globally integrated market economy. The national environmental authority (SEPA) continues to empower itself, while some key economic agencies such as NDRC expedite their greening process. Although this has brought about some conflicts in contesting the immediate environmental leadership, the trend may prove very constructive for long-term policy integration. There is also a continuous shift of policy-making power from the administrative bodies to the legislature, though the role of the judiciary remains weak. The advancement of the rule of law in China has started to affect environmental governance. Meanwhile, for various reasons, the state has gradually allowed for and expanded the involvement of business and civil society in industrial environmental policy-making processes. The continuous broadening of the policy instruments makes strict implementation of a basic functional monitoring and enforcement regulatory system even more necessary.

Linked to that, the second strategy involves mobilising and strengthening local governments to fulfil their environmental responsibilities, as the central institutions prove less and less capable of actually managing local industrial environmental problems.

As a final strategy, China's environmental state has adopted a proactive approach to foster bigger roles for non-state actors, institutions and mechanisms in environmental governance. But there are still major hurdles to be removed if the state wants to take full advantage of the market and civil society. Improving the processing, dissemination, disclosure of and access to reliable, timely, and pertinent environmental information is crucial. A better legal framework is needed to safeguard public participation and information access. Last, but not least, the state itself must take the lead in practising the rule of law.

Since President Hu Jintao and Premier Wen Jiabao took office in March 2003, the new Chinese government seems to have adopted a more balanced approach to industrial development. The so-called 'scientific development' paradigm not only focuses on industrial and economic growth, but also takes more account of the impact of such developments on Chinese society and environment. The ongoing integration of China's economy into the international arena has both positive and negative implications for China's environment. The sheer scale and pace of the industrial and economic growth, with all the dramatic environmental and natural resource consequences, often prevents us from seeing how global integration improves China's environmental governance. In the long term, greater openness and integration will be beneficial to the modernisation of China's industrial environmental governance. The question remains whether it will be enough to protect China's (and the global) environment; but there seems to be little alternative.

Acknowledgements

The authors would like to thank Arthur P. J. Mol, Neil Carter, Reid Lifset and an anonymous referee for their helpful comments on early drafts of this paper. The authors are responsible for any remaining errors.

References

Dasgupta, S., Wang, H. & Wheeler, D. (1997) 'Surviving success: policy reform and the future of industrial pollution in China'. World Bank Policy Research Working Paper. Available at http://www.worldbank.org/ (accessed August 2001).

Economy, E. (2004) *The River Runs Black: the Environmental Challenge to China's Future* (Ithaca, NY: Cornell University Press).

Editorial Board of the Chinese Environment Yearbook (1996–2003) *China Environment Yearbooks (1996–2003)* (Beijing: China Environment Yearbook Press).

Ho, P. (2001) 'Greening without conflict? Environmentalism, NGOs and civil society in China', *Development and Change* 32(5): 893–921.

Hu, J. (2005) 'Address by President Hu Jintao of China at the opening ceremony of the 2005 Fortune Global Forum, Beijing, 16 May 2005'. Available at http://english.people.com.cn/200505/17/eng20050517_185302.html (accessed 8 June 2005).

International Energy Agency (IEA) (2004) *Energy Statistics of Non-OECD Countries: 2001/2002–2004 Edition* (Paris: OECD).

ISO (2004) 'The ISO survey of ISO 9001:2000 and ISO 14001 certificates, 2003'. Available at http://www.iso.org/iso/en/iso9000-14000/pdf/survey2003.pdf (accessed 8 May 2005).

Jahiel, A. (1998) 'The organization of environmental protection in China', *China Quarterly* 156: 757–87.

Jordan, A., Wurzel, R. & Zito, A. (2005) 'The rise of "new policy" instruments in comparative perspective: has governance eclipsed government?', *Political Studies* 53(3): 477–96.

Khanna, M. (2001) 'Non-mandatory approaches to environmental protection', *Journal of Economic Surveys* 15(3): 291–324.

Ma, X. & Ortolano, L. (2000) *Environmental Regulation in China: Institutions, Enforcement and Compliance* (Lanham, MD: Rowman and Littlefield).

Mol, A. & Liu, Y. (2005) 'Institutionalising cleaner production in China: the Cleaner Production Promotion Law', *International Journal of Environment and Sustainable Development* 4(3): 227–45.

National Bureau of Statistics (NBS) (1996–2004) *China Statistics Yearbooks 1996–2004* (Beijing: China Statistical Publishing House).

OECD (2005) *China in the Global Economy: Governance in China* (Paris: OECD).

Pan, Y. (2005) 'Environmental protection and social justice', *Environmental Education* 1: 4–8 (in Chinese).

Rooij, B. van (2004) 'Towards compliance: recommendations for Chinese environmental law enforcement', *Van Vollenhoven Research Report* 4(6): 1–39.

SEPA (2004) 'National environmental statistics report – 2003'. Available at http://www.sepa.gov.cn/eic/649371571659472896/20040602/1050945.shtml (accessed 1 October 2005).

SEPA (2005) 'National environmental statistics report – 2004'. Available at http://www.sepa.gov.cn/eic/649371571659472896/20050610/8632.shtml (accessed 1 October 2005).

Shi, H. (2003) 'Cleaner production in China', in A. Mol & J. van Buuren (eds.) *Greening Industrialization in Transitional Asian countries: China and Vietnam* (Lanham, MD: Lexington), pp. 63–82.

Sinkule, B. J. & Ortolano, L. (1995) *Implementing Environmental Policy in China* (Westport, CT: Praeger).

Stockholm Environmental Institute (SEI) and UNDP (2002) *China Human Development Report 2002. Making Green Development a Choice* (Hong Kong: Oxford University Press).

Tietenberg, T. (1998) 'Disclosure strategies for pollution control', *Environmental and Resource Economics* 11(3–4): 587–602.

UNCTAD (2004) *Making FDI Work for Sustainable Development* (New York: United Nations Conference on Trade and Development and Sustainable Business Institute at the European Business School).

UNIDO (2005) 'Energy conservation and GHG emissions reduction in Chinese TVEs – phase II'. Available at www.unido.org (accessed 12 January 2005).

Wang, H., Bi, J., Wheeler, D., Wang, J., Cao, D., Lu, G. & Wang, Y. (2002) 'Environmental performance rating and disclosure: China's Green-Watch program'. Policy Research Working Paper 2889 (Washington, DC: World Bank).

Wen, J. (2004) 'The government work report 2004 of China'. Available at http://english.people.com.cn/200403/16/eng20040316_137651.shtml (accessed 20 August 2005).

World Bank (1997) *Clear Water, Blue Skies: China's Environment in the New Century. China 2020 Series* (Washington, DC: World Bank).

World Bank (2001) *China – Air, Land and Water: Environmental Priorities for a New Millennium* (Washington, DC: World Bank).

Yang, G. (2005) 'Environmental NGOs and institutional dynamics in China', *China Quarterly* 181: 46–66.

Zhang, L. (2002) 'Ecologizing industrialization in Chinese small towns', PhD thesis, Wageningen University.

Zhang, T. & Chen, J. (2003) 'Industrial environmental management in China', in A. Mol and J. van Buuren (eds.) *Greening Industrialization in Transitional Asian Countries: China and Vietnam* (Lanham, MD: Lexington), pp. 23–38.

Zhu, Y. (1998) 'Review on TVE development in China', in *China Economic Guide*, 10 April, Beijing (in Chinese).

Balancing Technological Innovation and Environmental Regulation: an Analysis of Chinese Agricultural Biotechnology Governance

Introduction

How is China managing the challenge of governing GMOs, a new technology that has proven problematic for political decision-making processes in many settings? China finds itself in an unusual situation in relation to GMOs. This is that China has a 'first-world' capacity in relation to biotechnology research and technology development. At the same time it remains a developing country with a large smallholder sector, many people living in poverty in rural areas and low levels of administrative and technical capacity at provincial level and below in many parts of the country. In addition, there is the particular dilemma of the Chinese political system where for some policy issue debates, openness and accountability are quite limited. Governing GMOs has proved a tough challenge for many countries. China, in general, faces many challenges in relation to governance. Are the dilemmas associated with GMOs, when governance is already an issue, likely to be too difficult to manage?

Making and implementing policy on GMOs can cause tensions for any nation. Difficulties include thinking about how to manage the international trade in GMOs, whether to invest in GM research and development, and how to regulate technologies. Cutting across these issues in some countries there will be questions about how to make these decisions, who to consult with, and how to build consensus between potentially conflicting stakeholders over appropriate courses of action.

In China these issues take a particular shape given the dominant role that the Chinese state plays in promoting innovation, and the iterative nature of developing regulatory systems for new technologies or products that are associated with high levels of uncertainty, and where the nature of risk is unclear. This happens alongside China integrating into the world economy, and balancing the rights and obligations linked to different global agreements and institutions it is part of. Consideration of GMOs also happens in the context of a particular domestic culture of policymaking, where certain forms of technical expertise are often privileged, where debate and deliberation are only possible within certain parameters and where achieving coordinated decision-making between ministries is problematic (Lieberthal & Oksenberg, 1988; Howell, 2004). The article maps the institutions involved in this terrain, and looks at how different biotechnology discourses have been played out through these political and institutional arrangements.

The State and Biotechnology Policy and Development in China

China's interest in modern agricultural biotechnology builds on a long history of plant-breeding, a Chinese Green Revolution and a long-standing concern with food security and agricultural productivity. Raising agricultural incomes is a central plank of current government policy reflected in '*San nong*' discourse, and the emphasis placed on agricultural in the key No 1 Policy Documents for 2004 and 2005.[1] Official documents and Chinese research frequently emphasise the challenge of feeding 22 per cent of the world's population on 7 per cent of the world's arable land. This land-base in China is generally thought to be shrinking due to changing land use patterns linked to urbanisation and rural industrialisation, and the conversion of arable land to forest or grazing land to meet environmental conservation objectives. Given these dynamics agricultural biotechnology is often presented in the policy narratives of government officials and scientists as essential for sustainable agricultural intensification and food security in China.[2]

Agricultural biotechnology policy (in the most general sense) was first developed in the 1980s as part of a policy of promoting rapid catch up with the West through science and technology-led development. Science and technology modernisation was one of Deng Xiaoping's Four Modernisations, and an aim of the Open Door Policy. In the mid-1980s key scientists returned to China from periods of study and research overseas and made a case to the senior leadership that high levels of investment in high-tech sectors was essential for China's modernisation and national security.[3] One product of these discussions was the formation of the 863 Committee (under the Ministry of Science and Technology, then the Science and Technology Commission). The 863 committee manages large programmes of investment in strategic areas of applied research with important potential benefits for Chinese industrialisation. Agricultural biotechnology was chosen as one of seven priority areas. The committee continues to be an important body: the officials in the agricultural biotechnology section and the networks of scientists the committee supports are a central part of what can be labelled a biotechnology discourse coalition in China.

In addition to 863, there are several other state programmes and organisations that fund different aspects of GM research and development. These include the National Natural Science Foundation, the Spark Plan and the 973 Committee (Huang & Wang, 2003). Chinese investment in agricultural biotechnology research from these, and other, sources has gradually increased, reaching US$500m per annum by 2005 (Huang *et al.*, 2002). The scale of this investment means that there is now considerable agricultural biotechnology research capacity in China, with over one hundred public sector institutes doing transgenic research. Chinese researchers have undertaken field trials for a range of crops, including cotton, rice, maize, potatoes and several horticultural crops. A range of different technologies for different traits have been developed. These include insect and disease resistance; drought, salinity and herbicide tolerance; and nutritional enhancement. The decoding of the rice genome by Chinese researchers in the Beijing Genomics Institute was heralded as a major international scientific achievement. High-profile programmes such as the Rice Genome Research Programme are now being implemented with the aim of developing applications relevant to rice production from genomics research. The development of the pollen tube pathway as an alternative to particle bombardment or bacteria transfer for gene insertion is another achievement demonstrating that Chinese biotechnology research has already made substantial progress.

A key feature of Chinese biotechnology policy processes is that biotechnology research and development is overwhelmingly a public sector project. Most research is not carried out by private corporations, and most applications for commercialisation of GM crops do not come from private companies. The majority of risk assessment applications are for technologies that are the outputs of research projects funded by the major public science funding bodies, and carried out by National Key Laboratories in state institutes (particularly institutes under the Chinese Academy of Sciences, the Chinese Academy of Agricultural Sciences and the Agricultural Universities, as well as some other key universities). This is a major contrast with development of GMOs in other countries where most applications come from life science companies.

It is important also to note that while the research system is in the public sector, it does encourage scientists to benefit from some of the returns on research investments. Scientists can patent their research achievements, and alone or with their institutes they can form companies to commercialise outputs. It is through these mechanisms that China is ultimately encouraging the development of its own private transgenic seed sector. This sector, however remains very small in China. Even within the seed industry large seed companies have only begun to emerge in recent years following the reform of the state controlled seed system and the introduction of the Seed Law in 2000. Most Chinese seed companies do not have transgenic research capacity (Keeley, 2003a). It is also very unusual to hear Chinese seed-company representatives quoted in the media discussing biotechnology. Even Monsanto, which has a very large share of the Bt cotton market, does not have the dominant role in biotechnology discourse that it does in other settings. As will be argued below it is an actor-network of biotech scientists which is the most vocal and active within biotech 'discourse coalitions' and policy processes in China (Latour, 1987; Hajer, 1995).

Regulatory Institutions and Risk-assessment Processes

Alongside promoting innovation and carrying out research, different parts of the Chinese state are also responsible for the regulation of biotechnology. China has had a series of different biotechnology regulations evolving with the development of the Chinese biotechnology programme, as well as developments in the wider international politics of biotechnology. The earliest biotech regulations, the Safety Administration Regulation on Genetic Engineering, were published in 1993 by the Ministry of Science and Technology (MOST). These were followed by Implementation Guidelines issued by the Ministry of Agriculture (MOA) in 1996. These guidelines created the Office of Genetic Engineering Safety Administration in the MOA (OGESA), and outlined in general terms a range of different safety classes linked to different risk assessment requirements.

In 2000 new Biosafety Regulations were issued by the State Council, and OGESA was expanded into a larger Biosafety Office. The new regulations announced a four-stage process for risk-assessment: field trials, environmental release, a new large-scale production trial stage and commercial release. The regulations also introduced new import and export regulations and declared the intention to set up a labelling system. In March 2002, Implementation Guidelines for the Regulations were announced.

The Chinese biosafety regulations place risk assessment responsibility with the Biosafety Committee under the Biosafety Office in the Ministry of Agriculture. The Biosafety Committee is a body of technical experts, including biotech scientists, entomologists and plant pathologists, and biodiversity specialists. It meets twice a year to review risk assessment applications. The recommendations of the Biosafety Committee are sent to the Biosafety Office where they are considered by officials in the Ministry of Agriculture alongside a range of non-scientific factors such as trade impacts and consumer acceptance. Final decisions should be taken by an Inter-Ministerial Committee with representatives from the Ministry of Agriculture, the State Development and Reform Commission, the Ministry of Science and Technology, the Ministry of Commerce, the Ministry of Health, the General Administration of Quality Supervision, Inspection and Quarantine, and the State Environmental Protection Administration. This body is responsible for researching and coordinating key problems in GMO safety management work; examining and approving permission for commercialisation for key GM crops; and, examining and approving import and export policies on key GM crops.

SEPA has responsibility for the Biosafety Protocol and has been the focal point for the Convention on Biological Diversity. On 19 May 2005 China ratified the Biosafety Protocol. Following ratification, SEPA issued a statement saying that a Biosafety Law will soon be passed.[4] The issue of the Biosafety Law has been controversial; it has been underway for several years (announcements were made in *China Daily* in 2002).[5] However, discussions with policy researchers close to the ministries suggest that the Ministry of Agriculture has strongly resisted the law, and particularly any transfer of responsibilities to SEPA. SEPA has been part of the National Biosafety Frameworks capacity building process supported by United Nations Environment Programme – Global Environment Facility (UNEP-GEF). It has also received bilateral donor support. In relation to practical implementation of risk assessment, however, SEPA engagement is very limited.

The Biosafety Committee contains many of China's most respected authorities on GMOs. All the members come from either ministries or state research institutes. At present there are no participants from civil society (either farmer representatives or consumer or environmental organisations). Some researchers within China have also raised concerns about the number of biotechnologists on the committee compared to ecologists or those from other scientific disciplines (Keeley, 2005). There are also no representatives from SEPA on the committee (at least according to the currently available list of members). One SEPA official complained that it is difficult for the ministry even to get to see the minutes of Biosafety Committee meetings.[6] For important decisions like the 2004 announcement allowing the import of Monsanto corn, cotton and soya beans MOA has the key role: it issues certificates, announces decisions and makes policy.

Some officials within SEPA and some researchers feel that the dominant role played by MOA in biosafety regulation is inappropriate because MOA funds and guides technology development, institutes under the MOA develop technologies, and firms owned in part by these institutes commercialise technologies. Some argue that risk assessment should be housed elsewhere, where there is no potential for conflict of interest. SEPA has pushed for a stronger role in domestic risk assessment, but MOA has resisted this, arguing that SEPA does not have the necessary range of research institutes and expertise. Despite this, SEPA has continued to maintain a presence in the domestic biosafety debate, organising major workshops on environmental biosafety issues in June 2002 and June 2004.

Details of the proceedings of the Biosafety Committee meetings at present are confidential. For a range of key issues there is a lack of publicly available information: these include which varieties and traits have been submitted for approval; who is applying; where trials are taking place; what data is being considered; what criteria are being looked at in the risk assessment process; reasons for turning down an application; and which applications have been approved by the Biosafety Committee. At present this information is restricted to an elite group of experts. Discussions surrounding the Biosafety Committee meeting in December 2004, for example, were treated as very sensitive and not for public consumption. Committee members were not allowed to remove documents from the meeting and were prevented from discussing proceedings with outsiders. The final decision of the meeting was also not made public (Liu, 2004).

Some information is available from the Biosafety Office about application procedures, but very limited channels exist to seek information about, or to make comments on applications. Critics of the current system argue for more transparency about where risk assessment trials are taking place, who is conducting them, and what is being investigated. Demands are also made for mechanisms to allow for the input of comments and objections and so on. These might potentially include opportunities to challenge decisions and to make an input into monitoring and evaluation processes (see Liu, 2004).

Chinese governance of GMOs then is characterised by a high-degree of state support for innovation fundings and research and development. Alongside this risk-assessment and regulation happen with limited transparency, availability of information and participation in decision-making. Does the push in favour of biotechnology on the innovation side meet sufficient critical analysis and deliberation on the regulatory side? Is an apparent lack of transparency and participation a problem that creates ineffective governance of GMOs? These issues are explored in the following sections.

Discourse Coalitions and the Politics of Expertise

To explore the tensions that exist in governing GMOs, particularly in relation to balancing innovation and regulation, the concept of discourse coalitions is useful. The concept directs attention to the ways in which ideas and perspectives are mediated both by particular networks of actors and by relationships between governance institutions. Hajer defines discourse as 'a specific ensemble of ideas, concepts, and categorisations that are produced, reproduced and transformed in a particular set of practices and through which meaning is given to physical and social realities' (1995: 44). Hajer argues that discourse coalitions are alliances between a range of different actors and organisations around a common approach to a problem, often expressed as a common story-line. The coalitions bring together many institutional and discursive practices: for example, some actors utilise economic discourses, others scientific institutional practices.[7]

The earlier section noted that parts of the Chinese state have played a strong role promoting biotechnology as an important potential contributor to Chinese agricultural problems, and also as a key area in the global knowledge economy where it is important for China to be at the international cutting edge. This section continues the theme that policy has been linked to a strong discourse coalition generally very supportive of biotechnology. This coalition has been successful in some areas (development and commercialisation of Bt cotton) but less successful so far in others (commercialisation of GM rice). A rather fragmented counter discourse coalition has also gradually become more evident in China, reflecting to some extent the slow but growing influence of global environmental discourse in China.

The state is at the heart of the biotech project in China. Scientists in state institutes, rather than representatives of commercial seed companies, have been the key advocates for China's biotech programme. This advocacy can be either behind the scenes or in public through the media. Zhang Qifa, for example, is a rice biotechnologist at Huazhong Agricultural University; he has developed a variety of insect-resistant rice which is reported to be close to approval for commercial release. Zhang made an important presentation to the senior government leadership in 2003 on the case for commercialising GM crops.[8] Others such as Chen Zhangliang are frequently heard in the media. Chen is President of China Agricultural University, and a biotech scientist who worked on some of the earliest GM crops to be commercialised in China, tobacco and GM peppers; he is also a director of a key biotech firm. Likewise, Zhu Zhen at the Institute of Genetics, another rice biotechnologist whose varieties are currently being considered for commercial approval, is an important spokes-person for the 'biotech discourse coalition'. A key figure in the 863 committee, he is also often quoted in the press making statements about the importance of agricultural biotechnology for China. When *China Daily* – the main English language newspaper – runs a story on GM crops it invariably quotes Chen or Zhu as authorities in their capacity as expert scientists. In contrast, seed company representatives are seldom interviewed. It is the scientists who play the key role as protagonists: this is significant because they are closely linked to the state either through the state institutes where they work, or the state committees on which they serve.

Biotechnology deliberations (around, for example, policy objectives, planning, allocation of funds, and priority setting) have been associated with a particular model of technical expertise. This is a model which emphasises expert committees (such as the 863 and 973 committees), and which makes assumptions about who is qualified to take part (academic experts from prestigious institutes), and about appropriate levels of transparency. A similar model holds in relation to biosafety decision-making. In relation to decisions about commercialisation of particular crops the discussion in large part focuses on varieties developed by Chinese scientists based in public sector research institutes. Chinese seed companies, as has been noted, have an interest but they play a less significant role than Chinese research scientists. Monsanto, by contrast, has a less direct influence over decision-making processes.[9]

Across these technical committees there are clear networks which can be understood as a biotechnology discourse coalition. One key figure on the Biosafety Committee, for example, is also in charge of allocating basic research funds as head of the biotechnology part of the 973 committee. Another senior official allocating funding on the 863 committee is also a key spokesman for biotech in China, his varieties of GM rice are currently being considered for commercial release. Another member of the Biosafety Committee is a member of the institute that developed Chinese Bt cotton; he is a director of the company commercialising this cotton, and also a member of the 863 committee.

The links between these key individuals are well-known among those working on biotechnology in China. For some these patterns of influence are a problem; as one Chinese ecologist commented: 'The promoters – X, Y, Z – they are all pro, a group. The 973 committee is like this. Funds are distributed politically, not according to science; it's like being boxer and referee at the same time...You can't have biosafety just to promote biotech'.[10]

Biotechnology policy-making is not of course insulated from the outside world, and these local networks are increasingly part of wider international networks, as science and technology development processes become more globalised. Chinese research on disease resistant rice, for example, has involved international partnerships that have resulted in rights to use the Xa-21 gene.

At the same time China has become increasingly exposed to global environmental discourse, which has contributed to the emergence of a fragmented counter discourse on GMOs. The environmental NGO Greenpeace has played a key role here. Greenpeace operates in China as a branch of Greenpeace Hong Kong. The NGO has frequently been the major voice quoted in the media offering critical perspectives on GMOs, in much the same way that a network of scientists and policy researchers are quoted arguing in favour of rapid deployment of new varieties of GM crops. The organisation has been strategic in employing a senior figure in the Biosafety section of SEPA as a scientific advisor. They have also published a newsletter 'International Biosafety' jointly with the Nanjing Institute of Environmental Sciences, a research institute under SEPA. The next section looks at how the dominant and counter discourses have played out in relation to two concrete GMO debates. The sections show the role of discourse coalitions in mediating discourse and how these link to different parts of the institutional architecture for governance of GMOs.

Bt Cotton: China's GM Success Story?

An analysis of Chinese experience with Bt cotton illustrates how discourse coalitions engage with the governance of GMOs in China. In particular it shows that one grouping has been important in promoting a discourse around Bt cotton as a successful solution to a certain set of agricultural problems in China. This activity has been facilitated by a particular political and bureaucratic context.

Insect-resistant Bt cotton is the only GM crop commercialised in China on a large scale. Bt cotton has spread widely in China, and is often presented as an example of a highly successful technological innovation. After the first varieties were approved for cultivation in 1998 its uptake has been rapid. In the provinces in the northern Yellow River cotton zone cultivation of Bt cotton is thought to be close to 100 per cent. Total acreage had reached 3.7 m hectares in 2004. This is 65 per cent of the total cotton area (James, 2004).

The development of Chinese Bt cotton varieties by Guo Sandui and his colleagues at the Biotechnology Research Institute under the Chinese Academy of Agricultural Sciences (under the MOA) is often presented in policy discourse as a milestone achievement of the national high-tech 863 programme supported by the MOST and the MOA (see 863 Committee, 2001; Fang *et al.*, 2001). The major company marketing Chinese GM cotton is Biocentury, a semi-private company partly-owned by the BRI and Guo Sandui, and a Guangdong based holding company. In company publicity brochures Biocentury is also presented as a success story for the 863 programme. Through joint ventures with a range of smaller seed companies the company has achieved a key position in the market for Bt cotton in a range of provinces.

The main rival to Biocentury is Monsanto, which operates in China through two joint ventures with local seed companies, Jidai and Andai. Their market share is similar to Biocentury, although it is hard to be precise because varieties for seed from both companies are widely pirated. There are also many much smaller companies marketing GM cotton in partnership with other research institutes (some of these varieties have been through the formal biosafety risk assessment process, but many have not).[11]

Bt cotton in China is often cited as an example of a popular and successful GM crop.[12] This happens both in international and domestic discourse around GM crops. A major reason for this is has been the dissemination of impact assessment studies carried out over three years by Huang Jikun and colleagues (Huang *et al.*, 2002, 2003; Pray *et al.*, 2002; Hossain *et al.*, 2004). Huang (a leading agricultural economist and policy researcher in China, and director of Centre for Chinese Agricultural Policy at the Chinese Academy of Sciences) and colleagues claim that Bt cotton leads to substantial reductions in pesticide use, and thereby to reduced input costs and labour savings, and improved incomes for farmers. There findings have been widely cited in the international literature (Nuffield Committee on Bioethics, 2003; FAO, 2004). Huang himself has become the pre-eminent non-scientific spokesperson in China on biotechnology.[13]

Latour (1983) argued that bits of scientific information are extended through actor-networks such that contingent facts can become claims of great size. Knowledge becomes 'black-boxed' and removed from the conditions of knowledge production, such as the processes and contingencies of a field survey. This can be argued in relation to the China Bt cotton economic impact studies. Huang's work has been widely used in the case for Bt cotton, nevertheless, aspects of his methodology and conclusions have been subject to criticism (Scatasta & Wesseler, 2004; Pemsl *et al.*, 2005). One concern is that the impact assessments are based on recall data, which some argue is not the most reliable method to gauge input costs. Also, for several provinces there are only Bt cotton samples and (given the near total uptake of Bt cotton in some provinces) no non-Bt comparator, some provinces are only sampled for one season. At the same time, in-depth studies of particular cotton counties monitoring with farmers pesticide applications over the course of a season have suggested that pesticide use remains uneconomically high even on Bt cotton. In this sense the technology is not necessarily the uncritical success it is often presented as being (Pemsl *et al.*, 2005; Yang *et al.*, 2005).

The counter discourse coalition on GMOs first became evident in China around the issue of Bt cotton. A key moment was the publication of a report by Greenpeace and Nanjing Institute of Environmental Sciences in 2002. This was linked to a conference (which received national and international press coverage) in which international Greenpeace experts spoke about the controversy surrounding contamination of Mexican maize landraces by GM seeds as well as other issues. The report on the environmental impacts of Bt cotton generated considerable debate, and hostility, especially as it emerged from a SEPA institute (Xue, 2002). This report summarised a range of different research outputs on environmental impacts of Bt cotton. The most significant was research suggesting a rise in non-target pests (which would perhaps lead farmers to continue to use high levels of pesticide, undermining the case that Bt leads to drastic falls in pesticide use). The report also noted that early resistance to Bt cotton had been found in laboratory studies. Reaction to this study was intense, including a public rebuttal by two key members of the Biosafety Committee, one of whom belongs to the institute responsible for developing Chinese varieties of Bt cotton (for a summary of the debate and reactions see Keeley, 2003b). These researchers argued that the 'Greenpeace report' was 'garbled'.

It is also significant that the widespread illegal planting of Bt cotton is acknowledged by the MOA (Ministry of Agriculture, 2004). Chinese researchers note that illegal Bt cotton is likely to express a low dose of the Bt toxin rather than a high dose. This undermines a key premise of the refuge theory (using non-GM crops also consumed by bollworms alongside Bt cotton to delay resistance) and could mean early insect resistance to Bt cotton (Xu *et al.*, 2005; Yang *et al.*, 2005). This might require the introduction of new more expensive GM technologies, or increased use of pesticides.

Despite the serious lack of capacity in enforcing regulation, the counter discourse coalition on Bt cotton has only made limited headway. Nobody has produced clear evidence showing that there is pest resistance in the field to Bt cotton, or more fundamentally refuting Huang's studies on the economic benefits of Bt cotton at anything more than an anecdotal level (Xue, 2003). In India there have been several studies by NGOs with large data sets claiming to show that Bt cotton has not led to higher yields or reduced costs for farmers. Similar studies have not yet appeared in China, perhaps because it would be politically difficult to carry out such research. Individual scientists may have reservations about Bt cotton, or doubt some of the evidence showing how successful it has been, but there is no grouping of people making a serious case that China should reverse its position on Bt cotton and restrict its continued use. The number of provinces in which it is being used has increased, more varieties have been approved, giving the overall impression that it is a *fait accompli*. Even Greenpeace no longer concentrates on Bt cotton in China; its efforts are now focussed on stopping the commercialisation of GM rice, the subject of the next section.

The Struggle over GM Rice

The push to have another GM crop approved for cultivation, and in particular a food crop, has concentrated on GM rice.[14] Rice is China's major food crop, and has great symbolic importance. World Food Prize winner Yuan Longping's work developing hybrid rice in the 1960s and 70s earned him the status of national hero. Current programmes to develop new high-yielding Super Rice with 863 support are well-publicised. Unsurprisingly, several of China's key biotechnologists have concentrated their research on rice. According to Zhu Zhen (biotech scientist and official on the 863 committee) 25–30 per cent of China's GM investments are in GM rice research.[15] China also has a stronger position in GM rice research relative to multinationals.

The conflict between different biotechnology discourse coalitions now focuses on rice. This helps explain why there was such media interest and secrecy around Biosafety Committee evaluations of Zhang Qifa and Zhu Zhen's varieties of insect-resistant rice, and Jia Shirong's disease-resistant rice. Huang Jikun has produced policy papers, made strategic presentations and numerous media interventions on the case for GM rice. Greenpeace have responded with a 'Rice is Life' campaign. This battle has found its way into the pages of *Science* with articles by Greenpeace Beijing and others rebutting an article by Huang in the journal (Huang *et al.*, 2005). An intensely Chinese policy debate has assumed a global significance in the battle between different discourse coalitions over the future of GM crops.

Huang Jikun and his colleagues presented a paper to the State Council making the case for commercialisation of GM rice, along with removal of China's labelling requirements (the latter presented as reducing the economic benefits of GM rice) (Huang & Hu, 2003). His arguments have been based on Global Trade Analysis and cost–benefit analysis of the economic impacts of GM rice seeds utilised by farmers participating in production trials. This latter data was recently published in *Science*, and has been widely quoted (Huang *et al.*, 2005).[16] Huang and colleagues collected data from farmers participating in production trials of GM rice varieties developed by Zhang Qifa and Zhu Zhen.[17] Huang and colleagues claim yield gains of 6–9 per cent for GM rice over non-GM varieties and 80 per cent reductions in pesticide usage. Again producer-recall techniques are used (about pesticide levels used) rather than monitoring. This research has been controversial because on this occasion the data comes from a field trial organised by scientists applying for commercialisation of GM rice. Different sides in the debate take different positions on whether this data reflects 'realistic' on-farm conditions.

The Global Trade Analysis meanwhile has been used to appeal to Chinese policy-makers nervous about the trade implications if GM rice were commercialised. Analysis claims that since only a relatively small amount of China's rice is exported, even if there are bans on Chinese imports in the EU and among other East Asian nations such as Korea and Japan, China still would be better off in economic terms commercialising GM rice (Huang *et al.*, 2004).

Since 2004 Huang and co-author Rozelle have been periodically quoted in the press announcing the imminent commercialisation of GM rice.[18] These claims were given credence by events surrounding the meeting of the Biosafety Committee in December 2004. According to an article in Southern Weekend (based on interviews with informants close to the decision-making process) this meeting gave approval to the rice biotechnologists' varieties (Liu, 2004). The varieties were deemed to have passed risk-assessment. None of the information associated with the applications has been made public. Of course a decision to commercialise GM rice is a political decision and involves more factors than the technical biosafety assessment. This is why Huang's papers claiming positive economic impacts are an important part of the argument, and the discourse around commercialisation of GM rice.

Even if the Biosafety Committee has given approval to GM rice, MOA officials in the Biosafety Office are not necessarily convinced. According to a leading official in the Biosafety Office: 'Rice – we doubt that this will be approved, because China is a centre of biodiversity for rice. Scientists argue – why don't you approve? We have been under pressure for two or three years. But we don't give in. Usually we agree with the recommendations [of the Biosafety Committee]. Rice is the one case where we don't agree'.[19] This MOA bureaucrat clearly perceived himself as being under pressure from a particular grouping of vocal biotech scientists.

Greenpeace has focused its GM campaign on drawing public attention to the risks associated with commercialisation of GM rice. Greenpeace activities have included a rice tour in Yunnan and a press conference in December 2004 linked to the Biosafety Committee meeting. The front-page article in Southern Weekend (based on interviews with Greenpeace as well as biotech scientists) put across some of the arguments against GM rice, and also raised the question whether there were some conflicts of interest among those who research and develop technologies while also assessing their safety. Some of the argument was repeated in *China Daily*.

Greenpeace also investigated production trials for GM rice in Hubei and Fujian provinces. According to Greenpeace reports, investigations and interviews with farmers and local traders revealed that GM rice is being grown beyond the restricted area associated with the trials (allegedly illegal seeds were found in a market in Guangzhou). Testing of rice seed by a German lab, Genescan, confirmed that some of the samples were genetically-modified. If Greenpeace's research is correct it would be a significant development, confirming that GE rice is being traded and grown illegally outside the field-trial area (SciDevNet, 2005).[20] Greenpeace publicity suggests it might force EU countries to consider bans on Chinese rice imports. So far, however, this has not happened.

For the counter discourse coalition these findings have important implications for the governance of GMOs because it is likely that, as with illegal cotton seeds, the MOA cannot effectively enforce biosafety regulations at the local level. China is a centre for biodiversity for rice, which makes claims by Chinese scientists about the inevitability of gene flow from GM rice to wild varieties important (Lu *et al.*, 2003). It is sometimes claimed that if GM rice were commercialised it would only be grown in areas where risks of out-crossing with wild varieties are low.[21] Such assertions (it is argued in the counter discourse) make unrealistic assumptions about the enforceability of regulations. It is likely that, as with cotton, seed would travel to prohibited areas if it was perceived to offer significant agronomic advantages, and it would be difficult to prevent this happening. Indeed, a Biosafety Committee member interviewed for this research acknowledged that the committee would have liked to have approved GM maize for North-East China but did not do so out of recognition that seed would inevitably be marketed illegally in unapproved provinces in North China where deployment of non-Bt maize is an important part of a refuge strategy to delay insect resistance to Bt cotton.[22]

Another aspect of the GM rice case is that the public seems to be showing more interest in the GM debate (comments on Sina and Sohu websites after a recent Greenpeace press launch ran to hundreds of pages). Rice as a food crop, consumed by a large part of the population in a largely unprocessed form three times a day, clearly generates interest where cotton does not.

The counter-discourse coalition appears then to be more articulate and substantial in relation to rice (as opposed to cotton). The biotechnology discourse coalition is clearly frustrated by what is seen as a failure to take action and capitalise on the achievements of China's substantial biotechnology investments. Despite this, to date the officials who make the decisions seem to have resisted pressure to commercialise a GM food crop. This is likely to reflect concerns about losing markets in the EU (linked to labelling and traceability requirements, and consumer demands for GM-free foods) and a lack of conviction that the potential benefits of GM rice outweigh the environmental risks and potentially hostile reactions of Chinese consumers. At present, then, despite the well-placed networks that link the innovation and regulatory roles of the state in relation to biotech, and the lack of transparency of the risk assessment system, the decision-making process around GM rice appears not to have been captured by a biotech discourse coalition committed to commercialisation at the earliest possible date.

Conclusion

This article set out to explore the paradoxes facing the Chinese state as it governs GMOs. The heart of the problem is that while China is at the international cutting edge of biotechnology research and development, it also faces a range of challenges that are either characteristic of a developing country (for example, capacity issues) or specific to China's political system (limited debate and transparency in some areas of policy-making). The question addressed was how China would face up to the challenge of managing a technology that has proved problematic in a range of different countries some of which do not face the wider governance dilemmas that China does.

In some respects there clearly have been problems coordinating the interests and remits of different institutions within the state. The difficulty in passing a Biosafety Law seems to illustrate the 'fragmented authoritarian' thesis of Lieberthal and Oksenberg (1988) where issues end in stalemate when ministries of equivalent rank engage in a clash to defend or expand their remits.

There are other aspects of governance with fundamental problems. It has proved difficult to enforce labelling regulations. Illegal varieties of Bt cotton have been grown in many places, and, allegedly, GM rice seed has escaped beyond the confines of controlled production trial areas into farmer seed markets.

The broader challenge of balancing innovation and regulation processes, however, has been negotiated more effectively than perhaps might have been predicted. If GMOs were proving a fundamental governance challenge for China it might be conjectured that the strong discourse coalition around biotechnology, exploiting the relative lack of transparency surrounding the regulatory system, and the very limited opportunities for other stakeholders to voice their concerns, would have succeeded in pushing through a series of commercialisations of new GM technologies with minimal consideration of risk and safety issues.

That no GM food crops have been approved for commercialisation on a wide scale is significant given the lobbying that has gone on in relation to GM rice, and the dominant perception that Bt cotton has on balance been a successful technology (in contrast with other countries where this is often a more contested view). For the time being at least the stance appears to be to 'wait and see' what happens globally in relation to trade and consumer acceptance of GMOs, with a particular eye on the EU. This could of course change quite rapidly, and new approvals for commercial planting may follow during 2006. In this sense assessments are necessarily provisional. At present, however, the Chinese state appears to have been able to balance the pressures to develop technological capacity in what is seen as a strategically important area with the need for circumspection in relation to the trade, environmental and food safety, and consumer acceptance uncertainties associated with commercialising GM varieties of crops of fundamental symbolic and strategic importance.

Acknowledgements

Thanks to Peter Newell, Jillian Popkins and Graeme Smith and anonymous reviewers for comments on an earlier version of this paper. The author is responsible for the final version. This paper draws on research material from the DFID-funded project 'Biotechnology Policy Processes in Developing Countries'.

Notes

1. *San nong* (three '*nongs*': *nongmin, nongye, nongcun*) is a common rural development policy term referring to farmers, agriculture and rural areas.
2. Deng Xiaoping for instance was quoted as saying: 'Solving tomorrow's agricultural problems in the end will come down to biotechnology, to relying on the most sophisticated technologies' (863 Committee, 2001: 36).
3. Interviews with officials in the Ministry of Science and Technology suggest that the proposed development of the Star Wars missile defence system was a key stimulus.
4. http://english.sina.com/china/1/2005/0519/31660.html
5. *China Daily* (2002) Nation to draft laws on biosafety, 8 April. More recently a statement was made on the SEPA Biodiversity website, 'Our country will implement a GMO biosafety law', 19 May 2005 ('Wo guo jiang zhiding: "Zhuan jiyin shengwu anquan fa"') (http://www.biodiv. gov.cn/swdyx/144398862075822080/20050520/7840.shtml).
6. SEPA official, personal communication (2004).
7. Hajer illustrates his argument using a case study of acid rain in UK and the Netherlands. He argues that two key coalitions are identifiable: a traditional pragmatist coalition and an ecological modernisation coalition. For analysis of the role of discourse coalitions in environmental policy processes see Keeley and Scoones (2003).
8. Personal communication, Chinese policy researcher, Beijing (2003).
9. The exact extent of Monsanto's influence is hard to gauge. Interviews with individual Chinese scientists suggest that informal links to Monsanto through study tours, periods of study at universities in the US, joint authorship of articles with Monsanto staff, or personal links with Chinese Monsanto employees can be quite strong. These links are generally not publicised. More generally foreign companies can push for influence through foreign trade talks. In relation to the trade in GM soya foreign companies were able to put substantial pressure on the Chinese government through US Secretaries for Trade and Agriculture.
10. Personal communication, Chinese ecological scientist (2002). Transparency in relation to funding proposals has been a problem and something that the Ministry of Science and Technology now claims to be addressing (see SciDevNet (2004) 'China to make research funding more transparent', 15 September).
11. Personal communications, Biosafety Committee member and SEPA official, Beijing (2002 and 2003).
12. 'GM cotton has become the "miracle crop" of China since its commercial growth was first permitted in 1996, and more than a half of China's cotton is now GM. One of the main reasons for this success, say its advocates, it that it has both helped farmers to cut their production costs by an average of almost 30 per cent, and reduce their exposure to chemicals' (SciDevNet (2004) 'China urged to step up GM efforts', 5 March).

13. See, for example, SciDevNet (2004) 'China urged to step up GM efforts', 5 March; *The Economist* (2002) 'Biotech's yin and yang', 12 December.
14. GM maize and soya bean imports are permitted, but only in processed form.
15. For maize multinationals such as Monsanto, Syngenta and DuPont would be in a more competitive position relative to Chinese researchers. In wheat, technologies are less developed.
16. See *The Economist* (2005) 'Genetically modified rice', 28 April; SciDevNet (2005) GM rice 'good for Chinese farmers' health and wealth', 29 April.
17. The varieties are Xianyou-63 an insect-resistant Bt rice developed by Zhang Qifa, and Youming-86 (insect resistant with the CPTI gene) developed by Zhu Zhen (Huang *et al.*, 2005).
18. *The Economist* (2004) 'Soya on rice to go: Brazil and China are set to commercialise genetically modified crops', 18 November.
19. Interview with Cheng Jinggen, Biosafety Office, Ministry of Agriculture (2002).
20. See SciDevNet (2005) 'China to assess claim illegal rice entered the food chain', 14 April; Greenpeace report available at http://www.greenpeace.org/international/news/scandal-greenpeace-exposes-il
21. Rice biotechnologist and Biosafety Committee member Jia Shirong comments: 'We have environmental safety reports. What is more, when we give the go-ahead China will take a cautious attitude, approving on a province-by-province basis, guaranteeing that GM rice varieties will not out-cross' (Liu, 2004).
22. Personal communication, Biosafety Committee member, Beijing (2002).

References

863 Committee (2001) *Jueqi: Volume Commemorating 15 Years of Achievements of the 863 Committee* (Beijing: 863 Committee).
Fang, X., Chang, D., Xu, J., Xu, R. & Fan, T. (2001) 'Commercial implementation of intellectual property rights of Chinese transgenic insect-resistant cotton with the Bt gene and Bt + CpTI genes', *Journal of Agricultural Biotechnology* 9(2): 103–106.
Food and Agriculture Organisation (FAO) (2004) *State of Food and Agriculture 2003–4: Agricultural Biotechnology, Meeting the Needs of the Poor?* (Rome: Food and Agriculture Organisation).
Hajer, M. (1995) *The Politics of Environmental Discourse* (Oxford: Clarendon).
Hossain, F., Pray, C., Lu, Y., Huang J., Fan, C. & Hu, R. (2004) 'Genetically modified cotton and farmers' health in China', *International Journal of Occupational and Environmental Health* 10(3): 296–303.
Howell, J. (ed.) (2004) *Governance in China* (Lanham, MD: Rowman and Littlefield).
Huang, J. & Hu, R. (2003) 'Jiasu nongye shengwu jishu chanyehua jiang dui wo guo jingmao liyi chansheng jiji yingxiang' (Speeding up commercial use of agricultural biotechnology will have positive economic and trade impacts for China). CCAP Paper 03(13) (in Chinese).
Huang, J. & Wang, Q. (2003) 'Biotechnology policy and regulation in China'. IDS Working Paper, Biotechnology Policy Series (4) (Brighton: Institute of Development Studies).
Huang, J., Rozelle, S., Pray, C. & Wang, Q. (2002) 'Plant biotechnology in China', *Science* 295 (25 January): 674–6.
Huang, J., Hu, R., Pray, C., Qiao, F. & Rozelle, S. (2003) 'Biotechnology as an alternative to chemical pesticides: a case study of Bt cotton in China', *Agricultural Economics* 29(1): 55–67.
Huang, J., Hu, R., Van Meijl, H. & Van Tongeren, F. (2004) 'Biotechnology boosts to crop productivity in China: trade and welfare implications', *Journal of Development Economics* 75: 27–54.
Huang, J., Hu, R., Rozelle, S. & Pray, C. (2005) 'GM rice in farmers' fields: assessing productivity and health effects in China', *Science* 308: 688–90.
James, C. (2004) 'Global status of commercialized biotech/GM crops: 2004'. ISAAA Brief No. 32, Ithaca, NY.
Keeley, J. (2003a) 'The biotech developmental state? Investigating the Chinese gene revolution'. IDS Working Paper 207, Biotechnology Policy Series (6), Brighton.

Keeley, J. (2003b) 'Regulating biotechnology in China: the politics of biosafety'. IDS Working Paper 208, Biotechnology Policy Series (7), Brighton.

Keeley, J. (2005) 'Interrogating China's biotech revolution: the developmental state meets the risk society', in: M. Leach, I. Scoones & B. Wynne (eds.) *Science, Citizenship and Globalisation* (London: Zed Press), pp. 155–66.

Keeley, J. & Scoones, I. (2003) *Understanding Environmental Policy Processes: Cases from Africa* (London: Earthscan).

Latour, B. (1987) *Science in Action: How to Follow Scientists and Engineers through Society* (Milton Keynes: Open University Press).

Lieberthal, K. & Oksenberg, M. (1988) *Policy-making in China: Leaders, Structure and Processes* (Princeton, NJ: Princeton University Press).

Liu, J. (2004) 'GM rice: who will really benefit?', *Southern Weekend*, 9 December (Nanfang Zhoumo: 'Zhuan jiyin shuidao yu shisan yi ren zhu liang de liyi xuan yi').

Lu, B., Song, Z. & Chen, J. (2003) 'Can transgenic rice cause ecological risks through transgene escape?', *Progress in Natural Science* 13(1): 17–24.

Ministry of Agriculture (2004) 'Notice on strengthening and regularising seed management work'. Ministry of Agriculture Regulation 30 (14 July) (Guanyu jin yi bu guifan he jiaqiang zhongzi guanli gongzuo de tongzhi) (Beijing: Ministry of Agriculture Office).

Nuffield Committee on Bioethics (2003) *The Use of Genetically Modified Crops in Developing Countries* (London: Nuffield Council on Bioethics).

Pemsl, D., Waibel, H. & Gutierrez, A. (2005) 'Why do some Bt cotton farmers in China continue to use high levels of pesticides?', *International Journal of Agricultural Sustainability* 3(1): 44–56.

Pray, C., Huang, J., Hu, R. & Rozelle, S. (2002) 'Five years of Bt cotton: the benefits continue', *Plant Journal* 31(4): 423–30.

Scatasta, S. & Wesseler, J. (2004) 'A critical assessment of methods for analysis of environmental and economic costs and benefits of genetically modified crops in a survey of existing literature'. Paper presented at the International Consortium on Agricultural Biotechnology Research, Ravello, Italy, 8–11 July.

Xu, X., Yu, L. & Wu, Y. (2005) 'Disruption of a cadherin gene associated with resistance to cry1ac endotoxin of Bacillus thuringiensis in Helicoverpa armigera', *Applied and Environmental Microbiology* 71(2): 948–54.

Xue, D. (2002) *A Summary of Research on the Environmental Impacts of Bt Cotton in China* (Hong Kong: Greenpeace and Nanjing Institute of Environmental Sciences).

Xue, D. (2003) 'Biodiversity impacts of environmental release of GM cotton: research, trials and countermeasures', *International Biosafety* 8: 26–31 (Zhuanjiyin mianhua huanjing shifang dui shengwu duoyangxing de yingxiang diaocha, shiyan he duice).

Yang, P., Iles, M., Yan, S. & Jolliffe, F. (2005) 'Farmers' knowledge, perceptions and practices in transgenic Bt cotton in small producer systems in northern China', *Crop Protection* 24: 229–39.

China, the WTO, and Implications for the Environment

ABIGAIL R. JAHIEL

Introduction

On 11 December 2001, China formally entered the World Trade Organization (WTO). This movement promised among other things to further liberalise the Chinese economy, accelerate economic growth, increase the country's international prestige, and in these ways enhance the flagging legitimacy of the Chinese Communist Party. While the implications of WTO membership for the economy, society, and politics have been heatedly debated in the period surrounding China's accession (see Wang, 2000; Fewsmith, 2001; Harwit, 2001; Langlois, 2001; Lee, 2001; Hsiung, 2003; Bhalla & Qiu, 2004),[1] far less attention has been paid to the environmental implications of membership.[2] Yet, two decades of rapid economic development under China's 'open door' policy prior to WTO entry intensified the country's earlier environmental degradation and resulted in serious strains on the country's resources and ecosystems. Today, China faces a host of domestic environmental problems and contributes mightily to global ones, posing potentially significant political challenges. The environmental implications of its entry into the WTO thus merit close study.

Prior to WTO membership, officials in the Chinese State Environmental Protection Administration (SEPA) discussed the challenges WTO entry might pose for environmental protection. On balance their conclusions were optimistic (interview, 0513 2002; Ye, 2002). Along with researchers at SEPA's Policy Research Center for Environment and Economy (PRCEE), they projected that industrial pollution would decrease and that the rural environment would benefit (*Guojia*, 2002; Hu and Meng, 2002). Though potential problems were noted, the consensus was that proactive steps could be taken to avoid negative outcomes.[3] These optimistic conclusions were not surprising given the pressures imposed by a Communist Party that repressed dissent, embraced neoclassical economics, and staked its future on the promised benefits of WTO membership. Today, however, it is clear that even as entry into the WTO has spurred economic growth, the ecological implications have been more harmful than most observers anticipated. Indeed, not only have these conditions exacerbated China's profound environmental challenges, but its political ones as well.

This article seeks to understand why by exploring the arguments on both sides of the trade and environment debate. It looks first at the theoretical literature on the subject, then at China's history with trade liberalisation prior to WTO entry, and finally at the environmental effects and related social and political repercussions of WTO membership. Throughout the article, the distinct impacts of economic growth, trade liberalisation, and other results of WTO membership are noted, but emphasis is placed on the composite effect of these factors as most important for the environment. The article concludes with an assessment of the political dilemma faced by the Chinese state in responding to these deepening environmental harms.

Trade and Environment: the Logic of Liberalisation

A sharp debate exists over the implications of trade liberalisation for the environment (Weber, 2001; Williams, 2001). On one side are those who, like the Chinese state, view free trade primarily as a catalyst for environmental improvement. These individuals argue that trade liberalisation:

1. leads to economic growth, which is a precondition for acquiring the technical and institutional capability to address pollution [*the wealth argument*];
2. reduces costs of imports and thus provides greater access to cleaner production techniques [*the technology argument*];
3. removes subsidies and trade barriers, encouraging structural changes to the economy and exchange on the basis of comparative advantage and efficient use of resources [*the structural change/efficiency argument*]; and,
4. promotes environmental legal reform to prevent rejection of products for sale overseas [*the 'regulatory race to the top' argument*].

On the other side are those who view trade liberalisation as antithetical to environmental protection. They argue that:

1. the expansion in output comes at a cost to the environment [*the scale argument*];
2. comparative advantage can negatively affect the environment if a country's industrial structure and natural endowments favour specialisation in pollution-intensive industries [*the 'pollution haven' argument*]; and,
3. trade liberalisation encourages the reduction of environmental standards as countries compete for foreign investment [*the 'regulatory race to the bottom' argument*].

While this article is not intended primarily to address this debate empirically,[4] these arguments provide a framework to understand and assess the environmental effects China has experienced as a result of increasing trade liberalisation, first under the 'open door' policy and then following WTO membership.

Trade Liberalisation and the Environment Prior to WTO Accession: 1978–2001

Central to China's vast economic expansion prior to WTO accession was the gradual liberalisation of trade and investment policies. Between 1978 and 2000, China's foreign trade grew 24-fold, from US$20 billion to US$474 billion; annual average foreign direct investment (FDI) reached US$42.7 billion; and by the beginning of the 21st century, exports and foreign investment generated 40 per cent of China's GDP.

These changes in China's political economy had a broad impact on the environment. China's 'open door' policy allowed for greater access to less-polluting technologies, pollution abatement equipment, and advanced environmental management practices (Hu & Yang, 2000; CCICED, 2001). Pursuit of comparative advantage encouraged China to 'reallocate its resources away from capital, land, and energy-intensive dirty industries to labour-intensive cleaner industries' (Chai, 2002: 30). This reallocation, in turn, led to a notable decrease in the pollution intensity of manufacturing industries between the early 1980s and the late 1990s – at least among state-owned firms and larger companies.[5] In addition, the 'open door' policy attracted foreign funds to address specific problems.[6] Increased contact in the international arena also heightened awareness of and commitment to addressing environmental problems. This contributed to China's efforts to strengthen its regulatory environmental regime by developing an extensive environmental protection apparatus and a host of environmental laws, regulations, and policies (Jahiel, 2000). In addition, by the 1990s China was urging firms to adopt international ISO 14000 standards to compete better internationally and was developing an organic foods industry and a green labeling process (Ross, 2000; Theirs, 2000).

In spite of these positive developments, the first two decades of rapid economic growth and trade liberalisation significantly expanded China's already notable ecological problems (Smil, 1993; Sanders, 1999; Edmonds, 2000; Muldavin, 2000). In a comprehensive study of the Chinese manufacturing sector from 1978 to 1999, Chai found that even as China shifted its export portfolio toward cleaner production industries and adopted cleaner technologies, the negative environmental effects of the vastly increased *scale* of trade far exceeded the positive. In fact, '[t]he rate of increase of water, air and soil pollution went almost hand-in-hand with that of Chinese manufactured export expansion' (Chai, 2002: 32).

Pursuit of the export market also led to vast exploitation of the country's natural resources. In order to feed and clothe overseas epicurean tastes for exotic herbs and cashmere sweaters, fragile grasslands in Inner Mongolia were over-cultivated and over-grazed. To increase cash crop yields, fertile lands in coastal areas fell subject to heavy applications of chemical pesticides and fertilisers. Delicate inland landscapes and hillsides were mined for non-ferrous metals and rare minerals, exposing populations to dangerous and even radioactive materials (Wang, 2001). And coastal zones were over-harvested to feed the world's rapidly growing seafood industry (Feigon, 2000; CCICED, 2001).

China also found comparative advantage in the transfer of pollution, both from dirty industries and the waste trade (Wang, 2001). According to a 1995 SEPA study, 30 per cent of all foreign-invested ventures in China were engaged in heavily polluting industries (*Guojia*, 2002) – including ones involved in the production and consumption of ozone-depleting substances (ODSs), whose manufacture and use were banned in the industrialised world under the Montreal Protocol (CCICED, 1997).[7] With regard to the waste trade, wastes (including plastics bags, bottles and agricultural sheets, dirty diapers, sanitary napkins, food, paper, hospital wastes, radioactive scrap metals, electronic wastes, and unidentified chemicals) imported chiefly from industrialised countries, were accepted by Chinese 'entrepreneurs' as lucrative business ventures; in others, wastes entered under the exporter's pretext that they were recyclable materials or resources (Greenpeace, 1997; interview, 0707 1997). Between 1990 and 1997 the value of imported hazardous wastes alone grew almost 140-fold from just under US$14 million to US$19 billion (Ren, 2001). Tough new laws implemented in 1997 made trade in certain wastes punishable by up to ten years in prison or a fine of RMB 500,000, yet still the waste trade persisted. In several coastal villages, China's poor continued to make their living scavenging through highly toxic, electronic wastes to retrieve precious metals and other materials, at great costs to their personal health and to the health of local ecosystems (BAN, 2002).

The situation between 1978 and 2001, *prior* to entry into the WTO, suggests, then, that early efforts at trade liberalisation and engagement in the global economy shifted the distribution of China's manufacturing industries somewhat away from the most heavily polluting industries and technologies, increasing the economy's efficiency. Greater global engagement further drew increased regulatory attention to the environment. However, these benefits to the environment were more than offset by the *scale* of growth and the international incentives to pursue China's comparative advantage in ecologically destructive ventures and dirty industries and trades. Moreover, even though trade liberalisation did not lead to a *regulatory* race to the bottom – the body of environmental law grew – an *environmental* race to the bottom took place as a result of failure to implement new laws and policies. In seeking comparative advantage, Chinese entrepreneurs – and complicit local government officials – were willing effectively to let China become a 'waste haven', reducing environmental quality and ecosystem health for financially prosperous ventures, even as central government officials were working to climb the environmental regulatory ladder. How, if at all, has this situation changed under WTO membership?

Accession to the WTO and its Environmental Impact: 2002 and Beyond

Initial Projections

Under its accession agreements, China was required to reduce its import tariffs, end all export subsidies, lower or eliminate import quotas, and open certain sectors of the economy to foreign trade. Structural changes to the economy were expected to follow, with short-term economic dislocations resulting from the failure of uncompetitive sectors and the development of other sectors with global comparative advantage. Expected to feel the hardship most were the capital-intensive heavy industries (e.g. automobile, shipbuilding, machine, steel, chemical, pharmaceutical, and petrochemical), the paper industry, township-and-village enterprises (TVEs), and the grain and cotton sectors of the agricultural economy (Sun, 2000; Lee, 2001; Harwit, 2001; Mai, 2002; Yeung, 2002). Projected to prosper were the labour-intensive industries and agricultural sectors (e.g. textile and garment, shoe, household electronics, bicycle, fruit, vegetable, horticulture, meat and fish) and the service and financial sectors (Wang, 2000; Fewsmith, 2001; Ren, 2001).

  Environmental officials and policy analysts from China and abroad anticipated notable ecological benefits. In keeping with the logic of trade liberalisation, they suggested that: 1) the elimination and reduction of subsidies, tariffs and the like would lead to the import of superior environmental protection equipment and less-polluting industrial and agricultural technologies (CCICED, 2001; *Guojia*, 2002; interview, 0513 2002); 2) heightened international competition would bring environmentally-beneficial structural adjustments to the Chinese industrial and agricultural economies (*Guojia*, 2002; Hu & Meng, 2002); 3) greater access to low-priced foreign goods would increase imports of consumer products and raw materials, reducing domestic energy consumption, pollution emissions, and impacts on natural resources through avoided production costs (Oberheitmann, 2002); and,

4) increased imports would force China to strengthen its legal code to avoid an influx of pollution-intensive or environmentally-harmful products (interview, 0528 2002; Ye, 2002), while 'green trade barriers' and the threat they posed to exports would convince industry managers to consider environmental issues as 'life and death issues for their firms' (*Guojia*, 2002),[8] and demand the adoption of stricter domestic environmental, health and safety codes based on international standards (Ferris & Zhang, 2002; interview, 0513 2002). As one report summarises the impact, echoing these optimistic projections, 'When trade and environmental policies are well coordinated, trade and investment liberalisation can be conducive to saving resources, improving efficiency, restructuring industry, improving the environment and sustaining the growth of China's economy' (CCICED, 2001: 7).

The Realities

For the most part, however, the overall environmental benefits projected have not materialised. Economic growth has indeed outstripped earlier projections, and certain structural adjustments, technological changes, and legal and cultural developments have been beneficial for the environment. Nevertheless, some of the greatest economic advances in both the industrial and agricultural sectors are seriously exacerbating China's most severe environmental problems – and some of the world's greatest ecological crises as well. Moreover, they are creating serious political challenges.

Within the first three years of WTO entry, FDI in China grew almost 30 per cent, foreign trade doubled, exceeding US$1 trillion, and China surpassed Japan to become the world's third largest importer. As a result, the economy has continued to expand rapidly, growing at an annual rate of 9.5 per cent. These macro-economic trends have propelled further restructuring of the economy. Low labour and material costs have provided the comparative advantage anticipated in a number of industrial and agricultural sectors. Growth has been particularly electrifying in the export-oriented, labour-intensive textile industry, where wages are 20–40 times lower than in developed countries and two to four times lower than in many developing ones, and where WTO-related protocols have brought an end to the three-decade-old quota system (Cheng and Shen, 2004).

Counter to predictions, China's automobile industry has also experienced rapid growth (Pan *et al.*, 2004). Competition associated with the sharp drop in automobile tariffs and increase in import quotas under the WTO,[9] as well as the influx of FDI in this previously inefficient sector and continued government support for this 'key' industry, have reduced prices for motor vehicles, increased consumer demand, and contributed to this industry's massive growth.

In agriculture, labour-intensive industries like fruit and vegetable production, horticulture, animal husbandry, and aquaculture have thrived, spurred on by favourable global economic incentives, preferential government policies, and increased foreign investment. Not only are farmgate costs for certain crops a fraction of costs in California (Rosen *et al.*, 2004), but the Chinese government has worked to accelerate the modernisation of agriculture by 1) promoting improved crop strains (including biogenetically engineered crops – see Keeley, this issue), high value products, and advanced technology; 2) encouraging the development of large-scale agricultural corporations; and 3) courting foreign investment in these efforts. The growth of the aquaculture industry, aided by a pronounced inflow of FDI, has been particularly striking: China is presently the largest producer and exporter of marine products in the world (Zhao *et al.*, 2004).

As for the environment, no comprehensive studies are yet available on the number of heavily polluting firms that have closed as a result of increased international competition. However, the government continues to encourage phase-outs and updates of outdated technology as well as plant closures in the metallurgy, construction, chemical industry and energy sectors. To stay competitive, the steel and automobile industries have also had to adopt newer technologies. In addition, economic expansion has been particularly robust in the less energy-intensive light industry sector, and China's environmental protection and cleaner production industries have continued to grow and attract foreign investment, as has the 'green food' sector.

Legal and cultural changes that favour the environment are evident, too. Many new environmentally beneficial laws and standards are being promulgated in response to pressures created by WTO trade liberalisation (as is discussed further below). International environmental organisations are becoming more involved in China's ecological preservation efforts, and public involvement in environmental NGOs, although still limited, is growing. The central government has indicated greater recognition of the severity of China's environmental situation in its trial adoption of a 'green GDP'. Finally, SEPA appears to be assuming a much more aggressive stance toward polluters, announcing in January 2005 a halt on 30 key projects (26 in the power sector) for failure to comply with environmental impact assessment laws.

Nevertheless, the *actual* environmental impact of those sectors that have prospered most under the WTO demonstrates the significant harm engagement in this trade regime has brought. I will explore the industrial and the agricultural sectors below.

The Industrial Sector

Unit for unit one would expect that as the economy has continued to move away from capital-intensive heavy industries to labour-intensive light industries and the service sector, pollution emissions would fall. But as Chai's study of the manufacturing sector during the 1980s and 1990s demonstrates, what is critical for the environment is the *scale* or extent of overall economic growth, not solely the shift in balance between various sectors. If the heavily-polluting, capital-intensive sector shrinks proportionate to the economy as a whole, but the less-polluting labour-intensive sector grows substantially, the total amount of emissions may nevertheless rise – even as the pollution intensity of individual firms decreases.

This phenomenon is, in fact, what we are witnessing. The scale of light industry growth is so large that it is having an overall negative impact on the environment. The sheer increase in output of this sector has caused a rapid increase in energy demand throughout the economy (Jiang *et al.*, 2004). Moreover, to meet this increased demand, economic pressures have encouraged the growth of that part of the energy sector that is *most* environmentally destructive: the small coal mining ventures or TVEs originally predicted to falter from increased competition following WTO entry (Jiang *et al.*, 2004).[10] The boom in the manufacturing sector is thus responsible for air pollution increases on some indicators (both regional and global), water pollution increases (with the exception of BOD) and further soil degradation due to its greater reliance on 'dirty' coal. But the growth of the manufacturing sector negatively affects the environment in many other ways as well, as is demonstrated by the cases of the textile and automobile industries.

Textiles

The ecological footprint of textile production is large. From chemicals used in the printing and dyeing processes to heavy consumption of water in the manufacturing process and the generation of large volumes of difficult-to-treat wastewater, the production of textiles creates many environmental problems. Even before it becomes fabric, cotton and synthetic fibre production takes its toll on the environment. Conventional cotton production requires high inputs of water and more pesticide use per unit of production than any other crop; a shift to genetically modified cotton, while potentially reducing pesticide use, holds unknown environmental impacts that have sparked huge debates about biosafety; the manufacture of synthetic fibres draws on limited petroleum reserves and produces toxic byproducts.

In China, the environmental impact of textile production is especially great. Due to inferior technology, '...water consumption per unit of production is about 50 per cent higher than in developed countries'. In addition, 'dyes made in China usually have lower dye uptake and...dye residual in wastewater is higher'. Thus, 'the sewer discharge per product is nearly double the amount discharged in developed countries', and the textile industry is one of the major contributors of industrial sewage (Cheng & Shen, 2004: 182).

It is possible that some of these problems may be mitigated in the future. With entry into the WTO, Chinese tariff rates for imports of foreign-produced dyes, cotton, and textile machinery are dropping and access to superior production technology and to foreign capital is improving. In addition, in response to the global trade regime, China has developed a series of environment-related standards for both finished products and production processes[11] and has encouraged technological changes which result in more environmentally-friendly production. For example, Chinese textile factories switched to EU-dyes when products with highly polluting Azo dyes were rejected from German markets, exacting huge financial losses (interview, 0515 2002).

Several factors, however, suggest that these benefits are limited, and that the continued surge in the textile sector will be environmentally harmful. First, cotton production in China is not slowing, though imports are increasing.[12] While Bt Cotton accounted for 66 per cent of Chinese production in 2004, potentially eliminating use of some potent pesticides, the long-term ecological impacts remain to be seen. Second, like the coal industry, within the textile industry small firms have prospered, accounting for about 85 per cent of all cotton textile manufacturers. The threshold for entrance into this sector is low due to limited financial and technical requirements; moreover, since WTO accession, foreign investment in small plants has increased (Cheng & Shen, 2004). But small firms are equipped with inferior technology and thus scholars believe that 'the...cumulative [negative] impacts on the environment [of such firms] may be even greater than those of larger enterprises' (Cheng & Shen, 2004: 201). Finally, the development of these firms is difficult to regulate and monitor, due to a shortage of rural environmental protection personnel and to economic pressures to approve projects quickly and overlook environmental factors. In May 2002, a Wuhan Environmental Protection Bureau official in charge of approving new industrial ventures explained:

> [With entry into the WTO, t]he approval process has to speed up...many companies want to set up apparel businesses...[or] dying factories. They set up very quickly, but they can't really deal with the environmental problems. There are numerous cases of such factories applying for approval...And the tenth five-year plan explicitly calls for expanding production in high quality textiles...So this creates a great challenge for us. The environmental impact assessment regulations require us to complete the process and notify the enterprise within 60 days. But companies want the approval much faster. There's a lot of pressure [on us]. (Interview, 0522 2002)

The difficulties for environmental officials are further aggravated by the dismantling of much of the industrial ministerial structure of the planned economy, in part as preconditions for admission into the WTO. In the past, the now defunct Ministry of Textile Industry acted as an institutional ally, aiding the EPB in enforcement (Cheng & Shen, 2004).

Automobile Industry

The environmental ramifications of the feverishly growing automobile industry are at least as daunting as the textile industry. In this case, however, while the manufacturing process is environmentally destructive, it is the consumption of the product that is most polluting. Car emissions are now *the* major source of pollution in China's large cities, contributing heavily to human health and atmospheric problems. Moreover, due to inferior technologies and congested roads, automobile emissions per vehicle are estimated to be ten times higher than those in developed countries. Yet, as noted elsewhere, the Chinese government continues to regard automobile production as critical to the country's economic development, and sales of automobiles are expected to rise (Pan *et al.*, 2004).

As with the textile industry, the environmental impacts of automobiles may be mitigated. Since entry into the WTO, the Chinese government has developed stricter emissions standards based on EU models. Beginning in 2002, all new cars were required to meet European I standards; in 2004, China began implementing European II standards; and European III standards have been set for enforcement in 2007 (Pan *et al.*, 2004; *China Daily*, 28 April 2005). These standards are notable improvements from previous regulations, though they do not strictly regulate trucks, whose numbers have also grown. It remains to be seen to what degree China will persevere in adopting – and especially enforcing – the highest international emissions control technologies and standards. Not only will the government have to contend with those within China who try to skirt the law in various ways (Pan *et al.*, 2004), but it will have to hold firm against foreign investors who try to reduce costs by transferring older technologies.

Even if more stringent regulations and newer technologies for the motor vehicle sector are enforced, a computer simulation of automobile emissions under present market trends leads Pan *et al.* to conclude that the sheer *scale* of increased production '. . . will result in heavier [air] pollution . . . simply because reduction [of emissions] per car is easily offset by the increase in the number of cars'. Coupled with the environmental impact of higher emissions is the increased demand for more of China's scarce arable land to build roads (Pan *et al.*, 2004: 110–111).

The Agricultural Sector

The impact on the environment of WTO-induced changes may be even more harmful in the agricultural sector. Here claims of the environmental benefits of structural shifts toward labour-intensive ventures are not well-supported; nor is it clear that technological modernisation will be an improvement. While WTO accession is even more likely to prompt legal reform in this sector (due to direct health concerns), again problems of scale, shortcomings of technology, and institutional weaknesses may have a far more destructive impact on the environment than the many changes in laws suggest.[13]

Fruit, Vegetables, Horticultural Products, Aquaculture and More

Prior to accession, WTO-induced market factors encouraging the development of labour-intensive cash crops, livestock and aquaculture ventures and discouraging production of land-intensive grain crops were widely projected to be beneficial to the environment (World Trade Organization, 1997; Sun, 2000; Ren, 2001; Wang, 2001, *Guojia*, 2002; Hamburger, 2002; Hu & Meng, 2002). In line with the logic of liberalisation, they were expected to:

1. minimise toxicity of chemical pesticides (as prices of low-toxicity foreign products dropped and strict environmental and health standards upheld by trading partners spurred legal changes in China);[14]
2. reduce application of environmentally-degrading chemical fertilisers (with the shift toward animal husbandry and aquaculture);
3. make rural environmental problems easier to control (as farmers shifted from ventures that generate non-point source pollution such as grain production to ones that generate point source pollution such as animal husbandry);
4. promote production of pesticide-free organic crops and biogenetically engineered crops;
5. inhibit population-induced pressures to extend farming on marginal lands (as grain imports increased); and,
6. encourage ecosystem restoration (as farmers abandoned grain production and followed policies to convert farmland back to forests or lakes).

All of these factors were projected to benefit water resources, rural ecosystems, and human health.

In most respects, however, the reality has been far different. Use of chemical pesticides and fertilisers has continued to rise since entry into the WTO. China is now a major importer, producer, and consumer of pesticides, and the largest importer, producer, and consumer of chemical fertilisers in the world (Hu, 2004). In 2004, Chinese farmers applied twice as much fertiliser to their fields as Americans (Earth Policy Institute, 2005), though the US has over four times the arable land. This rise in chemical inputs is due in part to the shift toward cash crops, which are far more chemical-intensive than grain crops, and also to the more limited supply of agricultural labour for weeding, as rural residents seek more lucrative off-farm work (Hamburger, 2002; interview, 0603 2004). It is paralleled by an increase in use of hormones and antibiotics in the growing large-scale livestock and aquaculture industries.

WTO membership may ameliorate the environmental harms of such agricultural chemicals. The increasing use of not only *potentially* hazardous pesticides, antibiotics and hormones, but *proven* toxins banned for use abroad – and in some cases in China – has created problems for trade and pressures to reduce use. Since accession, many Chinese agricultural exports have been prohibited entry to foreign ports. In 2001, half of China's tea exports were barred from sale in the EU because of new EU regulations reducing pesticide tolerance levels for tea by 100 times (Hamburger, 2002); in 2002, the EU suspended imports of *all* Chinese animal products (including farm-raised shrimp and fish) after detecting excess residues of veterinary medicines (*AFX.com*, 18 October 2004); later that year, Japan restricted imports of frozen spinach from China because of high pesticide residues (*Japan Economic Newswire*, 17 June 2003). Such actions have resulted in huge economic losses for China, amounting to billions of dollars (*China Daily*, 26 February 2005). As a result, international food safety and environmental health codes have begun to influence Chinese laws and policy practices. For example, in 2001, following the loss of US$125 million to tea farmers in Zhejiang, provincial officials there set up an organic certification programme (Hamburger, 2002), and central government officials initiated a national campaign to control pesticide residues and harmful substances. By 2003, with such incidents rising, the Chinese press reported that governments at various levels had initiated over 200 national and local laws, regulations and standards dealing with food safety (*Xinhua General News Service*, 27 November 2003).

Nevertheless, evidence suggests that institutional weaknesses impede implementation. These include a lack of environmental protection officials charged with monitoring agricultural work, generally poor central control over rural governance, and discrepancies between laws governing domestic and international trade. Interested in obtaining high yields, Chinese farmers still routinely use high doses of potent chemical pesticides and other toxic agents – especially on products for domestic consumption. In June 2003, the Ministry of Agriculture announced it was stepping up the pesticide residue campaign adopted two years earlier, apparently because compliance had been lax. Still, by March 2005, following a spate of dangerous domestic food scandals (some resulting in deaths), food safety remained a major concern of delegates to the National People's Congress (*Financial Times Information, Business Daily Update*, 10 March 2005); as a result, wealthy Chinese are now buying imported food (*Standard*, 16 August 2004) – and may well be justified in doing so. A close reading of regulations reveals that while entry into the WTO might encourage Chinese legislators to adopt stricter foreign food safety codes, international market constraints do not always translate to domestic markets. Regulations issued by Shandong Province to tighten control on pesticide residues specifically target '...businesses involved in vegetable *exports*' which are required to '...set up strong monitoring systems, and...only purchase vegetables from registered production bases' (*Xinhua General News Service*, 7 June 2003, emphasis mine). The same rules do not seem to adhere to domestic production.

As for the claim that an increase in large-scale animal husbandry ventures might make rural environmental problems easier to control, the US experience with a far more developed environmental regulatory apparatus would suggest otherwise. Large livestock ventures in the US have created huge solid waste, air, and water pollution problems with adverse impacts on rural ecosystems, drinking water supplies, and human health – and have proven difficult to regulate (Taquino *et al.*, 2002).

The negative impacts for the environment may be most pronounced in the aquaculture sector. Here massive quantities of nutrients and chemical byproducts from feed stock, veterinary products, and disinfectants in developed coastal regions have led to high levels of eutrophication, fish deaths, disruption of coral reefs, and a shift in the balance and type of phytoplantkton, causing red tides that drastically transform China's coastal ecosystems and affect the entire food chain. Moreover, Zhao and colleagues conclude, 'Not only is the frequency of red tides increasing and the size of the area affected growing year by year, but also poisonous species [which bioaccumulate] are becoming evident' (Zhao *et al.*, 2004: 90–91, 101). In fact, the number and intensity of such red tides along China's coasts has risen dramatically, with 96 reported in 2004, up 83 per cent from the previous year (*Xinhua Economic News Service*, 11 January 2005). These changes explain the increasing quantities of Chinese aquaculture products rejected by WTO trading partners.

Other projected rural environmental gains from trade liberalisation have not yet materialised. The scale of the organic agriculture sector is far too small to have a significant impact on pesticide use; genetically engineered crops, though increasing in number, pose unknown biosafety threats; and although international-environmental NGO work to preserve Chinese habitat has increased, it is clear that political and economic factors have had a greater impact on land use. Specifically, the economic gains to be made through development of the manufacturing and service sectors under a liberalised economy have led some local government officials to seize land from farmers to create 'development zones' or other endeavours, accelerating the loss of productive farmland.

In addition, WTO accession has increased the vulnerability of China's biodiversity. As trade has blossomed, so has the number of exotic and potentially invasive species unintentionally introduced into China. In 2001, flowers imported from the Netherlands inadvertently carried a non-native insect which spread throughout Yunnan province, affecting the unique ecosystem and devastating the new booming horticulture industry (Wu, 2002). Though SEPA has considered legal changes necessary to forestall the further spread of invasive species, with limited technology and manpower and vastly increased imports, it is hard to monitor this problem. The complex and fragile nature of ecosystems along with the difficulty of enforcing policies aimed at sustaining them, has led one agronomist to conclude that the ecological problems posed by accession to the WTO will be extensive and long term, and the overall negative impacts will far outweigh the positive (Liu, 2002).

Wider Implications

The Global Environment

It would be a mistake to view the ramifications of WTO entry solely with regard to its effects on China. The lowering of trade barriers, at precisely the time when China has reached mid-levels of development and income, is spreading environmental effects beyond the country's borders. Following severe floods in 1998 due to deforestation, the country enacted and enforced a strict forestry conservation policy. Yet, since WTO-entry, China has been able to meet its rapidly rising domestic demand for wood products *and* has become a major international base for furniture production and wood processing. This is because the reduction of tariffs and elimination of quotas under the WTO has allowed for a rapid growth in timber imports (Sun, 2004). While imports have eased pressures on *Chinese* forests, much of this wood comes from areas of the world practicing poor forest stewardship, such as Indonesia, Malaysia, Myanmar, Cambodia, Russia, and various South American and African countries, and is often illegally purchased (Sun, 2004; *Guardian*, 22 April 2005). As Sun sums up, 'Economic globalisation and trade liberalisation have promoted globalised resource allocation, and have made it possible that one country transfers stress on its forests to other countries via international trade' (Sun, 2004: 68). A 2005 World Wildlife Fund report highlights the severity of this transfer, warning that '. . . surging demand [in China] . . . threatens to have a devastating impact on forests around the world' (*Agence France Presse*, 8 March 2005).

Timber is but one example of how WTO entry has encouraged China to seek cheap raw materials overseas for processing at home. Increasingly, Chinese firms are tapping into natural resources in Africa, the Middle-East, South America, Southeast Asia and Russia, and investing in various mining and oil exploration ventures there. By doing so, certain environmental conditions in China may improve as the country's economy continues to grow (as happened with forests); but the voracious appetite of the Chinese manufacturing economy and its overseas customers from the industrialised world serves to exacerbate environmental problems elsewhere, much as development within the North has for decades brought ecological destruction to countries within the South and to the global ecosystem more broadly.

Socio-economic Changes

While the lowering of trade barriers created by WTO membership is *directly* responsible for many of the environmental harms discussed above, intensifying socio-economic changes brought about by WTO membership *indirectly* compound these problems. As a result of increased wealth and of structural adjustments to the economy since WTO entry, the income gap in China is widening, intensifying consumerism on the one hand, and relative deprivation on the other, both of which threaten the environment.

The aggregate growth of the economy and the boost in incomes for those who have benefited from WTO entry have meant that China has now surpassed the United States as the world's largest consumer (Brown, 2005). Wealthy Chinese, still a small proportion of the population, are notably responsible for the rise in atmospheric pollution from automobiles, the loss of arable land for roads and golf courses, the threat to various endangered species for culinary delights, and the increased consumption of electricity, water and other resources for large, modern houses full of electronic conveniences.

At the other end of the spectrum, the increase in relative deprivation (*Austin American Statesman*, 19 September 2004), with falling consumer purchasing power for many,[15] also poses environmental threats. Unemployment in both urban and rural areas remains high; in addition, Chinese farmers have to contend with new competition from international markets and with greater incentives for local officials to seek economic gains. Experience in other parts of the world and in China suggests that when people's livelihoods are threatened and they perceive uncertainty regarding their future, they often resort to strategies that degrade the environment in order to survive (Blakie & Brookfield, 1987; Redclift, 1989; Gadgil & Guha, 1995; Muldavin, 2000). Such threats in part account for many of the problems already identified.

Conflicting Political Imperatives

Socio-economic factors like these have for some time contributed to political imperatives propelling local leaders to engage in environmentally destructive ventures. The success of government officials in China is still measured overwhelmingly on the basis of local economic prosperity and social stability. Over the reform era, growth-oriented norms and economic opportunities have led local leaders to welcome polluting firms for the local employment opportunities and financial benefits they bring, as well as for the personal gains. Since WTO entry, in those parts of China 'left behind' and grappling with intensifying economic pressures, the political imperative to pursue such developmentalist strategies, even at a cost to the environment, has heightened. Throughout China, the opportunities to reap large financial rewards from investment ventures has also grown, leading to the previously mentioned local government seizure of farmers' lands for development zones or projects. Many such ventures have supported heavily polluting industries that have destroyed the soils and streams of surrounding communities. Recently, opposition chiefly to industrial pollution, land seizures, corruption, and income differentials has led to a massive rise in protests in the countryside, estimated at 74,000 in 2004 – up 28 per cent from the previous year (*Chicago Tribune*, 19 October 2005).

Politically, then, the Chinese government today faces a real dilemma. On the one hand, it has pursued developmentalist policies congruent with those of the WTO, policies which prioritise maximum efficiency and economic growth. On the other hand, these very policies have intensified socio-economic disparities, heightened self-serving actions by local political leaders and increased environmental harms in the countryside, leading to a surge of social discontent. Since at least the Tian'anmen Massacre in 1989, the Chinese Communist Party has rested its legitimacy and the regime's stability primarily on its ability to 'deliver the goods'. The need continually to expand economic growth factored heavily in the state's determination to enter the WTO. Now delivering these goods at the expense of farmland and the environment is precisely the factor undermining social stability and, with it, the state's legitimacy.

Conclusion

If the Chinese Communist Party hopes to maintain social order, and if China's contribution to local and global environmental degradation is to be reduced, the present development trajectory will need to be addressed. While this study demonstrates that membership in the WTO has increased wealth and brought with it technological and legal advances which might conceivably improve environmental quality, it also demonstrates that in important ways, other factors related to WTO membership have offset these benefits, and further challenged political stability. In particular, 1) the sheer *scale* of growth has overshadowed potential improvements from structural change; 2) *weaknesses in regulatory enforcement* have diminished the effects of legal advances; 3) environmental improvements at home, in some cases, have come at the expense of *environmental harms abroad*; 4) *socio-economic changes* have increased both environmentally destructive consumption and production; 5) and *conflicting political imperatives* have led local officials to undertake economic ventures with noted ecological costs – not to mention social and political ones. All of these developments have roots in the normative premise of the WTO – its prioritisation of economic growth – which has reinforced the ideological foundation of China's reform era (Jahiel, 2000).

Now at a crossroads, the Chinese regime has three avenues of resort. First, it could continue to pursue rapid economic growth under the WTO, satisfying the consumptive desires of a part of the population while attempting to stave off social unrest through repression, cooptation, and the transfer of ecological destruction to yet poorer parts of the world. Second, it could respond to popular protest with new measures aimed at strengthening regulatory enforcement, and prohibiting production in all environmentally destructive industrial and agricultural practices, even if these appear profitable under the present trade regime. Third, it could fundamentally shift its development trajectory in ways that benefit the local and global environments. This last alternative would include: 1) fully taking into consideration the environmental and human health costs of rapid economic growth when determining the country's comparative advantage; 2) prioritising environmental protection as an *equally* important measure of political success as economic and social prosperity; and 3) abstaining from practices overseas which would be environmentally destructive at home.

The central government appears wedded to the first alternative, while the State Environmental Protection Administration seems to be moving toward aspects of the latter two, threatening to hold large development projects to the law, urging greater attention to environmental achievements in administrative evaluation, but also discussing the need to calculate growth on the basis of a green GDP. As always, though, it remains to be seen if and how these measures will be implemented. Significantly, as yet there is no indication that these ideas are actively being linked to China's international trade policies and notions of comparative advantage, nor, fundamentally, to society's notion of prosperity. Moreover, WTO membership is unlikely to encourage these changes. Although, to date, the WTO has largely respected existing environmental laws, talk about incorporating the environment within the legal framework of the WTO under the Doha Round has not progressed. Moreover, the economic growth paradigm of the WTO has encouraged its members to '... support a greening of WTO rules only partially and only where it furthers their own interests' (Neumayer, 2004: 1), with continued adverse effects on the environment. China is now one of these members, and it is clear it is playing by the rules set by its predecessors. Unless China makes a strong commitment to pursue growth in its own best environmental interest *and* to prevent the transfer of environmental problems overseas – a commitment the industrialised countries have largely avoided – over time, even as the country responds to powerful political pressures by better managing its environmental impacts at home, we can expect it to cast a longer and longer environmental shadow abroad.

Acknowledgements

The author wishes to thank Arthur Mol, Neil Carter, Thomas Lutze, Alana Boland, and an anonymous reviewer for their very helpful comments at various stages of this article.

Notes

1. Several Western journals devoted entire issues to this topic. See *China Quarterly*, September 2001, 167(1); *Journal of Contemporary China*, August 2002, 11(32); and, *China Perspectives*, March/April and May/June 2002 (40 and 41).
2. Notable exceptions include Ferris & Zhang (2002), Oberheitmann (2002), CCICED (2004), and a special issue of *Sinosphere* 3(3).
3. For a counter argument see Jahiel (2002).
4. For empirical considerations see Desombre & Barkin (2002); Neumayer (2004).
5. Chai's data is based on SEPA statistics that do not generally include data from private firms and small rural enterprises.
6. For foreign-funded projects see 'Inventory of Environmental Work in China', in Woodrow Wilson International Center for Scholars, *China Environment Series*, 2002, 5: 137–227.
7. Between 1985 and 1996, foreigners invested US$2.18 billion in 1004 ODS-related enterprises (CCICED, 1997).
8. One of China's concerns was that environmental laws in other countries would increasingly be used to restrict trade, at great cost to the economy. In May 2002, the issue of protectionist 'green trade barriers' was brought up repeatedly by environmental officials and policy analysts I spoke with in Beijing, and by presenters at the *International Conference on China's Entry into the WTO: Economic and Ecological Challenges and Opportunities*, in Kunming. SEPA's 2002 report '*Jiaru* WTO' noted that environmental labeling laws in 50 countries had already affected Chinese products worth US$4 billion.
9. Tariffs have been falling from the original 80–100 per cent in 2001 to the required 25 per cent in 2006, while import quotas for foreign automobiles have increased by 15 per cent each year (Pan *et al.*, 2004).
10. In 2003, small coal mines, representing 17.6 per cent of the nation's coal output, accounted for over 46 per cent of the increase in production over the previous year (Jiang *et al.*, 2004)
11. These include 'Criterion for the Formaldehyde Content of Textile Products', 'Water Consumption Quota for Printed and Dyed Cotton Products', and 'Textile Requirements on Environment-friendly Textile Products'.

12. In 2003, the area sown to cotton grew by 22 per cent (Asia Pulse Analysts, 2004).
13. For a more detailed discussion see Jahiel (2003).
14. At the time of WTO entry, various pesticides used in China were prohibited from use in other industrialised countries. China had maximum toxicity levels for only 62 types of pesticides, compared to Japan's 96 and the US's 115; in addition, other countries had adopted fruit- and vegetable-specific residue and use standards, but China had not (Wang, 2001; Hamburger, 2002).
15. According to a World Bank study, China's rural poor have suffered a six per cent decline in living standards since WTO entry (*Agence France Presse*, 21 February 2005).

References

Asia Pulse Analysts (2004) 'Profile: China's cotton industry', January.

Basel Action Network (BAN) (2002) 'Exporting harm: the techno-trashing of Asia', February.

Bhalla, A. & Qiu, S. (2004) *The Employment Impact of China's WTO Accession* (London: Routledge Curzon).

Blakie, P. & Brookfield, H. (1987) *Land Degradation and Society* (New York: Methuen).

Brown, L. (2005) 'China replacing the United States as world's leading consumer', *Eco-economy Update 2005*, 1, 16 February. Available at http://www.earth-policy.org/Updates/Update45.htm (accessed 16 February 2005).

Chai, J. (2002) 'Trade and the environment: evidence from China's manufacturing sector', *Sustainable Development* 10: 25–35.

Cheng, L. & Shen, X. (2004) 'Textiles', in CCICED, pp. 179–206.

China Council for International Cooperation on Environment and Development (CCICED) (1997) *Pollution Havens and Ozone Depleting Substances Control in China, Report for the First Meeting of Phase II* (Winnipeg: International Institute for Sustainable Development (IISD)).

CCICED (2001) *China and International Cooperation on Trade and Environment: Final Report – Phase II* (Winnipeg: IISD).

CCICED (2004) *An Environmental Impact Assessment of China's WTO Accession* (Winnipeg: IISD).

Desombre, E. & Barkin, J. S. (2002) 'Turtles and trade: the WTO's acceptance of environmental trade restrictions', *Global Environmental Politics* 2(1): 12–18.

Earth Policy Institute (2005) 'Oil and food: a rising security challenge', *Environmental News Network*.

Edmonds, R. (ed.) (2000) *Managing the Chinese Environment* (Oxford: Oxford University Press).

Feigon, L. (2000) 'A harbinger of the problems confronting China's economy and environment: the great Chinese shrimp disaster of 1993', *Journal of Contemporary China* 9(24): 323–32.

Ferris, Jr, R. & Zhang, H. (2002) 'The challenges of reforming an environmental legal culture: assessing the status quo and looking at post-WTO admission challenges for the People's Republic of China', *Georgetown International Environmental Law Review* 14(3): 429–60.

Fewsmith, J. (2001) 'The political and social implications of China's accession to the WTO', *China Quarterly* 167(1): 573–91.

Gadgil, M. & Guha, R. (1995) *Ecology and Equity: the Use and Abuse of Nature in Contemporary India* (London: Routledge).

Greenpeace (1997) 'China: the waste invasion: hazardous and other waste imports to China and Hong Kong 1993–1999'. Available at http://www.eldis.org/static/DOC4499.htm (accessed 31 May 2005).

Guojia huanbao zongju, wuran kongzhi si (Pollution Control Department of SEPA) (2002) *Jiaru WTO dui wuran kongzhi gongzuo de yingxiang yu jianyi* (The impact of entry into the WTO on pollution control work, and suggestions), March–April, internal paper.

Hamburger, J. (2002) 'Pesticides in China: a growing threat to food safety, public health, and the environment', Woodrow Wilson International Center, *China Environment Series* 5.

Harwit, E. (2001) 'The impact of WTO membership on the automobile industry in China', *China Quarterly* 167: 655–70.

Hsiung, J. (2003) 'The aftermath of China's accession to the World Trade Organisation', *Independent Review* 8(1): 87–112.

Hu, T. (2004) 'Agriculture', in CCICED, pp. 25–44.

Hu, T. & Meng, F. (2002) 'Zhongguo jiaru WTO yu nongye de huanjing yingxiang' (China's accession to the WTO and the environmental impacts of agriculture). Paper presented at the International Conference on China's Entry into the WTO: Economic and Ecological Challenges and Opportunities, Kunming, China, 20 May.

Hu, T. & Yang, W. (2000) *Environmental and Trade Implications of China's WTO Accession: a Preliminary Analysis* (Winnipeg: IISD).

Jahiel, A. (2000) 'The organisation of environmental protection in China', in Edmonds (ed.), pp. 33–63.

Jahiel, A. (2002) 'The environmental impact of China's entry into the WTO'. Unpublished manuscript.

Jahiel, A. (2003) '"Green agriculture" and "green trade barriers": WTO benefits to the Chinese countryside reconsidered'. Paper presented at Annual Meeting of the Association for Asian Studies, 29 March.

Jiang, K., Hu, X., Guo, D. & Cheng, L. (2004) 'Energy', in CCICED, pp. 139–75.

Langlois, J., Jr (2001) 'The WTO and China's financial system', *China Quarterly* 167(1): 610–29.

Lee, K. W. (2001) 'China's accession to the WTO: effects and social challenges', *China Perspectives* 33: 13.

Liu, B. (2002) 'WTO and biodiversity protection'. Paper presented at the International Conference on China's Entry into the WTO, Kunming, China.

Mai, Y. (2002) 'The petroleum sector after China's entry into the WTO: can the Chinese oil giants survive market competition?', *China Perspectives* 41: 24.

Muldavin, J. (2000) 'The paradoxes of environmental policy and resource management in reform-era China', *Economic Geography* 76(3): 244–71.

Neumayer, E. (2004) 'The WTO and the environment: its past record is better than critics believe, but the future outlook is bleak', *Global Environmental Politics* 4(3): 1–8.

Oberheitmann, A. (2002) 'Energy production and related environmental issues in China', *China Perspectives* 40: 37–49.

Pan, J., Hu, H., Yu, F. & Cheng, L. (2004) 'Automobiles', in CCICED, pp. 107–36.

Redclift, M. (1989) 'The environmental consequences of Latin America's agricultural development: some thoughts on the Brundtland Commission report', *World Development* 17(3): 365–77.

Ren, G. (2001) 'Jiaru WTO dui Zhongguo huanjing baohu de yingxiang fenxi' (An analysis of the environmental protection impacts for China of entry into the WTO). Unpublished paper, Peking University.

Rosen, D., Rozelle, S. & Huang, J. (2004) *Roots of Competitveness* (Washington, DC: Institute for International Economics).

Ross, L. (2000) 'China: environmental protection, domestic policy trends, patterns of participation in regimes and compliance with international norms', in Edmonds (ed.), pp. 85–111.

Sanders, R. (1999) 'The political economy of China: environmental protection lessons of the Mao and Deng years', *Third World Quarterly* 20(6): 1201–15.

Smil, V. (1993) *China's Environmental Crisis: an Inquiry into the Limits of National Development* (London: M. E. Sharpe).

Sun, C. (2000) 'WTO and Chinese forestry: an outline of knowledge and knowledge gaps', *Sinosphere* 3(3): 18–23.

Sun, C. (2004) 'Forestry', in CCICED, pp. 47–72.

Taquino, M., Parisi, D. & Gill, D. (2002) 'Units of analysis and the environmental justice hypothesis: the case of industrial hog farms', *Social Science Quarterly* 83(1): 298–316.

Theirs, P. (2000) 'China's green food label and the international certification regime for organic food: harmonized standards and persistent structural contradictions', *Sinosphere* 3(3): 8–18.

Wang, H. (2001) 'Huanjing wenti: rushihou de waimao jiaodian: fangwen guojia huanbao zongju fujuzhang Wang Yuqing' (The environmental question: the foreign trade focus after entering the WTO: an interview with SEPA Vice Administrator Wang Yuqing), *Keji Ribao* (*Science and Technology Daily*), November.

Wang, S. (2000) 'The social and political implications of China's WTO membership', *Journal of Contemporary China* 25: 373–405.

Weber, M. (2001) 'Competing political visions: WTO governance and green politics', *Global Environmental Politics* 1(1): 92–113.

Williams, M. (2001) 'Trade and the environment in the World Trading System: a decade of stalemate?', *Global Environmental Politics* 1(4): 4–6.

World Trade Organization, Commission on Trade and Environment (CTE) (1997) 'Environmental benefits of removing trade restrictions', 7 November.

Wu, X. (2002) 'The implications of China's entry into WTO on environmental protection'. Paper presented at the International Conference on China's Entry into the WTO, Kunming, China.

Ye, R. (2002) 'China's entry to the WTO and environmental protection'. Paper presented at the International Conference on China's Entry into the WTO, Kunming, China.

Yeung, G. (2002) 'The implications of WTO accession on the pharmaceutical industry in China', *Journal of Contemporary China* 11(2): 473–93.

Zhao, Y., Zheng, H., Bai, M. & Lin, X. (2004) 'Aquaculture', in CCICED, pp. 75–104.

Author Interviews

0707 (1997) SEPA official responsible for solid waste, Beijing.

0513 (2002) Senior SEPA official, Beijing.

0522 (2002) Municipal EPB official, Wuhan.

0528 (2002) SEPA official, Division of Law and Regulation, Beijing.

0515 (2002) Hu Tao, senior policy analyst, PRCEE, Beijing.

0603 (2004) Lu Chuntao, Henan Provincial Agricultural Research Institute, Zhengzhou.

China and the Environment: Domestic and Transnational Dynamics of a Future Hegemon

NEIL T. CARTER & ARTHUR P. J. MOL

The Harbin Disaster

The environmental disaster in the Songhua River, centred on the city of Harbin in the north-eastern province of Heilongjiang in November 2005, provided an illustration of the current trends and tensions that characterise China's system of environmental governance. At first sight it looked like a classic example of an industrial environmental accident that could happen anywhere when old facilities, poor risk management and the limited environmental capacities of state and private agencies come together. An explosion at a large petrochemical factory released a huge spill of highly toxic benzene into a major river, threatening the water supplies and river-based economic activities not only of various Chinese cities and villages along the river, but also of towns downstream on the Russian border. Only a decade ago, such accidents might have received little publicity, or have been reported only as a successful example of disaster management by the local authorities. Now, however, the immediate media coverage in China focussed not only in great depth on the disaster itself, but even more on the attempt by local officials to conceal details of the pollution threat and then to release misleading information about it. Moreover, citizens held their local government directly responsible and accountable both for its inadequate response to the incident (particularly its failure to safeguard water supplies) and for the attempt to cover up the disaster. This kind of local political and bureaucratic response in the face of an environmental crisis is hardly unique to China, and few sinologists were surprised by these actions (Economy, 2005). Surprisingly, however, shortly afterwards it turned out that local officials had been willing to give full details of the disaster to the media and public, but that the State Environmental Protection Agency (SEPA) was withholding the information until public unrest forced it to act otherwise. In the end this led to the resignation of the minister responsible for SEPA, Xie Zhenhua, an action increasingly required by China's top leaders if ministers and other high officials fail (as with Severe Acute Respiratory Syndrome (SARS) and various corruption cases). The rapid spread of the news to the wider world is also a major change from a decade ago, putting additional pressure on Chinese leaders to act and underlining the increasing integration of China in the world. The incident demonstrated the conflicting pressures on environmental governance in China: whilst the knee-jerk official instinct is still to suppress and conceal bad news, the attention of the global media contributed to a change of tack that resulted in a more positive and open response by the national authorities. In a nutshell, the Harbin disaster and its aftermath indicate many of the ingredients of the current (dynamic) state of China's environmental governance system:

- the inadequate environmental capacities of state and economic organisations;
- instability in the relations between central and lower levels of government;
- an active citizenry that increasingly holds officials responsible and accountable;
- local and national media reporting which is becoming more independent from local and national authorities;
- the increasing integration of China into international and global networks.

This developing environmental governance system confronts a huge task, as has become clear from this volume. The environmental crisis in China, probably unmatched for its sheer scale and for the speed with which it is unfolding, increasingly attracts the attention of both sinologists who see the significance of these environmental challenges for wider Chinese politics, and environmental scholars who recognise the importance of China in global environmental politics. China's industrial growth has placed a heavy burden on its natural resources – coal, oil, forests, water, biodiversity – and increasingly those of other countries. The litany of environmental problems afflicting China today has become familiar through detailed analyses by, for example, Elizabeth Economy (2004) and Jianguo Liu and Jared Diamond (2005). There is a widespread belief that a major part of the environmental battle for 'spaceship

Earth' will be fought in China. Sometimes, the doomsayer reports that were a defining feature of 1970s environmentalism, but had been replaced by a sustainable development discourse in the 1980s and 1990s, seem to have re-emerged in the coverage of contemporary China. It is indeed tempting to fall back into these conventional reflexes as there seems to be widespread evidence to justify such alarmism. In this issue, for example, Aden and Sinton show that despite the installation of particulate controls in many industrial facilities and the imposition of tougher emission standards for road vehicles, the rising (and projected) levels of coal use, industrial activity and car ownership have resulted in significant increases in particulate emissions. Worryingly, the energy intensity of economic growth has worsened since 2001; in other words, energy consumption grew more quickly than GDP. In short, China is already a major polluter and it has the potential to get far worse before it gets any better.

However, this volume has moved beyond simple alarmism and has adopted a more balanced perspective. As Liu and Diamond (2005) rightly observe, 'China is lurching between accelerating environmental damage and accelerating environmental protection' (p.1186). Much of the literature on China's environmental situation has, to date, focused on the 'damage' side of the equation. Without neglecting the seriousness of the environmental challenges posed by China's economic development or ignoring the deleterious state of her environment, the contributions to this volume have focused instead on the contemporary transformations in China's environmental institutions. The aim has been to identify and assess China's preparedness for the continuing environmental challenges that will inevitably arise in a still developing country where, understandably, the dominant desire is to prolong the economic growth trajectory. In this final contribution we integrate more general insights about these current developments in China's environmental governance, with some reflections on its future direction. Drawing upon the various contributions to this volume we start by reviewing the extent to which China's environmental governance transition is just a matter of catching up with the West. While, as we will illustrate, there are clear tendencies towards environmental governance homogenisation, China still has its particularities and local characteristics. This becomes all the more relevant now that the one-way flow of environmental governance practices and institutions from OECD countries to China may very well be reversed in the near future. While China's hegemonic aspirations will start in the domains of economics and politics, it will spill over to the environment. So, secondly, we examine the opening up of China to the world, and the various consequences that the new superpower in-the-making has for global environmental politics.

Changing Environmental Governance in China – Catching Up?

It has become clear from this volume that a major transformation in environmental governance in China is under way. In assessing the nature of this governance transition we see that some of the developments are very much in line with what is happening in many other countries, whilst in other respects a distinctively Chinese approach to environmental governance is in evidence. If OECD innovations in environmental governance can be captured by the concept of ecological modernisation, then China's environmental reforms can be labelled as a variant, or different style, of ecological modernisation (see Mol, 2006). To some extent, China is indeed catching up with more developed countries in designing and implementing a more advanced system of environmental governance to meet current and future challenges, and here we see the similarities with, for instance, the EU and the US. But by the same token China is still different, and its environmental governance system carries the consequences of the national particularities of a transitional state with a different cultural background.

Similarities

As noted in the various contributions to this issue, the general direction of Chinese environmental governance is in many respects broadly similar to experiences elsewhere: there is greater decentralisation and flexibility, a shift away from rigid hierarchical command-and-control system of governance, an increasingly 'hands-off' approach to regulation (reflecting the growing role of the market in economic decisions), all of which is underpinned by more stringent and rapidly developing environmental legislation. The following examples also illustrate that such progress in environmental reforms comes along with its own problems, and that there are great variations between and within regions; an observation that is all too familiar for Western scholars studying the unequal distributions and effects of environmental risks and reforms.

First, several legislative initiatives have contributed to a general strengthening of the environmental state. Lo and Tang note the dramatic impact of national and local laws requiring a range of industrial upgrades, involving the closure of small cement, metal and glass factories that used highly polluting low-tech burners. Jahiel, although critical of the overall impact of WTO membership, concedes that it is directly responsible for many new laws setting industrial standards in the textile and automobile industries. Furthermore, recent and upcoming legal initiatives and innovations on Cleaner Production (see Mol & Liu, 2005), Environmental Impact Assessment, renewable energy and the Circular Economy (in development) show that China is far from a laggard in environmental legislation. However, whilst there is no regulatory race to the bottom, WTO membership seems to have done little to prevent the previously established environmental race to the bottom, which has seen China become a waste haven for the import of recycled plastics, shipwrecks and electronics (Smith *et al.*, 2006), among other materials from rich industrialised nations such as Britain and the United States.

Second, the numerous legislative, institutional and policy initiatives discussed in this volume demonstrate the expansion in China's environmental capacity. Yet, as Lo and Tang argue, it is still very underdeveloped both in terms of the regulatory structures in place, and the effectiveness of those structures. In short, ineffective implementation is a major problem, not unlike many other developing, and even developed countries. Shi and Zhang highlight how environmental protection bureaux (EPBs) lack the authority, capacity and resources to monitor and enforce industrial compliance. With half of all industrial activities remaining outside the inadequate EPB monitoring systems in 2004, it is not surprising that pollution regulation is often ineffective. Similarly, Jahiel notes the paucity of officials available to enforce regulations governing the use of pesticides and other toxic substances, especially in rural areas where the reach of central government is generally less effective, which has resulted in serious food safety issues. Keeley describes the failure to implement regulations concerning the labelling of GM crops and the existence of many pirate and illegal crops outside the trial zones. Indeed, it was the recognition of these weaknesses that contributed to the delay in official approval being given to GM rice. Nickum and Lee show that the reluctance of officials to implement politically sensitive reforms, such as increased water fees and wastewater treatment charges, which in turn has put off potential private investors, means that chronic financial shortages have limited investment in new facilities and resulted in inadequate operations management of existing infrastructure. Implementation failures are also a result of corruption. Jahiel observes that prior to WTO entry, despite improved environmental legislation, Chinese entrepreneurs and complicit officials allowed China to become a waste haven. Shi and Zhang argue that the pressure on EPBs to raise their own funds has reduced their credibility and neutrality and led to some corruption.[1]

Third, Lo and Tang's study of EPBs illustrates the gradual shift from environmental regulation to environmental governance, as illustrated by the 'two separate lines for revenue and expenses', the different types of service organisation, the environmental quality administrative leadership responsibility system and the growing role of non-state actors in environmental regulation (see below). One key indicator of emerging environmental governance is the use of a wider range of policy instruments. It is clear that the Chinese government has decided that it must move away from the expensive, and largely ineffective, command and control and end of pipe approaches. The old industrial pollution regulation regime, for example, targeted state owned enterprises (SOEs), but it proved expensive and unreliable. Shi and Zhang identify a number of economic instruments, voluntary instruments and information disclosure programmes that have been introduced over the last 15 years. Another clear benefit of the shift to governance is improved accountability, which was largely lacking until recently in China's environmental governance system. Thus the environmental quality administrative leadership responsibility system involves a range of 'new public management' style incentives, including performance indicators and responsibility contracts, whilst the separation of revenues and expenses has resulted in the responsibility for (and, crucially, the financing of) pollution control now to be located solely with individual enterprises. However, the changes have also encountered problems. The lines of accountability seem to work better in richer regions where leaders tend to be more committed to environmental protection; in poorer areas the reforms may even have reduced the amount of resources available for the EPBs. Moreover, even when local leaders are given incentives to give greater importance to environmental concerns, there is also a wide range of other incentives that encourages them still to give greater priority to economic growth. As long as the environment is just one (minor?) component of the target system, then the economy is likely to trump environmental concerns.

Fourth, one critical element of effective environmental governance that China, like most other countries, has struggled to improve is environmental policy integration. Sometimes the lack of integration simply reflects political interests. The absence of a SEPA representative, or anyone from civil society, on the Biosafety Committee responsible for deciding whether to release GM crops reflects the dominance of agricultural interests in this policy area. Elsewhere, as Nickum and Lee show, some efforts have been made to improve coordination. The transboundary nature of water has led to repeated conflicts between administrative jurisdictions (provinces and municipalities) and functional units (flood control, water supply, drainage facilities, wastewater treatment). One institutional initiative intended to improve the coordination of the various water bureaucracies has been the introduction of water service bureaux (WSB). Some WSBs have undoubtedly achieved economic and efficiency benefits, but their impact on policy coordination is less apparent. Many have been allocated only some water functions and rather than resolving bureaucratic conflicts they have often simply added another layer to them. So, significant institutional barriers continue to impede the integration of water policy. Finally, Aden and Sinton observe that energy policy-making has been characterised by serious inter-sector conflict due to the partial liberalisation of energy pricing, which has resulted in prices that are market-driven for coal and crude oil, but state-controlled for electricity and refined oil. The central government moved to improve coordination of energy policy by restructuring the policy-making and regulatory structure in 2005. It is too early to judge the success of the new system, but the presence of the director of SEPA on the key cabinet committee does suggest that environmental considerations are now an important factor in energy politics.[2] In conclusion, although some important steps towards better environmental governance and integration have taken place, several contributions to this volume make clear that new environmental institutions and initiatives repeatedly run up against powerful economic interests. Thus SEPA and the EPBs remain institutionally weak, often excluded from key decision-making bodies, or simply ignored by a leadership still focused on pursuing the path of rapid economic growth.

A final example of growing similarities with western style environmental governance might arguably be found in the increasing role and involvement of civil society. Several contributors identify the absence of public participation and the general weakness of civil society organisations as a major obstacle to improved implementation, which certainly fits with established theory in this area (see Weidner & Jänicke, 2002). Indeed, it would appear that the Chinese government has adopted a limited version of this approach; for it has encouraged NGO and civil society activity primarily as a means to improve support for and the effectiveness of policy measures, rather than as a step towards a more active, democratic society. But it might prove difficult to have one without the other. The successful introduction of phone lines for environmental complaints in all cities has resulted in wide-scale citizen reporting of environmental non-compliance incidents, a policy supported by prominent public awareness campaigns aimed at encouraging citizens to monitor local environmental performance. The growing evidence of popular protests against environmental hazards suggests to Shi and Zhang that the public is indeed increasingly assisting in improving the effectiveness of implementation by putting pressure on local EPBs to respond and on local polluters to clean up. Other initiatives have further enhanced participation of civil society, including public hearings in EIA processes, the wider use of civil lawsuits against polluting enterprises and the institutionalised use of public hearings at water price settings on a local level. Martens argues that these and other opportunities for public participation in China, whilst still limited and constrained, are expanding rapidly. It is true that most of the developments she discusses, such as green consumerism and sustainable household practices, are, as yet, only a minority taste. Nevertheless, although the first environmental NGOs were only formed in the mid-1990s, their 'official status' has allowed them to carve out a small but legitimate role in improving the effectiveness of policy delivery, but also in pressing for wider concerns of transparency, accountability and public participation. It is perhaps significant that the rapid growth of these NGOs is taking place in a context of growing discontent about localised environmental hazards. If the newly legitimate environmental NGOs were to build stronger links with these popular protests (with up to 74,000 environmental protests recorded in 2004) then it is not impossible that, as in the former Soviet bloc, environmental NGOs could become a Trojan horse for wider democratic reforms.

Differences

In other respects, specific Chinese peculiarities are still very much in evidence in environmental governance, showing some major deviation from environmental governance systems in most OECD countries. The central role of the state is one of the most eye-catching differences. The development of GM crops in China, for example, is a state-driven project. Keeley reports that the state is a powerful proponent of GM crops, although also here we see signs of inner-state conflicts and lack of integration. But all GM research takes place in generously funded state research institutes, all GM technologies are developed in state institutes and patented by the state, and applications for the commercialisation of new GM crops come almost exclusively from the state sector. Hence, the strong private advocates for these technologies, which play a vital role in the USA and elsewhere, are largely absent in China.

Despite the gradual relaxation of media reporting of environmental issues there are still significant constraints on open debate, which inevitably limits accountability and hampers effective environmental governance. Thus the lack of transparency surrounding GM crops has allowed the powerful pressure for innovation to trump the case for tight regulation, particularly with regard to the authorisation of Bt cotton. Yet, conversely, the particular symbolic importance of rice in the national diet fuelled a more effective alternative counter discourse that has resulted in an open and intense policy debate over GM rice, which has reached an international audience through the publication of articles from both camps in *Science*. The Chinese leadership's strong commitment to the expansion of nuclear power is certainly not unique, but its capacity to deliver the policy successfully is unusual, for the absence of democratic rights and public participation will minimise the civil society resistance and planning problems that have obstructed the industry in many western liberal democracies. Similarly, unlike much of the developed world, where the capacity for large-scale hydro-electric projects is now largely used up (and there is strong conservationist opposition to further environmental despoliation), the Chinese government can still plough ahead with massive schemes such as the Three Gorges, riding roughshod over domestic and international criticism. But even here we see the limitations of that approach emerging, for instance in the case of the plan to build 13 dams in the Nu river in Yunnan province, which was put on a hold in 2004 by premier Wen Jiabao, following strong media and NGO protests. While it is still the state, or rather the Party, which sets the parameters for these new freedoms, greater transparency and more active public participation, any reversal of these reforms comes at a high price, as the Tianamen episode has proven. However, compared to the 1980s, today's developments have won more widespread approval from the highest echelons of the state and party.

Privatisation has been an important feature of the changing environmental governance in China. Of course, privatisation is not unique to China, although nowhere else outside the former soviet bloc has it been so extensive in such a short time. In Britain, for example, the Thatcherite privatisation of core utilities such as the water industry had the important unintended consequence of opening up established procedures to critical scrutiny, generating institutional upheaval and requiring new regulatory procedures (Carter & Lowe, 1998). So, too, in China, with mixed effects. One disadvantage is that some relatively successful environment programmes established in the 1980s were based on the planned economy, so the regulatory structures were geared to SOEs, but privatisation has made them dysfunctional. Furthermore, environmental managers were often the first to lose their jobs as privatised companies adjusted to the newly competitive landscape. However, the privatisation of SOEs has made it easier to monitor and enforce environmental regulations. Shi and Zhang show that privatisation removes the distinctive Chinese problem that an environmental official of a lesser rank has no authority to require a more senior (or equal) official in a SOE to comply with an order. Lo and Tang report that while EPBs no longer have to negotiate with other government units, they now have the additional burden of collecting the private company's pollution data, and often encounter evasion tactics, clandestine emissions or even physical opposition.

One final feature that has attracted little attention abroad, yet is potentially of great importance, is China's growing role as an innovator in environmental governance institutions. These include a National Environmental Model City programmme, the piloting of a green GDP scheme, the use of tradable emission permits, environmental quality administrative leadership responsibility system, the recent activities around what the Chinese label the 'circular economy'[3], and a widespread system of hotlines for reporting environmental offences to the authorities and prioritising governmental action. Several contributions in this volume have reported on them. Although we do not yet see any serious interest from OECD countries in these innovations, increasingly China is seen as an environmental innovator by at least some of the East and Southeast Asian countries. With the expected growth in importance of the environment in the ASEAN + 3 regional cooperation, China may very well become a net exporter of environmental governance innovations, greatly helped by its hegemonic status.

While the differences with OECD systems of environmental governance are eye-catching for western scholars, China's environmental governance arrangements are also markedly different from other transitional economies. China's dynamism in developing a new system of environmental governance becomes even more remarkable when compared with the sheer stagnation and even deinstitutionalisation of environmental governance in Russia, the other major world power in transition. The transitional processes in Russia have not seen the parallel development of new environmental institutions, more economic and market actors on the environmental stage, increasing levels of environmental R&D, more liberties for civil society or a decentralisation of environmental powers. Clearly, there is no inevitable relationship between the emergence of environmental governance and wider transitions in the economy and polity.

The International Dynamics of Environmental Governance Transformation

While there have been, and continue to be, clear domestic, endogenous developments, pressures and triggers for environmental governance innovation and stagnation, the remarkable opening up of China to the outside world has also provided a powerful force for change. Although the initial opening up to the world was certainly not environmentally motivated, it did allow and enhance foreign – public and private – development assistance on the environment to move in, playing an increasing role in domestic environmental governance innovations. Increasingly, with the perception of China as a superpower in-the-making, attention is shifting from the role of foreign assistance on domestic environmental reform, to China's outward role in global environmental politics.

There is also great interest in the growing importance of China as a leading actor in the making of global environmental politics. In recent years China has signed up to more than 50 multilateral environmental agreements. For example, it ratified the Biosafety Protocol in 2005, which was essential for the success of this treaty. In particular, as we noted in the introduction, China's compliance with the ozone treaty has proven critical in ensuring that it remains one of the few genuine success stories of environmental diplomacy. China was early in signing the Kyoto Protocol in 1998, but only approved it in 2002. But as the second largest producer of carbon emissions after the USA – and destined to become the largest emitter in around 2020 – the fact that China is not an Annex 1 country and has thus no emission reduction obligations, has worried many parties. During the December 2005 United Nations Framework Convention on Climate Change Conference of the Parties meeting in Montreal on a post-Kyoto protocol phase it became clear that China (and India and Brazil) will become key players in these new rounds of negotiations. China clearly indicated that discussions on post-Kyoto targets will no longer meet a veto. Within China, debates on climate change are currently vibrant, preparing the country to take a role in any post-Kyoto policy.[4] In short, future environmental diplomacy concerning almost every environmental issue will depend heavily on the role played by China. And China is increasingly becoming aware of its shifting position in global environmental politics.

Rapid economic growth has brought international pressure to adopt higher environmental standards, particularly since the entry of China into the WTO in 2001. Jahiel, although pessimistic about the overall impact of WTO membership on environmental governance, does identify a number of beneficial effects. In particular, WTO membership is directly responsible for the introduction of clearer, more even and tougher environmental standards that were essential if China was to export her goods to western markets. Jahiel identifies the adoption of cheaper imported cleaner technologies in the textile industry, tougher vehicle emission standards and new food and agricultural production regulations, as a direct consequence of WTO membership. While her overall assessment of WTO membership is negative, it may be that many continuing problems are a consequence of the rapid economic development of China coinciding with freer trade, rather than through the specific regulatory framework following the WTO. Certainly, as a recent member of the WTO, China is also playing a significant role in the current Doha round of negotiations and China's position on, for instance, trade and environment will become crucial. The stalemate position on the trade–environment dossier, which has hardly moved forward since Seattle, 1999, can accelerate once China puts its full (economic and political) weight behind it. Some observers see signs of China moving away from a defensive position of focussing on green trade barriers, towards a more offensive one, along with its active domestic policies on greening production and products (for example, the developments in eco-labelling programmes, ISO 14000 certifications and cleaner production).

The impact of the opening up of China is not restricted to the arena of governmental policies and politics; it also affects the market and civil society domains. Foreign owned transnational and multinational corporations investing in China are making a significant contribution to developments in environmental governance. Elizabeth Economy highlights the contributions of some big corporations, including Coca Cola, Shell and Dow Chemicals, in setting higher standards, technology transfer and the use of environmental impact assessments. She argues that the China–US Center has played an energetic facilitating role encouraging multinational involvement in environmental projects. Martens points to the growing importance of international environmental NGOs, such as Greenpeace, in highlighting pollution problems afflicting Chinese cities and spreading green ideas such as sustainable consumption. And Keeley demonstrates that the impact of international market and civil society links can be complex: whilst international partnerships with foreign companies have enhanced the development and use of new genes, China has also been increasingly exposed to a global environmental discourse that has fuelled a fragmented counter discourse on GMOs. Greenpeace and other NGOs have pointed to the potential implications for trade to caution Chinese policy-makers from agreeing to the commercial use of GM rice.

Also in the market domain (but hardly discernible yet in civil society), we can identify the growing influence of China in the world, including through the outward foreign direct investments of Chinese companies.[5] But here the signs are not that positive. Chinese natural resource extraction companies seem to follow the example set by Japan in the past two decades.[6] More stringent domestic policies on deforestation following the 1998 flooding (Lang, 2002) have forced many Chinese logging companies abroad, both in the East Asia region and beyond. There is mixed evidence concerning the impact of this migration. While they are reported to be among the worst environmental performers in Indonesia and Myanmar, they seem to do reasonably well in Surinam (van der Valk & Ho, 2004). Few, if any, Chinese companies abroad are among the environmental frontrunners, but they do bring home international experiences and new demands for a harmonisation of standards up to international levels.

One further international catalyst for change, as illustrated by the Harbin pollution incident, is the growing influence of the international media. Of course, domestic factors have strengthened the influence of the international media, notably the growing openness of Chinese society and the development of an increasingly bold Chinese media. The Beijing Olympics in 2008 will provide further opportunities for media scrutiny. Nickum and Lee report that the Olympics have focused top-level attention – and significant resources – on the need to improve the quality and quantity of water supply to Beijing. Similarly, the development of local public transport and cleaning energy production units has been triggered by the Olympics. But perhaps even more important, though often not that visible, are developments with respect to the new media, especially the Internet. Less than two hours after the municipality of Harbin announced the closing of its public drinking water network 'for maintenance reasons', news on the industrial pollution was spreading widely through the (Chinese) Internet. In 2003 China ranked first in the world in the number of mobile phones and second in the number of Internet users (Harwitt, 2004). Chinese environmental NGOs have been quick to use the Internet, also because of the political restrictions and tighter state control over the other media. More than half of the environmental NGOs in China have set up websites with environmental information, bulletin boards and Internet campaigns. Some NGOs, such as the Green-web and Greener Beijing operate only through the web and are unregistered.[7] They publicise environmental information, set up discussion groups, mobilise volunteers, organise activities and campaigns,[8] and catalyse offline campaigns. These information flows – and those which come from outside – generally do not stop at national borders and so they further integrate China within the global information society.

While increasingly, and in many different ways, becoming integrated in the world, China's environmental governance developments maintain a remarkably constant emphasis on national (environmental) security. Current Chinese leaders are much more open to global developments and have adopted a broader definition of China's interests and longer term threats than did their predecessors two decades ago. However, their decisions and actions – at home and abroad – strongly reflect well-perceived domestic interests and priorities (sovereignty and security being among the most important), and there is little evidence of an acceptance of a wider global environmental responsibility as a future global hegemon. But then that sentiment is also absent from the current hegemon, the United States.

The Future?

If we are to draw lessons from this volume about the future, neither naive optimism nor alarmist pessimism makes much sense. While there is no doubt that we must now place China centre stage in any serious analysis and assessment of future global sustainability, a simplistic framing of the situation in alarmist *Limits to Growth* terms wrongly presents the idea that China is on an exponential growth path – unaware, indifferent, unwilling and inactive regarding the domestic and global environmental threats arising from it. This volume has presented sufficient insights into the dynamic developments in China's environmental governance and provides evidence that China has left a simple modernisation trajectory, to become more reflexive about the environmental side-effects of its economic growth. That said, it would be foolish simply to frame future environmental developments in terms of optimist scenarios that only require the evolution of existing environmental institutions, regulations and practices, not least because it would underestimate the seriousness, magnitude and geographical scale of the environmental crisis in-the-making. It would also take insufficient account of the complex mix of domestic economic, social and political dynamics, the fundamental institutional transitions, and the changing global relations and power balances, which together make the outlook highly unpredictable and indeterminate. While we can report that much is being done in China with respect to putting in place serious environmental governance arrangements, there is no reason to be overly optimistic about their capacity to contain the environmental crisis.

What has emerged from this issue is that a number of key areas will be crucial in shaping China's ability to deal with the environmental challenges at home and abroad. It is these areas that deserve the future attention of sinologists and environmental social scientists:

- the position and role of China in global politics, economics and informational processes;
- the domestic developments in political liberalisation, the building of a stronger civil society with countervailing powers and high levels of participation, and the increase in transparency, accountability and access to information and the media;
- environmental capacity building towards modern environmental governance with more emphasis on implementation inspection and enforcement, the rule of law, low levels of corruption and informality, further expansion of market dynamics, and the separation and articulation of tasks and responsibilities;
- dealing with the large inequalities (and related tensions) within the country with respect to economic opportunities, social welfare, environmental threats and quality of life.

These processes and developments will not only determine China's environmental governance and performance. All signs indicate that China is a new hegemon in-the-making and that this hegemon will – by definition – strongly influence and structure global environmental politics and governance, and via that the domestic governance arrangements in Europe. So that is all the more reason for western environmental social scientists to turn their attention to the east.

Notes

1. In the global corruption perception index of Transparency International, China consistently takes up a position in the middle of all countries, clearly above most African and some other Asian countries but well below most OECD countries. Chinese companies investing abroad are also more likely to pay or offer bribes than companies from most other OECD countries, according to the Transparency International Bribe Payers Index 2002 (see for both http://www.transparency.org/policy_and_research/surveys_indices/).
2. In October 2005 China announced plans to more than double its reliance on renewable energy by 2020, which could make it a leading player in the wind, solar and hydropower. It would aim

to provide 15 per cent of its energy needs from non-fossil fuels within 15 years – up from 7 per cent today, and 50 per cent more than its previously stated goal of reaching 10 per cent by 2020. Of course, not all renewables are beyond environmental debate, as we know from the Three Gorges Dam controversy.

3. Following the examples of the Japanese and German Recycling Economy laws, and intellectually inspired by the notion of Industrial Ecology, Chinese academics and leaders have strongly promoted the idea of a circular economy on the research and policy agendas. China's 11th Five Year plan on the national economy (2006–2010) has identified the circular economy as one of the key elements, and the National People's Congress is preparing legislation on the circular economy.

4. Many of these debates take place within the China Council for International Cooperation on Environment and Development (CCICED), but also between policy-makers and universities and within the media. The CCICED is a high-level advisory body that makes recommendations for consideration by the Chinese government on environment and development issues. The Council, launched in 1992, consists of about 20 senior Chinese officials and the same number of international experts.

5. China's fast-growing economy and economic liberalisation are fuelling an accelerating burst of overseas investment. Overseas direct investment reached US$33.2 billion over 2003 and US$62 billion in 2004. Mainland enterprises had established 7470 companies in more than 160 countries or regions by the beginning of 2005, with Hong Kong capturing nearly 75 per cent of the total. Over 90 per cent of firms investing overseas were in the mining, manufacturing, wholesale, retailing and commercial services sectors. See also Wong (2006).

6. Cameron (1996) analyses two waves of Japanese foreign direct investment in Southeast and East Asia. The first wave of Japanese FDI in the 1970s can be explained by internal developments in Japan; it was basically the industrial practices that were no longer tolerated in Japan – or could not compete – that were relocated to other Southeast and East Asian countries, taking advantage of weak environmental and other social regulations and giving little consideration to the local environment. The second wave in the late 1980s (especially in tourism and natural resource extraction such as mining and logging) is similarly analysed by Cameron in terms of what might be called a 'colonisation of Southeast Asia's environment' or Japan's 'ecological shadow' (Maull, 1992). Cameron is quite sceptical and pessimistic regarding the contributions of this outward Japanese FDI to ecological improvements in industrial developments in these NICs.

7. In China, NGOs need to be registered (see Mol & Carter, this volume). Web-based groups can escape the regulations on registration. In a useful overview Guobin Yang (2005) distinguished seven different types of environmental NGOs in China, of which web-base groups is one category.

8. For example, Guobin Yang (2005) reports on an online campaign in 2002 organised by Green-web, which successfully stopped the building of an entertainment complex that threatened a wetland.

References

Cameron, O. (1996) 'Japan and South-east Asia's environment', in M. Parnwell & R. Bryant (eds.) *Environmental Change in South-east Asia: People Politics and Sustainable Development* (London: Routledge), pp. 67–93.

Carter, N. & Lowe, P. (1998) 'Britain: Coming to terms with Sustainable Development?' in K. Hanf & A.-I. Jansen (eds.) *Governance and Environment in Western Europe* (Harlow: Longman) pp. 17–39.

Economy, E. (2004) *The River Runs Black* (Ithaca, NY: Cornell University Press).

Economy, E. (2005) 'The lessons of Harbin', *Time Asia*, 5 December.

Guobin Yang (2005) 'Environmental NGOs and institutional dynamics in China', *China Quarterly* 181: 47–66.

Harwitt, E. (2004) 'Spreading telecommunications to developing areas in China: telephones, the internet and the digital divide', *China Quarterly* 180: 1010–30.

Lang, G. (2002) 'Deforestation, floods, and state reactions in China and Thailand', in A. Mol & F. Buttel (eds.) *The Environmental State under Pressure* (Amsterdam: Elsevier/JAI) pp. 195–220.

Liu, J. & Diamond, J. (2005) 'China's environment in a globalizing world', *Nature*, 435, 30 June: 1179–86.

Maull, H. (1992) 'Japan's global environmental policies', in A. Hurrell & B. Kingsbury (eds.) *The International Politics of the Environment* (Oxford: Clarendon Press), pp. 354–72.

Mol, A. (2006) 'Environment and modernity in transitional China: frontiers of ecological modernisation', *Development and Change* 37(1): 29–56.

Mol, A. & Liu, Y. (2005) 'Institutionalising cleaner production in China: the Cleaner Production Promotion Law', *International Journal of Environment and Sustainable Development* 4(3): 227–45.

Smith, T., Sonnenfeld, D. & Pellow, D. (eds.) (2006) *Challenging the Chip: Labor Rights and Environmental Justice in the Global Electronics Industry* (Philadelphia, PA: Temple University Press).

Valk, L. van der & Ho, P. (2004) 'Van kaalslag naar duurzaam bosbeheer? Het Surinaamse bosbeleid in beweging', in A. Mol, J. Mol & B. van Vliet (eds.) *Suriname Schoon Genoeg. Hulpbronnengebruik en Milieubescherming in Een KleinAamazoneland* (Utrecht: Jan van Arkel/ International Books), pp. 133–52.

Weidner, H. & Jänicke, M. (eds.) (2002) *Capacity Building in National Environmental Policy: a Comparative Study of 17 Countries* (Berlin: Springer-Verlag).

Wong, J. (2006) 'China's outward direct investment: expanding worldwide', *China: an International Journal* 4(2): 273–301.

Index

accountability: improved 186; promotion 48

achievement; National Environmental Model City 30

Aden, N. 17

administrative reform; key aim 53

agricultural biotechnology governance 145–9

agricultural incomes; increase 146

agricultural sector 171–4

agriculture: growth of 167–8; labour intensive 171–2

air pollution; in villages 114

air quality 109

airborne emissions 110

allocation systems; quota-based 93

arrangement; enterprise refund 49

Asian financial crisis; effects on exports 108

authority 9

automobile industry 167, 170–1; growth of 167

automobiles; environmental impact of 171

awareness; environmental 2–3

BASF 34

Beijing: Guanting Reservoir 86; Miyun Reservoir 86–7; water resources in 85–8

Beijing Olympics (2008) 83–4, 87, 192

Bell, R. 37–8, 39

Biocentury 153

biodiversity; vulnerability of 174

biofuels; surfeit of 114

biogas digesters 114

biomass: by-products 112; usage of 115

Biosafety Committee 149–50

Biosafety Law; difficulties with 158

Biosafety Protocol 149–50, 191

biosafety regulations 148–9

biotechnology governance; agricultural 145–9

block water pricing 93

boundaries; dealing across 91–2

Bt cotton 152–5, 170, 189; illegal planting of 154

carbon dioxide emissions 110

Chai, J. 165, 168

challenges 26; economic 38–9; environmental 38–9

China Business Council for Sustainable Development (CBCSD) 139

Chinese characteristics; public participation 63–79

Chongqing 75

circular economy 185, 190

citizen: action 101; complaints 71; consumer role 69–77; environmental behaviour 72; power of 141; reporting system 71

citizen consumers; environmental management 63–79

city: Guangdong 45; Guangzhou 44–5

civil environmentalism: channels for 77; contextual approach 66–9

civil society: beyond state and market 12–15; role of 140

clean-up process 35

coal: availability of 114; liquefaction
119
coal industry growth; environmental
consequences of 109–11
coal mining; safety of 108
coal production: Shanxi Energy Base
107; stimulation of 106–7
coal sector reform 106–11
complaints; citizen 71
complaints system 13
concentration; regulation
enforcement 49
construction; natural areas and
reserves 70
consumer class; expanding 77
consumer role; citizen 68–9, 69–77
corruption; preventing 48
cotton; GM 152–5

Dam construction; protest
against 65
De Burgh, H. 13
debates; limits 64
decentralisation 7–8
developing economies; environmental
governance 25–6
development: economic 1–3, 23–4;
governance 17
Diamond, J. 184
discourse coalitions 150–2
Doha; negotiations 191
domestic production; different
regulations for 173
Dongjiang: and Hong Kong 89–91;
water quality in 90
Dow Chemical 35
downsizing; state 44
Dudek, D. 37
dynamics; state and political 25

eco-labels 73; reliability of 73
ecological modernisation; concept of
185
economic actors 138–9; domestic 11;
market incentives 10–12
economic agencies; greening of 133

economic development:
environmental impact 24;
environmental protection 24–5,
27–8
economic growth; political challenges
of 167
economic innovations; governance 27
economic performance;
environmental protection 55
economics of scale 95
economisation; environmental
governance 24–5, 26–7
economy: circular 185, 190;
environmental governance 25–7;
restructuring of 167
Economy, Elizabeth 17
effective regulatory mechanism 120
effluent; untreated 92
embedded; institutions 44
emission permits; tradable 36–8
emissions; SO_2 36–7, 39
energy: quantitative targets of 120;
renewable 185
energy and environmental politics;
developments in 117
energy consumption; decline of 109
energy elasticity 105
energy inputs; availability of 102
energy intensity 105
energy market; liberalisation
102, 121
energy policy: environmental
implications of 100–22; three ways
100–6
energy resources: domestic 102;
internationally-traded 104
energy-saving; household practices 68
energy sector: future determinants of
120; growth of 105–6, 169
energy sector growth; environmental
implications of 105–6
energy shortages 117
enforcement 38
enterprise refund; arrangement 49
enterprises: foreign 57; privately
owned 57–8

environment: global 174–5; media
13–15; public concern 69
environment; and trade 163–71
environment state; transformation of
136–8
environmental behaviour; citizen 72
environmental capacity;
growth of 64
environmental challenges; key areas
in 194
environmental complaint
systems 78
environmental conflicts; safeguarding
interests in 129
environmental damage; criminal
penalty for 135
Environmental Development
Model City Scheme; Japan-China
30–1
environmental enforcement 138
environmental governance
123–42, 128–32; changing
184–90; developing economies
25–6; domestic 27; economic
innovations 27; economisation
24–5, 26–7; economy 25–7;
state and political dynamics
25; trends in 125; western
style 187
environmental governance regime
131–2
environmental governance system;
features of 183
environmental governance
transformation; international
dynamics of 190–3
environmental hazards; popular
protests against 188
Environmental Impact Assessment
185; laws 168
environmental institutions;
development of 128
environmental management; citizen
consumers 63–79
environmental model city;
environmental expense 32

environmental movements;
key role of 78
environmental policy: development
of 128; innovative 135–6;
integration 187
environmental politics;
modernisation 9
environmental problems; negative
publicity 55
environmental protection: economic
development 24–5, 27–8;
Guangzhou 54; system 3–4
Environmental Protection and
Resource Conservation Committee
(EPRCC) 135
Environmental Protection Bureau
(EPB) 26–7, 49, 129;
underfinancing of 132
Environmental Protection Law 4
environmental protests;
government-organised 12–13
environmental quality; deterioration
of 124
environmental reform strategy 3–4
environmental regime 128–9; failures
in 129–31
environmental regulation 128–32,
145–9
environmental regulators; local
132–3
environmental risks 123
environmental state: apparatus 124;
birth of 3–6; institutions 132;
transitions 7
European Union (EU); banned
imports to 172–3
evaluation; responsibility systems
55–6
expenses: environmental model city
32; revenues 45–51
expertise; politics of 150–2
export market 165
extra-budgetary revenues; retention 43

farmland; government seizure of 176
fees 10; and fines 58

fertilisers 172
Five Year Plan; Sixth 107
food safety; laws and regulations 173
foreign assistance program 16
foreign direct investment 127–8
foreign investment 192; outward 192
forestry conservation policy 175
forestry sector; biomass contribution
  of 112
frame; environmental 67–8
frame construction; state role 68
Friends of Nature; Global Village of
  Beijing 66
future hegemon 182–94

genetically modified organism (GMO)
  145–6; governance of 150
Geping, Q. 39
global economy; integration 16
global environment 174–5
global environmental politics; shift
  in 191
global sustainability; China's role
  in 193
Global Trade Analysis 156
Global Village of Beijing 76; Friends
  of Nature 66
global warming 68
globalisation; effects of 138
globalised resource allocation 175
GM cotton 152–5
GM research 147, 188–9
GM rice: commercialisation of 156–7;
  illegal growing of 157; policy
  debate over 189; struggle over
  155–8
governance: developments 17;
  environmental 3–4; state and
  market 6–12
governing institutions; subtle changes
  42–3
government-organised environmental
  protests 12–13
government-organised
  non-governmental organisations
  (GONGOs) 66

governmental control; media 14
Green Company Image 72–4
green energy supply; absence of 74
green gross domestic product (GDP)
  27–30, 39; international actors 28;
  political interests 29; political
  product 28–9
green products 73
Green Revolution 146
Green-web 193
Greener Beijing 193
greenhouse gas emissions 110
Greenpeace 35, 76, 152; and Nanjing
  Institute of Environmental
  Sciences 154; Rice is Life campaign
  155
GreenWeb Info 73
Guangdong; city 45
Guangdong Province 54; local
  environment management 42–61
Guangzhou 48; city 44–5;
  environmental protection 54;
  National Environmental Model
  City 31
Guanting Reservoir 86

Hajer, M. 150–1
Harbin disaster 182–4; accountability
  for 183
heavy industry; state-owned 125
Hong Kong; and the Dongjiang
  89–91
household practices: energy-saving
  68; sustainable 74–5
household waste; reduction and
  re-use of 75
Hu, R. 155–6
Huang, J. 154, 155–6
hydro-electric products 189
hydropower 115–16; obstacles to
  115–16; social and environmental
  costs of 116

impact: assessment 72; economic
  development 24
industrial; structural changes 56

industrial environmental management 131; roles in 124

industrial growth 123

industrial ownership; reform of 126

industrial plants; privatisation 60

industrial privatisation; negative environmental impacts of 126

industrial sector 168–71

industrial transformation 125–7

industry; location 58

institutional reform; recent trends in 91–6

institutional restructuring; effects of 104

institutions; embedded 44

integration: global 15–16; global economy 16

International Business Community; engaging 32–6

International Conventions and Treaties; participation in 75–7

international environmental organisations 168

international relations; improvement in 136

internet: developments through 193; forum for debate 64; green pages 73; media 14

investment; foreign direct 127–8

Jahiel, A. 17

Jänicke, M.; and Weidner, H. 60

Japan; banned imports to 172–3

Japan-China; Environmental Development Model City Scheme 30–1

Jiasheng, X. 29

Jingping, Z. 29

Keeley, J. 17

Khanna, M. 131

Kuznets curve 100–1

Kyoto Protocol 191

labelling regulations; enforcement of 158

labour intensive agriculture; benefits of 171–2

large-scale enterprises; dominance of 125

Latour, B. 153

Lee, Y. 17; and So, A. 33, 35

legislative and judicial institutions; rising role of 133

Lo, C. 17

local authority 43

local environment management; Guangdong Province 42–61

local schools; nature education 70

location; industry 58

Lui, J. 184

market-based solution 37

market demand 10–11

market incentives; economic actors 10–12

market orientated growth model 3

market trends; international 11

Martens, S. 17

media 14; cases of pollution 14; environment 13–15; governmental control 14; growing influence of 192; internet 14; reporting 189; role of 141

Mineral Resource Law 107

Ministry of Civil Affairs (MOCA) 66

Miyun Reservoir 86–7

modernisation: environmental politics 9; political 7, 43, 59

Monsanto 152, 153

multinational corporations 33, 39, 127

Nanjing Institute of Environmental Sciences; and Greenpeace 154

National Energy Leadership Group 117

National Environmental Model City 8, 30–2; achievement 30; Guangzhou 31; programme 39; Shenyang 31

National Environmental Protection Agency (NEPA) 4

National Environmental Protection Office 4

national protection; nature and biodiversity 70–1
natural areas and reserves; construction 70
nature education; local schools 70
nature protection 78
negative publicity; environmental problems 55
newspapers; role 68
Nickum, J. 17
nitrogen oxide emissions 110
non-governmental actors; limited role 60
non-governmental organisations (NGOs) 192; Chinese 65; environmental 12; government-organised 12–13; international 12
nuclear power; promotion of 119

occupational diseases; death from 111
outward foreign investment 192
ownership changes; regulatory enforcement 56

Pearl River Delta 88–9
permits; tradable 39
pesticides 172, 173
policy: initiatives and innovations 26; Total Emissions Control (TEC) 36–7
political imperatives 176
political interests; green gross domestic product (GDP) 29
political liberalisation; need for 78
political modernisation theory 43
political product; green gross domestic product (GDP) 28–9
politics; public participation 64–6
pollution: control 49; local control 71–2
pollution abatement; basis of 129–32
pollution control 139–41
pollution-related protests 140
power transmission and distribution 113

privatisation 189; industrial plants 60
project culture; reliance on 84
promotion; accountability 48
property rights reform 104
protection 33; key evaluation indicator 44
protection goals 36
protest; environmental 65
public authority; service organisations 52
public concern; environment 69
public health; concerns 32–3
public participation: Chinese characteristics 63–79; new ways of 140; politics 64–6
Pye, L. 64–5

Qifa, Z. 151

reform; economic (1970s) 4
regulation enforcement; concentration 49
regulatory decentralisation 107
regulatory enforcement; ownership changes 56
regulatory institutions 148–50
regulatory system; environmental 4
relative deprivation; increase in 176
renewable energy 185; promotion of 119
reporting system; citizen 71
research institutes 52
responsibility system 54–6, 59–60
retention: extra budgetary revenues 43; pollution fees and fines 45, 48
revenues; expenses 45–51
rice; GM 155–8, 189
rice genome; decoding of 147
risk assessment 147, 148–50
rivers; cleaning 55–6
Rock, M. 26, 30, 44
Royal Dutch Shell 33
Rozelle, S. 156
rule and codes of conduct; social norms 15
rural energy 111–15

rural energy problems; solutions to
112–14
Russia; transitional processes in 190

Sandui, G. 153
service organisations: definition 51;
public authority 52; spinning off
51–4; types 51
Shapiro, J. 2
Shenyang; National Environmental
Model City 31
Shenzhen Reservoir 90
Sinopec 72–3
Sinton, J. 17
Smil, V. 26
So, A.; and Lee, Y. 33, 35
social connections (*guanxi*) 15
social norms; rule and codes of
conduct 15
social unrest 140
socially responsible investments 139
socio-economic changes 175–6
spaceship Earth; environmental battle
for 183–4
stakeholder participation 97
state; central role of 188
state and political dynamics;
environmental governance 25
State Development Planning
Commission (SDPC) 5
State Economic and Trade
Commission (SETC) 5
State Environmental Protection
Agency (SEPA) 4, 34, 183
state-owned enterprises: pollution
intensity of 126; privatisation of
reform 125–6
structural changes; industrial 56
structural reforms 108
sulphur dioxide/SO_2 110–11;
emissions 36–7, 39
sustainability 193
sustainable household practices
74–5
sustainable industrial development
138

Tang, S-Y. 17
technological innovation 145–9
textile production: ecological
footprint of 169; environmental
impact of 169
Thames Water PLC 35
Tietenberg, T. 131
Total Emissions Control (TEC);
policy 36–7
township and village enterprises 126
trade; and environment 163–71
trade liberalisation 163–71; and the
environment 164–6; rural
environmental gains from 174
transformations; industrial 56–9

unemployment 176
United States of America (USA);
livestock ventures 173
Urban Environmental Quality
Examination System 8
urban regions; growth in 83–4
urban water; institutional change in
83–97
urbanisation; rapid 96
US Centre for Sustainable
Development 34

Vermeer Manufacturing 34
villages; air pollution in 114
volume 16–18

Wang, J. 14, 36; and Wheeler, D. 10
waste management; responsibility for
75
wastewater treatment 89, 96
water: transboundary nature of 187;
urban 83–97
water conflicts 96
water consumption issues 74
water cycle 84
water disputes; transboundary 91–2
water enterprises; market-orientated
85
water pricing 92–4; block 93;
increases in 93–4

water quality: deterioration in 89; in Dongjiang 90

water resources bureau 94–5; objectives of 95

water services bureau 85, 94–6

water supply; state system in 84

Weber, M. 163

Weidner, H.; and Jänicke, M. 60

Western social democracies; decline in political participation 65

Williams, M. 163

World Trade Organisation (WTO): accession to 166–8; implications for the environment 162–77

World Wildlife Fund (WWF) 175

Xianchun, X. 28

Yang, D. 60

Yang, G. 12, 14

Yangtze River 70, 115

Yue, P. 29

Zhangliang, C. 151

Zhao, Y. 174

Zhen, Z. 151

Printed in the United Kingdom
by Lightning Source UK Ltd.
129366UK00007B/24/A